OSAMA BIN LADEN: A CASE STUDY

SANDIA NATIONAL LABORATORIES

REPUBLISHED BY NIMBLE BOOKS LLC

Nimble Books LLC
1521 Martha Avenue
Ann Arbor, MI, USA 48103
http://www.NimbleBooks.com
wfz@nimblebooks.com
+1.734-330-2593

Version 1.0; last saved 2011-05-07.

Printed in the United States of America
ISBN-13: 978-1-60888-128-4

The paper used in this publication meets the minimum requirements of the American National Standard for Information Sciences—Permanence of Paper for Printed Library Materials, ANSI Z39.48-1992. The paper is acid-free and lignin-free.

[redacted]

Osama Bin Laden: A Case Study

Part I: Summary and Analysis

Abstract

This document provides an open-source examination of the threat posed by Osama bin Laden, his al Qaeda organization, and allied terrorist organizations. It includes a summary of the relevant history, the lessons learned from the 1998 African embassy bombings and from the follow-on cruise-missile strikes, the threat of future attacks using weapons of mass destruction, and a set of observations, conclusions and recommendations.

[redacted]

Sandia National Laboratories
P.O. Box 969
Livermore, CA 94551-0969

[redacted]

[redacted]

[redacted]

EXECUTIVE SUMMARY 4

INTRODUCTION 7

Caveats 8

OSAMA BIN LADEN 13

General observations 13
The man 13
Strengths 13

AL QAEDA 15

Motives and Philosophy 15
Composition and Recruitment 15
Strengths, Assets, and Capabilities 16
Weaknesses 17

THE 7 AUGUST 1998 AFRICAN EMBASSY BOMBINGS 18

The Good News 18
The Bad News 19
The bottom Line 20
DoS Findings 20
DoS Recommendations 21

THE 20 AUGUST 1998 CRUISE MISSILE STRIKES 23

The disadvantages of retaliation 23
The advantages of retaliation 24

WMD THREAT ASSESSMENT 26

Level of Interest 26
The good news 27
The bad news 27
Nuclear weapons 28
The future 28
Risk Assessment 30
Conclusions 48

RESPONSE OPTIONS 52

[redacted]

[redacted]

INTELLIGENCE AND LAW ENFORCEMENT OPTIONS 52
OPTIONS FOR REDUCING OUR VULNERABILITY 54
MILITARY OPTIONS 54
TARGETING BIN LADEN 54
DIPLOMATIC OPTIONS 55
MISCELLANEOUS OPTIONS 57
OPTIONS FOR THE SPONSOR STATE 57
THE BIG PICTURE 60

[redacted]

Executive Summary

This study represents an attempt to assess the threat posed by Osama bin Laden, his al Qaeda organization, his associates, and affiliated organizations. The report consists of two parts. Part II, which was completed first, consists of a detailed compilation of open-source historical information related to the lives and activities of Osama bin Laden and of other relevant individuals and organizations. The data compiled in Part II are organized by timeframe, by topic, or by region and are presented in a viewgraph format. Part I consists of a high-level summary of Part II, an analysis of the overall level of the threat, lessons learned, and options for the future. Part I is presented in a report format.

The study and the findings of this study can only be understood properly when examined in context. To this end, several constraints and caveats are important:

- The study consists of an analysis of existing data that was gathered from existing reports: No new data was collected or generated as a part of this study.
- The study relies exclusively upon second-hand sources of information (e.g., news media).
- The study relied exclusively upon open-source information.
- The completeness of the study was resource-limited.
- When this study was first started, there was no intent to publish. For that reason, source citations and archives are incomplete.
- The historical summary contains some inconsistencies. Resource limitations precluded the effective resolution of all such inconsistencies.
- The findings and conclusions are subject to change as new data emerges over time.

Findings

- Osama bin Laden is not a new threat. He is a capable adversary with many strengths. Likewise, his al Qaeda organization poses a significant threat and possesses many strengths and assets. However, it also has a number of exploitable weaknesses.
- The 7 August 1998 African embassy bombings should not be taken to imply that our intelligence and physical protection programs are a failure. On the contrary, many positive findings emerge after examining the full story in detail. On the other hand, there are many lessons learned and recommendations for future improvement.
- The 20 August 1998 retaliatory cruise missile strikes did little to help solve the problem posed by bin Laden and may ultimately prove to have done more harm than good. However, the issue is complex, and there are a wide range of possible advantages to retaliation which motivate such strikes.

- The risk of future attacks by Osama bin Laden or his associates using weapons of mass destruction (WMDs) is not insignificant. We find that the risk is greatest for radiological dispersion incidents, followed by use of low-end chemical or biological agents. A detailed set of findings and a quantitative assessment of various options is included in the body of this report.
- Many options exist for our future response to the bin Laden threat (and to the terrorist threat in general). The body of this report contains a list of options for intelligence collection and law enforcement, vulnerability reductions, military options, diplomatic options, options for sponsor states, and more. It is our finding that the root cause of the Islamic militant threat is the widespread and deep-seated discontent among a large segment of the Islamic world, as opposed to the actions or agitation of any one individual or group of individuals. As such, the diplomatic options are likely to provide the broadest and most effective long-term reduction in the threat. However, the threat can never be, and never will be, eliminated completely.

General conclusions

- Terrorism is not dead (although it has shifted from Marxist-oriented to religious-oriented)
- State sponsorship of terrorism is not over (although it has shifted from Soviet-dominated to third-world-dominated)
- Terrorism can be unpredictable and future threats may evolve from very unexpected sources
- Terrorism is a global phenomenon
- Our problems with terrorism are exacerbated by our position and by our image in the world
- Religion is a powerful motivational factor in modern terrorism
- Religion is a protective shield which complicates counter-terrorism
- Killing is an explicit goal of many modern terrorists
- Modern terrorism is not easily countered
- Despite repeated attacks over a period of many years, the truck bomb remains a very potent weapon and remains difficult to defend against
- Despite repeated warnings over a period of many months, the Nairobi bombing was not prevented
- Although the African bombings represent a failure of sorts, we do NOT find negligence to have been a significant contributing factor
- Although we may have underestimated the local threat in East Africa, we were more the victims of resource constraints than of poor intelligence or of a poor threat response
- Our overall counter-terrorist capabilities are strong
- We have a record of successes that we can be proud of
- However, the terrorist can always seek out the weakest targets
- The "war" against terrorism will never be "won": terrorism will always be a world problem
- We are seeing increasing attention domestically to terrorism as a threat to national security

- We are seeing increasing worldwide recognition of terrorism as a global phenomena
- We are seeing improvements in the global response to terrorism

WMD terrorism

- Current terrorist interest in WMD agents and weapons suggests a trend toward new terrorist capabilities in the future
- However, the timing of any evolution towards new methods and capabilities is highly uncertain
- Furthermore, the current effectiveness and availability of explosive devices make it likely that the vehicle bomb will remain a dominant tool for some time yet
- In addition, the apparent inability of al Qaeda to acquire and employ WMD agents or weapons (even after years of trying and with significant resources at their disposal), suggests that the threat of WMD terrorism may be smaller at the present time than we currently seem to imagine
- Nonetheless, the obstacles standing in the way of WMD acquisition and employment are not insurmountable and some forms of WMD employment must be considered quite plausible in the future

[redacted]

[redacted]

Introduction

This study began immediately following the tragic bombings of the U.S. embassies in Nairobi and Dar es Salaam in August of 1998. It follows in the footsteps of several earlier studies in which analysts at Sandia National Laboratories attempted to piece together a complete and coherent picture of various terrorist groups in order to understand how terrorist threats were evolving and what that meant for those of us tasked with the protection of nuclear explosive devices from seizure and use by such groups. In the course of these studies, we have found that the first and most difficult task is simply to gather together and organize the vast wealth of information which becomes available following any international terrorist incident.

Even though we all follow events in the media, it is difficult, if not impossible, to get a clear and coherent understanding of major terrorist events, and what they mean for the future, by following the news in the order in which it becomes available. Different bits of information which are closely related may emerge months apart. Some bits of information do not even seem to be related when they are digested months apart, but it becomes apparent that they are related, and that the relationship can lead to important lessons, when they are seen side-by-side. For that reason, we begin a painstaking process of gathering huge amounts of data as it becomes available and assembling it in an order that makes sense. Once this process is complete, it is as if a large puzzle has been assembled: a big picture often emerges which was not recognizable from the pieces alone. In fact, many different pictures, or lessons, emerge from various corners of the puzzle.

An example might help to illustrate the value of this process. Consider the Aum Shinrikyo cult and their involvement with various chemical and biological agents. Most observers, including the vast majority of site security personnel, security systems designers (scientists and technologists), and military officers know very little about the cult, their capabilities, and what they tried to do. Many, in fact, remain unaware that the Tokyo sarin incident was not the only attempt to use chem/bio agents nor that the cult was involved with many agents other than sarin. A good compilation of the facts reveals many things, among them the fact that the cult was involved with many agents other than sarin alone, that they tried biological agents before turning to chemical agents, and that they were capable of more sophisticated attacks than that for which they are best-known, namely the punctured plastic bags on the Tokyo subway trains.

A similar story exists for Osama bin Laden. Most people had never heard of him prior to the August 1998 African embassy bombings and still know nothing of his involvement in a wide variety of other terrorist acts and of his affiliations with various guerilla groups. An examination of bin Laden's activities makes it clear that bin Laden has been involved in fighting for Islamic causes since long before the East African embassy bombings, that he has had significant state support (as opposed to being the freelance agent sometimes portrayed in press articles), and that he is far more of a terrorist sponsor (and instigator) than an arms-carrying terrorist himself.

Although this type of knowledge will not be striking to those with long experience tracking these organizations, these observations are largely unknown among the wider military and technical community. More importantly, it is one thing to state these conclusions and quite another to draw them for oneself. By assembling the necessary background information, and *especially by putting together effective presentation materials based upon such information,* we have been able to educate audiences in a way that makes these lessons not only clear, but obvious, because the viewer can see for him/herself that the conclusions follow naturally from the facts. In fact, the better we do our job at assembling these histories, the more the conclusions we present will seem to be obvious, as opposed to being the result of some insider's insight.

This is exactly what we have sought to do: to characterize the threat posed by Osama bin Laden, his al Qaeda organization, and affiliated guerilla and terrorist organizations by assembling the huge volume of background information into a coherent package. The result is a two-part package. One part consists of an extensive set of facts assembled in viewgraph format. (This is the "puzzle" in the analogy used earlier.) This collection of information is presented in viewgraph format so that talks can quickly be assembled that cover any of various events and regions. The other part is a set of findings (observations, conclusions, and recommendations) which have been drawn from the assembled facts. (These are the "pictures" which we found when we examined the many facts). The latter material is presented here, in a short document labeled Part I. The former material, consisting of nearly 400 pages of viewgraphs, is compiled separately, and presented as Part II. The reader with very little time will want to read this document, and perhaps to scan the huge set of viewgraphs. However, we strongly encourage those with the time to read through the full package, since some pictures may emerge from the puzzle which we have not captured. This is especially true for readers with different backgrounds, who will look at the data from a different perspective.

Caveats

There are a number of caveats which the reader should be aware of when examining this two-part set of documents.

Analysis of existing data

Sandia National Laboratories is not an intelligence collection agency, and does not and cannot compete with such agencies at collecting intelligence information related to threat groups of any type. Therefore, this study involved no data collection activities of any kind whatsoever. In other words, no new information was uncovered or generated in the course of the study. Rather, the study involved a gathering together of existing information (which had already been collected by others), the compilation of that information into a coherent picture, and an analysis of the result.

Second-hand data sources

This summary draws upon news media and other broad sources of second-hand information. It was not, and was never intended to be, an investigation, in which original information sources were contacted or questioned. For example, there were no direct interviews of the witnesses to events of interest. As such, the summary is inherently second-hand in nature: raw information had already been generated, processed, and published in summary form (e.g., news articles) before it was examined for the purposes of this report.

Reliance upon open source material.

The sensitivity of the information collected by intelligence agencies seriously complicates its usefulness for our purposes. Much is too sensitive to access and what we can access we often cannot share (or at least not without the permission of the originating agency), a fact which seriously degrades our ability to inform and educate our staff, our leadership, and the organizations that we work with. Therefore, this study relied entirely upon open sources for all of the information gathered. Fortunately, however, a great deal of information, including some of that generated by our nation's intelligence agencies, is widely available from various open sources. These sources include the news media, law enforcement agencies, private companies and analysts, and even the intelligence community itself (in the form of unclassified releases and leaks to the press). Although this collection of open-source material does not knowingly include any classified information, it is nonetheless a very substantial body of information, worthy of examination in its own right, even if only as part of a larger examination which will later include more sensitive information sources.

Reliance upon open sources is not the handicap that it may seem. The news media in a free and open society are highly motivated and highly capable at gathering information. In fact, in some sense, the worlds news agencies collectively form the worlds largest intelligence organization, tasked with much the same task as any national intelligence agency, namely to uncover information, including information which is being held secret. Although they suffer from many disadvantages relative to a national intelligence service (such as a lack of sophisticated technology), they do have the advantage of being welcomed into places where any known intelligence operatives would be killed. For example, many journalist have had the opportunity to sit face-to-face with bin Laden himself. Furthermore, by providing an outlet for intelligence sources to reveal what they know (either for egotistical reasons or in an attempt to influence events), they ultimately have access to much of what has been collected by the technology they lack, although typically only in a broad and general sense. The bottom line is that there is a great deal of useful information available from open sources alone. In fact, with the easy availability of that information via the internet, the problem is often one of too much information rather than a problem of not enough.

Whatever the relative value of open-source data, the fact remains that no classified material of any kind was examined in the process of compiling this report. That is bound to mean that this report is incomplete in some areas and may mean than some of the conclusions will require modification when more is known.

Completeness

The enormous body of information generated on Osama bin Laden, the al Qaeda organization, and affiliated terrorist and guerilla groups is truly daunting. This study was originally started for internal use only, by Sandia National Laboratories, to provide information with which laboratory management and staff can make more informed decisions regarding our own programs. It was never intended to be 100% complete, so long as enough of the puzzle was assembled to allow the big picture to emerge.

Perhaps the greatest challenge in these studies is to avoid becoming so swamped with information that it cannot be assembled coherently or examined in a meaningful fashion. This difficulty is compounded by several facts. For one thing, new information becomes available almost on a daily basis. For another, we find that many sources report the same basic facts, which means that there is a great multiplicity in the reporting which seems to balloon the set of available data. Given this situation, we could not possibly hope to keep up with the flood of information with the resources available. Therefore, we have found it necessary to sample the sources available, using an experienced eye to try to avoid overlooking unique or important information. The result, however, is certain to be the loss of some meaningful data.

In the long run, it is unlikely that any data overlooked would seriously affect the outcome of the study. Most of the missing data is likely to be of a sort that bolsters the conclusions we have already drawn, provides additional support for those conclusions, or fills in narrow gaps, as opposed to bringing new revelations that seriously contradict what we have seen in the huge quantity of data that was examined. We would expect the result to be rather like a puzzle with a few pieces missing. Hopefully the big picture can still be seen with or without a few missing pieces. However, the possibility cannot be entirely ruled out that some key data may be missing.

Other limitations

This study was not originally intended for publication. For that reason, as the study began, sources were not documented. In fact, many of the original sources were not even archived for later retrieval. Instead, a fact would be retrieved from a document or web site, added to the large data summary, and the source would then go unrecorded and unsaved. Midway through the study, however, an outside sponsor provided additional funding, at which point the author began a more rigorous system of citations and of source archives. The large data summary (Part II) now consists of entries with and without citations.

The careful reader will also note that some inconsistencies have been left in Part II (the large viewgraph-format data summary). This is because an efficient use of the resources available did not permit each and every discrepancy to be tracked down and resolved. Some of these inconsistencies (such as determining the exact dates of certain events, for example) are noted explicitly in the summary text. Others will only be obvious upon careful examination and cross-checking of the data.

Furthermore, we must point out that the world situation evolves daily. It was necessary at some point to cut off the data gathering and collation and to begin the examination of the data in order to draw useful conclusions and to make recommendations. This cut-off occurred on or about the beginning of November 1999. To the extent that new information becomes available after that date, this report will become increasingly incomplete and it is possible that some of the conclusions or predictions would require modification in the future as more information becomes available.

Miscellaneous comments

Perhaps the best way to think of Part II of this report is as an electronic scrapbook. It contains excerpts from a vast number of articles and reports that have been pasted together into a coherent package. However, they key point is that they have been "pasted" together with very little editing. Like any scrapbook, the emphasis was on completeness, and on neatness of appearance, as opposed to consistency of style. For example, the spellings used in Part II are exactly those that were used in the original sources. Therefore, the reader will quickly note that there are many different spellings of names and places, in particular. This is because there are several different transliteration schemes in general use for Arabic names. The only exception to this was that Osama bin Laden's name was spelled consistently throughout (except where his aliases are mentioned) and that "al Qaeda" was spelled consistently in that body of the work which was generated after it had changed from an internal product into a deliverable for an external customer.

Another result of the "cut-and-paste" nature of this scrapbook-style compilation is that many different grammatical styles appear throughout. Although text was often edited for brevity, and was further edited in some cases because of the loss of context that results from the extraction from a larger article, in most cases we have left the text as close as possible to the original in order to avoid introducing any subtle changes in meaning.

We must also point out that a few items in Part II may lack relevance. In examining the history of these events, we occasionally found information about various events that may or may not have been connected with the primary individuals or incidents of interest. We have included such information in the compilation so that the product will be complete if it later turns out that these events were connected in some way. If history ultimately proves that these items are irrelevant, then the worst we have is a small amount of extraneous information buried within the whole.

Finally, we cannot overstate the value of examining Part II. Busy readers who are tempted to read only this summary report will miss a great deal. The history of Osama bin Laden and al Qaeda is rich with many minor lessons and subtleties that can only be grasped by immersion. No broad overview can possibly capture the richness and the texture of this great human drama. Part I of this report is like a short review of a Broadway play. Part II is the full production.

Osama bin Laden

General observations

- Not a new threat: He has had direct or indirect ties to many terrorist events in recent years
- A former ally: The moral is that our friends today may be our enemies tomorrow
- A significant threat (as opposed to being just a "Gucci terrorist with a fat wallet and a big mouth")
- More of a sponsor of terrorism than a terrorist himself: his real genius is his ability to tap into a bottomless reservoir of ethnic and religious discontent and funnel it against the U.S.
- Enjoys a huge following from which losses can quickly be replaced: bin Laden is said to command forces numbering 3,000 and has influence over many thousands more
- In many ways he is more of a guerilla warlord, overseeing a rag-tag army, than a more traditional urban terrorist
- More like Arafat (a would-be statesman), less like Carlos the Jackal (a shadowy criminal)
- Has enjoyed significant state support (as opposed to being an independent "free-lance" terrorist)

The man

- Large and inflated ego: Sees himself as a player on a very large and very old historical stage (e.g., he sees himself resisting the latest Crusaders)
- Seeks publicity, craves attention
- Charismatic
- Viewed as a hero in much of the Islamic world
- Has achieved near-legendary status
- Likely martyr-symbol if killed
- Therefore, the threat is unlikely to die when bin Laden does

Strengths

- Good at instigating and inciting others
- Recognizes the value of the media
- Skillful at media manipulation
- Good organizational skills: His real genius is in recruitment, publicity, and organization as opposed to planning and execution
- Effective at stroking politicians (e.g., building homes for the politically powerful)

- Effective at building alliances with politicians: what he offers evidently appeals to the leaders of pariah states
- Effective at stitching together Islamic alliances even across old and deep divisions
- Good logistical and financial skills
- Not a micro-manager: is willing to "spin off" ideas and teams which then operate semi-autonomously
- Effective delegation of authority
- Surrounded by several layers of protection, providing relatively good security
- Would not be easy to snatch or kill without the complicity of other nations

Al Qaeda

Motives and Philosophy

- Very anti-American but not exclusively so
- Seek a withdrawal of American forces from Saudi Arabia
- Seek to diminish American influence in the world
- Seek the overthrow of numerous regimes seen as overly secular or anti-Islamic (e.g., Egypt, Saudi Arabia)
- Seek the establishment of Islamic states (e.g., in the Philippines and the Caucasus)
- View their struggle globally (as opposed to just a struggle for leadership in any one country)
- Will join or support almost any Islamic cause or fight
- Present a global threat
- Expect to "lose some" along the way: Won't be easily deterred by setbacks
- View their struggle as righteous: What they do is moral because Allah wishes it to be so
- Very patient: View their struggle as a long one
- View their struggle as a war (as opposed to civil disobedience)
- View their struggle as religious-based: All infidels are the enemy
- Will kill indiscriminately (as opposed to making distinctions between combatants and non-combatants)
- See body counts as their primary leverage against the West
- Seek high body counts
- Interested in WMD agents and weapons
- Very broad-minded about WMD acquisition routes; not limited to any one idea or approach
- Very high risk of eventual WMD acquisition
- Relatively high risk of eventual WMD use (see WMD risk assessment later in this report)

Composition and Recruitment

- Not a "vertical" organization characterized by top-down leadership or blind adherence to orders from above
- Effective at recruiting others, which is both a strength (builds numbers) and a weakness (easier to penetrate)
- Large numbers with unlimited future replacement potential: can essentially tap a bottomless pit
- Recruit internationally
- Nearly endless access to personnel

- Global presence, not limited to nations that are primarily Muslim
- Global presence, not limited to nations that are primarily anti-Western
- Primarily attracts knuckle-draggers (those who are discontent and willing to fight) as opposed to philosophers
- However, also attracts sympathy across all socio-economic levels
- Taps a huge reservoir of discontent (from Muslim villages in the Philippines to wealthy families in the Gulf)
- A product of Islamic frustrations (as opposed to the creator thereof)
- Bin Laden and Islamic fundamentalism are the product of a lack of democratic traditions among Muslim nations: many Muslims lack any other effective voice than the voice of violence

Strengths, Assets, and Capabilities

- Excellent infrastructure (e.g., large and well-protected bases and camps)
- Numerous front companies
- Nearly endless access to funds
- Large numbers of active members
- Large numbers of active and inactive supporters provide excellent replicating ability (i.e., ability to replace losses)
- Even bin Laden himself may be replaceable (especially given his close ties to many other well-led terrorist organizations)
- Multi-national facilities and ties
- State support of many types, especially safe haven
- Although offered sanctuary by Afghanistan, the lack of a clear nation-state as a backer of bin Laden's attacks complicates our ability to strike back
- Seek and use insiders (e.g., military personnel, those with American passports, etc.)
- Can be expected to be well-armed
- Can be expected to be well-trained in guerilla warfare
- Can be expected to be tough and determined
- Can be expected to be willing to die for their cause
- Religion connections provide some legal protection (e.g., from law enforcement surveillance)
- Religion connections provide some cover (e.g., for recruitment and fund-raising)
- Religion connections provide public sympathy and moral arguments to bolster support
- Potential future access to chemical weapons (or other WMD; see WMD risk assessment later in this report)

Weaknesses

- Primarily appeals to Muslims, making it hard to recruit non-Muslims
- Active recruitment and large numbers imply ease of penetration, especially by Arab/Muslim intelligence agencies whose agents come with the correct religious, ethnic, and language backgrounds
- Large numbers imply that some finite subset will be disgruntled, dissatisfied, or disillusioned and might be turned
- Dependence upon large bases and training centers provides easy-to-locate targets for surveillance
- Dependence upon large bases and training centers provides easy-to-locate targets for retaliation
- A global personnel network necessitates international travel and international communications, with a high risk of interception
- Poor COMSEC, which provides indications and warning of future attacks
- A global financial network necessitates more easily traceable global financial transactions
- Global terrorism, not directed against just one country, means that many world governments, who might otherwise be at odds with one another (e.g., America and Russia), are motivated to cooperate against the common threat
- Global terrorism, not directed against just one country, means that many world governments, even those who are not direct targets of attacks, are motivated to cooperate with investigative activities (e.g., tracing financial activities)
- The high profile of bin Laden, and the open and public invective of the group, makes it difficult for sponsor states to plausibly deny that they are aiding terrorists
- The high profile of bin Laden, and the open and public invective of the group, makes it easier for intelligence and counter-terrorist agencies to procure the funding, authority, and resources needed to fight back
- The high profile of bin Laden, and the open and public invective of the group, makes it easier to justify pre-emptive or retaliatory military action
- The high profile of bin Laden, and the open and public invective of the group, provides information (such as statements) that could be used as evidence in a court of law
- Bin Laden's craving for media attention could be used against him by tracking journalist contacts

[redacted]

The 7 August 1998 African Embassy Bombings

The Good News

- Long before bin Laden came to public attention he and his group were a well-known threat and the subject of significant attention: We were definitely NOT "blindsided" by a new threat
- Much was known about al Qaeda and its cells and operations prior to the embassy bombings
- Specifically, Al Qaeda was known to have a global reach and anti-American hatreds which made them a potential threat to any and all U.S. installations overseas
- Much had already been done to limit their effectiveness (disruption) and to preclude specific attacks
- In fact, the existence of the East African al Qaeda cell was known
- Many members of al Qaeda in East Africa had been identified
- Al Qaeda operatives in East Africa were under intense scrutiny
- There had also been informant warnings about their activities in the region
- In response, there were active and ongoing surveillance, threat evaluation, and disruption operations
- The East African cell was feeling the heat of this scrutiny and felt themselves to be "at 100% danger"
- It was believed that this campaign of disruption had done much to dissipate the threat, and it is likely that it had
- In retrospect, there were also specific indications of a bomb plot
- Embassy personnel in Nairobi acted on the threat warnings by making improvements to security and by notifying Washington that they felt vulnerable
- More than one team from the States visited Nairobi in order to evaluate the threat and to re-examine the vulnerabilities
- The attackers were not successful in getting as close to either embassy structure as they had sought
- The attacks were not very successful in killing Americans (the intended targets): Most deaths were among innocent Kenyans in the building next to the Nairobi embassy (which collapsed)
- Several other planned bombings of U.S. installations had successfully been prevented (e.g., in Albania)
- In fact, the number of success stories (bombings prevented) far exceeds the number of failures (bombings that were not prevented)
- The attacks resulted in an escalation of the already-massive campaign to expose bin Laden, to build a legal case against him, to destroy his terrorist network, and to prevent future attacks; a campaign which has already had some success and which is likely to continue to bear fruit in the future
- Spurred on by the attacks, we were very quick to identify the perpetrators and to apprehend a number of them
- The large number of embassy closings since the bombings would seem to indicate that we are now more willing to accept some loss of productivity in response to false alarms as a tradeoff for minimizing the risk to our personnel

[redacted]

The Bad News

- In retrospect, it appears that we may have underestimated the threat (or overestimated the success of the disruption campaign that was targeted against the threat)
- Because the U.S. embassy in Sudan had been closed in response to the threat level there, and because the Sudanese embassy personnel had been moved to Nairobi, perhaps we should have anticipated a higher level of threat to the Nairobi embassy than we did (and have placed it higher on the priority list for improvements in the areas of security and physical protection)
- The signs of a bombing plot did not add up to as clear an indication of target and intent as might be surmised after the fact
- Much of the early warning data was from human informants, whose sincerity and motives can be impossible to ascertain
- Furthermore, warning signs came buried in a great deal of background noise (other signs, indications, warnings, and threats) that greatly complicated threat authentication and response prioritization
- For example, many warnings are received by U.S. facilities annually which turn out to be false alarms: this has the effect of instilling a degree of skepticism and caution in examining evidence of new threats
- In retrospect, it seems as if threat assessment personnel in Washington did not take the warning signs as seriously as did the embassy personnel in Nairobi
- The threat elsewhere seemed greater at the time so that, in the perspective gained by looking at the big picture, Nairobi was not high in priority for major improvements
- We cannot close or move installations at every threat: to do so would place control of U.S. installations in the hands of our adversaries
- In retrospect, the targeted embassies were not as well-prepared as they might have been for truck bomb attacks
- However, resource constraints did not allow instant fixes to all vulnerabilities
- Any physical security improvements would have been subject to countermeasures which could have limited their effectiveness (such as larger bombs to offset against greater standoff): there is no perfect security that can definitively prevent the loss of life and no assurance that the requested changes would have prevented an equivalent level of damage and casualties
- The attacks killed many innocent people
- The attacks caused massive property loss
- The attacks imposed significant future costs (both to rebuild locally and to upgrade security worldwide)
- The attacks generated enormous publicity for bin Laden and raised him to the level of a worldwide icon for frustrated Muslim fundamentalists

The bottom Line

- Even though the embassy attacks make America look weak, the many success stories imply that the U.S. capability to combat terrorism is far from feeble
- If the embassy attacks are viewed as one battle in a long war, the overall war is going well for America (even though some losses have been inevitable along the way)
- Because the small size of the total number of American casualties was not as well publicized as the larger number of total casualties, and because the thwarted bombing plots get less attention than the successful ones, the impact of the attacks has been magnified and has fed a perception that we were somehow negligent in prevention and protection
- If we view terrorism as an ongoing war, in which some non-zero level of casualties is unavoidable, then the full sequence of events on and around August 1998 can be viewed as much as a demonstration of our strengths, as a demonstration of our weaknesses

The U.S. State Department Accountability Review Boards have published two very nice analyses of the African embassy bombings. After examining those documents in detail, we have concluded that it is worthwhile to summarize the results of these studies here. What follows is a much-condensed list of the findings and recommendations for the reader who lacks the time to read the DoS reports in their entirety. In these summaries, we have taken the liberty of including some findings and recommendations from the body of the reports which were not actually labeled as findings or recommendations in the reports themselves, and of neglecting some findings and recommendations which were too narrowly focused to be of interest here. Therefore, these lists are less of a straightforward summary than they are a set of the lessons we have gleaned from a reading of the two reports.

DoS Findings

(The findings of the U.S. State Department, "Report of the Accountability Review Boards on the Embassy Bombings in Nairobi and Dar es Salaam on August 7, 1998", January 1999)

- Physical security at the sites generally met or exceeded levels prescribed by the DoS for posts at medium or low threat levels
- However, these standards were insufficient to protect against large vehicular bombs
- Neither embassy building met the DoS standard for a 100 ft setback/standoff zone: Because both were "existing office buildings", occupied before this standard was adopted, a general exception had been made
- The widespread use of such exceptions reflects the reality of funding levels that are inadequate to replace sub-standard buildings rapidly
- Security systems and procedures at both sites were properly implemented
- In Nairobi, the bomber failed to penetrate the embassy's outer perimeter because local guards refused to open the gates
- In Dar es Salaam, the bomber also failed to penetrate the perimeter, stopped by guards and blocked by an embassy water truck

- Neither site's Emergency Action Plan anticipated a car bomb scenario: Therefore, personnel were not trained to react properly and guards did not have adequate equipment
- In general, the DoS has systematically failed to recognize the threat posed by vehicle bombs and to react accordingly
- There has been a collective failure of the U.S. government for a decade to provide adequate resources to reduce the vulnerability of U.S. diplomatic missions to terrorist attacks
- There was no credible intelligence that provided immediate warning of the bombings
- Some intelligence was discounted because of doubts about the sources
- Some intelligence, while taken seriously, was imprecise, changing, and non-specific
- Actions by intelligence and law enforcement authorities to confront and disrupt suspect persons and groups were believed to have dissipated the threat
- Intelligence has allowed the US to thwart a number of similar terrorist threats

DoS Recommendations

(The recommendations of the U.S. State Department, "Report of the Accountability Review Boards on the Embassy Bombings in Nairobi and Dar es Salaam on August 7, 1998", January 1999)

- Provide a "special alarm signal" to warn of large exterior bombs
- Institute duck-and-cover practice drills
- Provide special equipment to perimeter guards to counter vehicular bombs
- Assume that all posts are potential targets of vehicular bombs
- Improve perimeter stand-off
- Improve counter-surveillance
- Close posts for which adequate enhancements cannot be made
- Provide training and equipment, where needed, to local governments and their police forces
- Place more weight on terrorism in the DoS "Composite Threat List"
- Increase the number of posts with full-time Regional Security Officers
- Augment the number of Marine Security Guard Detachments
- Provide Regional Security Officers with training on terrorism, terrorist methods, explosives, etc.
- Reduce the number of embassies by establishing regional embassies
- Review physical security standards on a priority basis
- When building new chancelleries abroad, collocate all U.S. government agencies in the same compound
- Obtain funding for capital building programs
- Clarify responsibilities for security

- Encourage better coordination among persons with security responsibilities
- Ensure that a single high-ranking officer is accountable for all security matters
- Build public support for increased resources for foreign affairs
- Advise all posts of the threats posed by WMD
- Provide crisis management training for mass casualty and mass destruction incidents
- Establish a revitalized program for on-site crisis management training
- Create and exercise a team and equipment package configured to assist in post-blast crises
- Acquire a modern, reliable, air-refuelable Foreign Emergency Support Team aircraft
- Improve procedures for mobilizing aircraft and aircrews to provide more rapid and effective assistance
- Ensure that all posts have emergency communications, excavation tools, medical supplies, emergency documents, next of kin records, and other necessary equipment at secure off-site locations
- Enhance the flow of intelligence
- Assign a State Department official to the Counter Terrorism Center
- The FBI and DoS should consult on ways to improve information sharing

The 20 August 1998 Cruise Missile Strikes

The disadvantages of retaliation

- Cost a lot of money
- Was questionable morally
- Generated a storm of international and domestic criticism
- Killed only (or nearly only) individuals who were innocent of the embassy bombings
- Killed some individuals who were innocent of any wrongdoing whatsoever (e.g., the Al Shifa night watchman)
- Put at risk the citizens of nations (e.g., Pakistan) that were not intended targets (but were overflown)
- Punished and embarrassed the leaders of a country (Afghanistan) whose poor control of the nation may mean than they should not bear responsibility for the acts of those on their soil
- Was questionable legally (particularly under international law)
- Undermined the rule of law by sidestepping due process
- By mirror imaging aspects of al Qaeda's own attacks (they bombed targets in independent third-world countries without concern for the sensitivities of the nations involved and we bombed targets in independent third-world countries with a similar disregard for the nations involved), we may have only muddied moral distinctions and given away the moral high-ground
- Bolstered the notion that our struggle with bin Laden is a war as opposed to a legal matter: This, in turn, provides moral weight to bin Laden's actions (and minimizes criticism of civilian casualties) by implying that they are acts of war as opposed to cowardly criminal acts
- Was poorly justified to the world (which only strengthened all of the concerns listed above)
- Damaged the Clinton administration (for not consulting more widely within the military and the government and for appearing weak in response to criticisms)
- Was unilateral (no obvious international consent or participation)
- Damaged U.S. relations with our allies (who were not consulted)
- Damaged the U.S. reputation as fair, law-abiding, and compassionate
- Damaged U.S. relations with developing nations, who fear unchecked American power
- May damage U.S. relations with Arab or Muslim nations if it bolsters opinions that the U.S. is anti-Arab or anti-Muslim
- Was of questionable effectiveness in eliminating (killing or wounding) would-be terrorists
- Was of questionable effectiveness in destroying or disrupting al Qaeda's physical infrastructure
- Was ineffective at eliminating or silencing bin Laden himself

- May have diminished the future deterrence of the U.S. armed forces by demonstrating how little we could achieve (e.g., limited physical damage)
- May have diminished the future deterrence of the U.S. armed forces if the resulting condemnation and moral questions undermine our willingness to use force again in the future
- May have diminished the future effectiveness of U.S. forces by depleting expensive ammunition stocks
- May have diminished the future effectiveness of U.S. forces by providing potential adversaries an opportunity to observe the workings of the attack and any vulnerabilities, shortcomings, or signatures of our own forces
- Resulted in some embarrassment (e.g., errant and malfunctioning missiles)
- May have diminished the future deterrence of the U.S. armed forces by bolstering the impression (held by bin Laden and others) that we are unwilling to use any forms of force other than those that pose no risk of U.S. casualties
- May have reduced future military options by driving bin Laden into better-protected bases
- Evidently did little or nothing to deter future acts of terrorism by bin Laden and his followers and supporters (who promptly set up several attack plots)
- In fact, the attack evidently provoked a new round of terrorist bombing plots
- The fact that the attack was so overwhelming, as opposed to a symbolic attack using only a handful of missiles, may escalate the level of future violence by prodding terrorists to retaliate on a larger scale than was characteristic of their earlier attacks
- Provided a bonanza of publicity for bin Laden, who appeared to many as an underdog standing firm in the face of bullying aggression
- Made bin Laden a revered hero to many Muslims who feel oppressed by U.S. dominance in the world
- Bolstered recruitment and support for al Qaeda worldwide

The advantages of retaliation

- Can be justified under domestic law (by the Antiterrorism and Effective Death Penalty act of 1996)
- Followed precedents set by previous presidents (e.g., bombings of Libya and Iraq)
- By calling attention to Afghan support for bin Laden, the attack seems to have significantly tarnished the Taliban's (already bad) international image at a time when they desperately seek international recognition
- By tarnishing their image, the attack complicated the Taliban's future ability to justify their support for Muslim fundamentalist groups
- May have forced the Taliban to constrain bin Laden in ways that truly degrade his capabilities: For example, the well-publicized policy of forcing bin Laden into a form of "internal exile" which the Taliban tried to promulgate shortly after the attack may have had some grain of truth to it, to the detriment of bin Laden
- May ultimately play a role in forcing the Taliban to surrender or expel bin Laden

[redacted]

- Because covert cooperation with the U.S. may be a more attractive option than unchecked U.S. military action on or over a nations' sovereign territory, the attack may have played a role in prodding some nations (e.g., Pakistan) into greater future cooperation in fighting terrorism
- Further enhanced the already-considerable amount of attention to terrorism as a serious global problem
- Brought attention to the need for greater worldwide cooperation in combating terrorism
- Demonstrated U.S. strength
- Demonstrated the global reach of U.S. military power (i.e., that there is no sanctuary)
- Demonstrated U.S. resolve
- Demonstrated that the U.S. considers terrorism a matter of national security (as opposed to a mere criminal matter)
- Demonstrated world leadership
- Punished a party guilty of international crimes
- May prove to be the only effective form of punishment (if bin Laden cannot be apprehended)
- May prove to be the most effective form of punishment (if bin Laden can be apprehended but cannot be convicted)
- May have been the most cost-effective reaction (e.g., cheaper than moving or hardening many embassies)
- May have been the lowest risk reaction (if apprehending bin Laden is likely to result in U.S. casualties)
- Appeased domestic calls for action against international criminals
- Provides strong incentives for nations to cooperate in fighting terrorism if for no other reason than to check unilateral moves by the U.S.
- May ultimately play a role in deterring future terrorism (even among groups yet unknown)
- May ultimately play a role in deterring future state sponsorship of terrorist groups
- Probably enhanced intelligence collection by forcing the adversary into movements, rebuilding activities, and stepped-up communications while under intense scrutiny
- May have enhanced future military options by forcing bin Laden to operate differently (e.g., if he now moves more often)
- May have diminished the future capabilities of the targeted group(s) by forcing them to operate differently
- May have diminished the future capabilities of the targeted group(s) by forcing them to spend more (money and manpower) on defense and hardening
- May force some supporters to distance themselves from bin Laden in the future because he has become too controversial

[redacted]

WMD Threat Assessment

Level of Interest

(Covering interest in any and all WMD agents and weapons by bin Laden, al Qaeda, and affiliated groups)

- They very clearly want WMD agents or weapons
- This interest is not new (dating back at least to 1993)
- They explicitly seek to use WMD against U.S. installations
- Bin Laden has made numerous statements confirming his interest in WMD
- Bin Laden has made numerous statements justifying his interest in WMD
- Bin Laden has made numerous statements justifying the deaths of innocents and the use of WMD
- It seems clear that the goal is to employ WMD, as opposed only to possessing them for status or blackmail
- They are interested in all three types of WMD (chemicals, biological agents, and nuclear devices) as opposed to any one type or any one agent
- This broad interest implies a desire-centered approach (they started with a desire for a WMD capability and are looking for any way to get it) as opposed to a capability-centered approach (where they would have started with some capability or some expert know-how and be seeking to utilize what they have)
- Bin Laden himself has been directly involved in the quest, as have several of his associates
- They have searched worldwide, including Sudan, former Soviet countries, and the former Warsaw Pact
- They have attempted to acquire assistance from one or more sponsor nations
- They have apparently had financial and personal relationships with companies capable of producing chemical agents
- They may have already tested, or participated in tests, of chemical agents and/or dispersal devices
- They have apparently acquired one or more biological agents (of unknown quantity and virulence) from an "East Asian" commercial source
- They have apparently attempted to purchase one or more Russia nuclear warheads on the black market
- Although there have been reports of success in purchasing Russian nuclear warheads, this seems highly unlikely for a number of compelling reasons
- They have apparently sought fissile material for use in the development of a nuclear device
- They have apparently sought nuclear weapons "components"

The good news

- They have apparently encountered scam artists attempting to take advantage of their interest in nuclear explosives
- Because they have apparently encountered scam artists who were merely attempting to take advantage of them, it would seem that they lack even a rudimentary knowledge of nuclear explosive theory (which would have prevented them from getting involved in obvious scams)
- From what is known about the membership of al Qaeda and affiliated groups, it would seem that they appeal to, and recruit among, disaffected individuals lacking in advanced technical skills or education: For example, they draw recruits from religious schools

  [In contrast, the Aum Shinrikyo cult emphasized recruitment of scientific personnel and of graduate students from universities]
- From what is known about the training of al Qaeda and affiliated groups, it would seem that they emphasize military skills and training as opposed to providing any form of advanced technical training
- From what is known about the tools and tactics employed by al Qaeda and affiliated groups in previous attacks, it would seem that they lack a high degree of technical sophistication and rely primarily upon brute force to achieve their objectives
- Based upon these observations, it seems unlikely that they currently posses the necessary skills and expertise to manufacture high-end chemical or biological agents
- In addition, the successful weaponization and employment issues associated with many chemical and biological agents (storage, transport, packaging, virulence, morbidity, mortality, shelf-life, particle size, dissemination, etc.) are likely to require technical skills beyond their current capabilities
- Based upon these observations, it seems highly unlikely that they currently posses the necessary skills and expertise to design and manufacture nuclear explosive devices (NEDs) of any kind
- Based upon these observations, it seems highly unlikely that they currently posses the necessary skills and expertise to bypass the arming and firing, safety, and use control features of a modern nuclear weapon
- Given the risks, it seems unlikely that any state sponsor of terrorism will wish to provide WMD agents or weapons to these organizations unless their own survival is at risk

The bad news

- They have the capability to search far and wide
- They have sufficient resources to take advantage of any useful purchases that are available
- Because low-end chemical and biological agents can be very simple to manufacture (e.g., Cholera), it is possible that such agents could eventually be within the reach of these groups

- Because the motives of individual humans are so difficult to predict, the ultimate "wild card" in any assessment is the possibility that the leader of a sponsor state, or a disgruntled Muslim insider in any nation's military or industrial base, could turn over the know-how or materials that would provide al Qaeda with a WMD capability

Nuclear weapons

Nuclear weapons purchase

While purchases of various chemical and biological supplies or agents are not unrealistic (especially since there are so many legitimate industrial uses for various agents and precursors), the prospect of an outright purchase of a nuclear explosive device seems outlandish for several reasons. For one thing, no nuclear nation has disintegrated to the point where nuclear weapons are actually for sale or accessible for easy theft (although this could change if, for example, Russia were to split into warring states). In addition, there are several nations known to have a strong interest in acquiring nuclear weapons whose resources and contacts would make it seem far more likely that they would purchase any available device before a terrorist or individual could do so

State Sponsors

Perhaps the greatest threat posed by bin Laden's interest in WMD, is the role which he could play in the hands of a state sponsor. For example, he could serve as an acquisition agent on behalf of a third-world country, paid and assisted by that nation (such as Iraq). Such an arrangement could serve to further the nuclear ambitions of both bin Laden and the sponsor state. It is also conceivable that he could serve as a clandestine employment agent on behalf of a sponsor state (such as Iraq, were Iraq to construct a nuclear device), although it seems highly unlikely that any nation would want to trust him with such a responsibility rather than using their own agents.

Bin Laden and the Islamic bomb

Given that Pakistan already has a nuclear capability, is a hotbed of Islamic fundamentalism, and is home to many supporters of bin Laden, the future stability of Pakistan should be of particular concern. If a fundamentalist party were to seize power there (or seize nuclear assets), bin Laden's principle role might be to advocate and instigate nuclear use in support of any one of the several Islamic causes which he and the Islamic hard-liners support (such as use to pressure America out of Saudi Arabia, to attack America or Israel, to "liberate" Kashmir, or to defeat the Russian forces which are "oppressing" the Muslim peoples of the Caucasus). In fact, if the current post-coup leadership of Pakistan acts against the interests of the Islamic hard-liners, bin Laden and his supporters may carry their terrorist war into Pakistan itself.

The future

- Current terrorist interest in WMD agents and weapons suggests a trend toward new terrorist capabilities in the future
- However, the timing of any evolution towards new methods and capabilities is highly uncertain

- Furthermore, the current effectiveness and availability of explosive devices make it likely that the vehicle bomb will remain a dominant tool for some time yet
- In addition, the apparent inability of al Qaeda to acquire and employ WMD agents or weapons (even after years of trying and with significant resources at their disposal), suggests that the threat of WMD terrorism may be smaller at the present time than we currently seem to imagine

Risk Assessment

In the section above, we have presented a number of findings and observations regarding bin Laden's quest for various weapons of mass destruction. Unfortunately, this is one area where the reliance upon open sources alone may be weak. Unlike the embassy bombings and many other events, where we have benefited from extensive reporting, the available evidence regarding the quest for WMD is quite limited, and primarily in the form of carefully-worded hints and allegations quoted from intelligence officials. (The only exception to this is in establishing a motive, where there is extensive evidence in the form of bin Laden's own numerous comments on the subject.) Therefore, it behooves us to re-state that no classified reporting has been accessed for the purposes of this report.

Nonetheless, based upon our findings above, and upon our knowledge of the technical challenges associated with WMD design, manufacture, and employment, we will try to address the probability that al Qaeda (and/or its affiliates) could succeed in employing such agents or weapons in the near future. We have chosen seven different measures by which to estimate that probability, each of which is actually a complex combination of factors:

1. Motivation: The probability that the adversary would be motivated to acquire and use a given type of agent or weapon

   This measure is fairly self-explanatory. However, we must be careful to point out that what an adversary desires and what he/she will actually do are two different things. For example, an individual who is highly motivated to commit murder may very well be deterred by the risk of apprehension and incarceration. Therefore, we must be careful not to assume that what an adversary wants to do is what he/she actually will do.

2. Funding: The probability of sufficient funding

   One factor in the overall probability of success would be the availability of funding in quantities sufficient to support the full range of activities associated with success: travel costs, equipment costs, fabrication costs, storage costs, employment costs, etc.

3. Information: The probability of access to necessary know-how

   Another factor in the overall probability of success is the availability of information that is required in order to acquire or manufacture, store, and employ the agent of interest. This would include such things as knowledge of chemical "recipes", familiarity with the processing steps, experience with equipment operation, an insiders "know-how" of the processing dangers, etc.

4. Equipment : The probability of access to necessary equipment & supplies

   Another factor in the overall probability of success is the availability of the equipment which would be required to manufacture, store, handle, and disseminate an agent.

5. Fabrication: The probability of success in fabrication & storage (or the availability of the agent or weapon, if purchase or theft is the route or interest)

   Another factor in the overall probability of success is the ability of the adversary to successfully fabricate and store the agent of interest. Even with all the money required, all of the necessary equipment, and a step-by-step set of instructions, the inexperienced adversary may well fail to store the agent in a manner that preserves the agent effectively and is safe to those who must handle it. This is one example where the difference between a novice and an experienced expert could come into play.

   By referring to storage here explicitly, we are making the point that there is much more to using dangerous agents than just to "cook" them up. Storage, handling, and transportation can all pose significant challenges of their own. These challenges include not only the obvious dangers, but issues of shelf-life and stability as well. The term "storage" here is meant as an abbreviated reference to this full set of post-fabrication issues.

   If the acquisition route of interest is to purchase or steal an agent or weapon which has already been fabricated by someone else, then this value will reflect the probability that such an agent or weapon is available and accessible for purchase or theft.

6. Stealth: The probability of success in avoiding detection

   Another factor in the overall probability of success is the probability of detection. The greater the number of unusual supplies and equipment required, the greater the probability of detection. Similarly, the more unusual the precursors required, the greater the probability of detection. Here we turn this probability around, and estimate the probability of success in <u>avoiding</u> detection (as opposed to the probability of detection).

7. Employment : The probability of successful employment

   Another factor in the overall probability of success is the probability of successful and effective employment. For some agents, this is not much of an issue. Sarin, for example, could be effective if just poured onto a crowded floor (especially on a hot day). For other agents, however, particle size and dispersion can be important factors. For a purchased nuclear weapon, the issue would be whether or not the adversary could bypass the safety and use control features of the weapon.

Using the seven measures laid out above (into which many complex issues are condensed), we now wish to make estimates of the probability that an adversary associated with bin Laden or his group could succeed in acquiring and using various agents or weapons. But first, we must identify the agents and weapons that we think he might seek. Unfortunately, the list of potential chemical and biological agents alone is enormous, running into the hundreds or thousands. It is well outside the scope o this report to attempt to list and classify all such agents. Instead, we have chosen to classify all agents and weapons which are referred to as weapons of mass destruction into one of seven distinct categories:

1. Low-end chemical agents

   This term will be used to refer to those chemical agents which are the simplest to acquire or manufacture. Blister agents such as mustard, for example, could be easily mixed up by any biker gang with the skills to manufacture methamphetamines. Phosgene might be considered another low-end agent because it is widely used for industrial purposes and is, therefore, very widely available.

2. High-end chemical agents

   This term will be used to refer to those chemical agents which are more difficult to acquire or manufacture. Some of the nerve agents, for example, require more than just "bucket chemistry" and could seriously challenge a non-chemist.

3. Low-end biological agents

   This term will be used to refer to those biological agents which are the simplest to acquire or manufacture. An example here would be a simple infectious disease such as Cholera, which can be acquired simply in the form of the body fluids of an infected patient (who must be kept hydrated to prevent death). As one expert has put it, you "put Gatorade in one end and agent comes out the other end".

4. High-end biological agents

   This term will be used to refer to those biological agents which are more difficult to acquire or manufacture. A wide range of issues comes into play here such as access to seed stock, growth, extraction and purification, virulence, effective particle size, etc.

5. A radiological dispersion device (RDD)

   This term will be used to refer to any device involving the use of explosives for the primary purpose of scattering radiological contamination. An example of such a device would be a stolen radio-nuclide strapped to a bomb. Alternatively, the RDD could be "assembled" at the time of use by bringing a truck bomb up against a nuclear waste container or a nuclear-laden vehicle.

6. A pre-built nuclear explosive device (NED) which must be purchased or stolen

   This term will be used to refer to an existing nuclear explosive device, which has been designed and manufactured by a nation state and then purchased or stolen by the sub-sate adversary. Such a device would most likely be a militarized weapon, although the possibility also exists of buying or stealing a test device. (The theft or purchase of a test device would, of course, be far more dangerous because of the fact that such devices lack the safety and security systems of a modern warhead.)

7. A manufactured nuclear explosive device (NED)

   This term will be used to refer to a nuclear explosive device (NED) which has been designed and manufactured by the adversary.

Clearly, the distinctions between these categories is a blurry one. Is sarin, for example, a low-end chemical agent or a high-end chemical agent? We could argue the case either way. Certainly to manufacture pure sarin, in the exact chemical form used in the past by the U.S. military, would be far more of a challenge than to manufacture a sarin-like chemical in an unpurified form (which may be every bit as useful as the "real thing"). Rather than get bogged down in nit-picking over such distinctions, we have simply chosen examples which we feel illustrate well the potential challenges (or lack thereof) for each category. Categorizing the many agents and the difficulties associated with their acquisition, manufacture, storage, handling, and employment is a large task that lies outside the scope of this report, and which we have addressed in other studies.

The following pages contain tables in which the author has provided an expert guess at the probability of success for each of the seven measures and for each of the seven agent/weapon categories. The difficulty with such tables is that they contain a fair number of estimates and it is difficult to get the big picture and to easily compare one agent type to another. To assist in this, the pages immediately following the tables contain data plots, in which the various estimates are grouped together in a visual form and with which comparisons between different categories of agents or weapons are made easy.

Several final cautions are in order for the reader who examines these tables and plots:

1. These represent the estimates of only a single individual. Estimate may vary (even widely so) among other experts.

2. All quantities are estimates. None of the variables of interest can actually be measured (with the possible exception of interest itself, where we have quotes and experience to go by in establishing a direct interest).

3. All probabilities are probabilities that WMD use could happen, not the probability that it actually will happen. A simple example will illustrate the difference: The probability that I could be murdered by my spouse is very high (because the weaponry and opportunities are readily available on a daily basis). However, the probability that I will be murdered by my spouse is low (or so we would surmise, given the low incidence of spousal murders relative to the population as a whole). Another way of illustrating the difference is to note that it is entirely possible that an adversary might acquire a WMD capability that he/she would not use (at least not immediately). For example, the adversary may wish to hoard a precious resource for later use, may fear retaliation, may be restrained by a sponsor, may be restrained by supporters, etc. Therefore, the probability that they could acquire and employ such agents or weapons is not the same as the probability that they actually will.

One final point is very important. There is a bias which can enter into any risk assessment and skew the results. This bias can result from the fact that the probability of a given occurrence is the product of the probabilities of success for each sub-step in the process. For example, the probability that A and B will occur is the probability that A will occur, multiplied by the probability that B will occur:

$$P(A \text{ and } B) = P(A) \times P(B).$$

Now let us think about the probability of manufacturing and employing a chemical agent. We could express this probability as a product of two numbers:

P(of manufacture and employment) = P(of successful manufacture) x P(of successful employment).

Alternatively, we could break down the number of sub-steps further:

P(of manufacture and employment) = P(of success obtaining a good recipe) x P(of success obtaining precursors) x P(of success in following the recipe) x P(of successful storage and handling) x P(of escaping detection) x P(of obtaining good dispersion on employment)

Now, if all of these probabilities are measurable quantities, then either formula should be correct. However, human capabilities and fallabilities cannot be measured, they can only be estimated. When based upon imprecise estimates, even when all estimates come from the same expert, the two formulas are likely to give different answers. In fact, this problem is exacerbated by a tendency to avoid setting any probabilities equal to one. To do so would imply that the expert is certain, and few experts would allow themselves to be pinned down into stating that something is absolutely certain (probability one). Instead, any events that are highly likely would typically be assigned a probability that is high, but is less than one (e.g., 0.9). Given this bias away from certainty, then as the number of sub-steps considered goes up, the overall probability will go down. For example, the result for two very probable sub-steps might be:

$$P = 0.9 \times 0.9 = 0.81$$

But, if the same probability is broken down into eight very probable sub-steps, we might get:

$$P = 0.9 \times 0.9 \times 0.9 \times 0.9 \times 0.9 \times 0.9 \times 0.9 \times 0.9 = 0.43$$

For this reason, we have chosen to re-normalize our results at the end of the table. Instead of simply tabulating the products of the various probabilities, we have taken this product for each agent or weapon and divided it by the product which we obtained for the radiological dispersion device (RDD). In other words, it is the opinion of the author that the RDD is the most probable route for successful attacks involving weapons of mass destruction. Therefore we have re-normalized in a manner which makes this probability one, and the probability of successful acquisition and employment for any other agent or weapon is expressed relative to this. The first of the various charts displays these relative probabilities in bar-chart form.

While the bar chart provides the most succinct, and to-the-point illustration of the results, other ways of displaying the data can also be instructive. For example, it might be useful to have an easy visual means to compare the probabilities of the various sub-steps that are called out in the tables. To help in this regard, we have also included a set of radial plots in which the estimated probabilities of success for each of the various sub-steps (as laid out in the tables) are displayed. Looking at the plots, one can see that the larger the area encompassed by the plot, the greater the threat (i.e., the greater the overall estimated probability of success). Although these radial plots help to identify the different obstacles facing the adversary for the various agents and weapons, and make it easier to compare the estimates from one agent type to another, we must caution the reader that these radial plots are illustrative only. In other words, the areas covered by the various plots are not proportional to the overall probabilities of success (which would be the products of the probabilities of success for the various sub-steps).

		Probability that adversary would be motivated to go this route		Probability of sufficient funding	
CAPABILITY OF INTEREST	**EXAMPLE**	**MOTIVATION**	**RATIONALE**	**FUNDING**	**RATIONALE**
Low-End Chemical Agent Manufacture	Mustard	1.00	All of these are widely mentioned in open literature and well known Furthermore, we have seen evidence of interest by bin Laden	1.0	Bin Laden has a lot of money at his disposal
High-End Chemical Agent Manufacture	Tabun	1.00		1.0	
Low-End Bio Agent Manufacture	Cholera	1.00		1.0	
High-End Bio Agent Manufacture	Anthrax	1.00		1.0	
Chem/Bio Purchase or Theft	Any	1.00	Easiest route of all: Already tried by bin Laden's associates	1.0	
Radiological Dispersion	Truck bomb next to waste shipment	0.60	Less appealing than fast-killers	1.0	
NED Purchase or Theft	Russian device	0.95	Collateral damage and retaliation concerns	0.9	High acquisition cost and potential bidding competition from rogue states
NED Manufacture	Homemade gun-assembled device	0.80	Less appealing because it is obviously much more difficult than purchase	0.2	Many costs: nuclear material, components, experts, etc.

[redacted]

		Probability of access to necessary know-how		**Probability of access to necessary equipment & supplies**	
CAPABILITY OF INTEREST	**EXAMPLE**	**INFORMATION**	**RATIONALE**	**EQUIPMENT**	**RATIONALE**
Low-End Chemical Agent Manufacture	Mustard	0.80	Only requires elemetary chemistry or an explicit recipe	0.90	Many industrial chemicals are widely available
High-End Chemical Agent Manufacture	Tabun	0.60	Requires more chemistry	0.60	Harder
Low-End Bio Agent Manufacture	Cholera	0.60	Requires some biology	1.00	Only need a sick patient
High-End Bio Agent Manufacture	Anthrax	0.30	Requires complex biology	0.60	Harder
Chem/Bio Purchase or Theft	Any	0.80	Only requires the identification of a reliable seller	1.00	None necessary for purchase or theft
Radiological Dispersion	Truck bomb next to waste shipment	0.90	Only requires knowledge of a nuclear material location	1.00	Only need a truck bomb (to place beside existing nuclear material)
NED Purchase or Theft	Russian device	0.50	Requires enough to separate reliable sellers from scam artists	1.00	None necessary for purchase or theft
NED Manufacture	Homemade gun-assembled device	0.05	Requires extremely well-trained scientists	0.05	Weapons grade material in sufficient quantities is not often for sale

[redacted]

		Probability of success in fabrication & handling (for manufacture) OR availability (for purchase/theft)		Probability of success avoiding detection	
CAPABILITY OF INTEREST	**EXAMPLE**	**FABRICATION OR AVAILABILITY**	**RATIONALE**	**STEALTH**	**RATIONALE**
Low-End Chemical Agent Manufacture	Mustard	0.80	Relatively easy	0.80	Easy to make with few external signatures
High-End Chemical Agent Manufacture	Tabun	0.35	Relatively hard for non-scientists	0.50	May need material that is less commonly available
Low-End Bio Agent Manufacture	Cholera	0.80	Relatively easy	0.80	Easy to make with few external signatures
High-End Bio Agent Manufacture	Anthrax	0.25	Relatively hard for non-scientists	0.50	May need material that is less commonly available
Chem/Bio Purchase or Theft	Any	0.80	Requires front company charades	0.70	Many sources available worldwide but they are subject to surveillance (and informants)
Radiological Dispersion	Truck bomb next to waste shipment	1.00	Very easy	1.00	High if nuclear material is not acquired in advance (e.g., truck bomb at nuclear facility)
NED Purchase or Theft	Russian device	0.05	Highly unlikely to become available	0.30	Nuclear weapons are well protected and well watched
NED Manufacture	Homemade gun-assembled device	0.01	Extremely difficult	0.01	An extrememly extensive program would be required

[redacted]

		Probability of successful and effective employment			
CAPABILITY OF INTEREST	EXAMPLE	EMPLOYMENT	RATIONALE	PROBABILITY PRODUCT	PROBABILITY PRODUCT (normalized)
Low-End Chemical Agent Manufacture	Mustard	0.9	Even an Aum Tokyo-type attack could be significant	0.415	0.853
High-End Chemical Agent Manufacture	Tabun	0.9	Even an Aum Tokyo-type attack could be significant	0.057	0.117
Low-End Bio Agent Manufacture	Cholera	0.6	Potential problems with particle size, morbidity rate, mortality rate,	0.230	0.474
High-End Bio Agent Manufacture	Anthrax	0.3	More problems with particle size, morbidity rate, mortality rate,	0.007	0.014
Chem/Bio Purchase or Theft	Any	0.9	Even an Aum Tokyo-type attack could be significant	0.403	0.830
Radiological Dispersion	Truck bomb next to waste shipment	0.9	As easy as any truck bombing: only obstacle is obtaining close	0.486	1.000
NED Purchase or Theft	Russian device	0.2	Must bypass safety and use control features; also timing issues	0.001	0.003
NED Manufacture	Homemade gun-assembled device	1.0	If it can be built (the hard part), then detonation is the easy	0.000	0.000

[redacted]

[redacted]

Probability Products (normalized)

Overall relative probability for beginning-to-end success (including acquisition and employment)

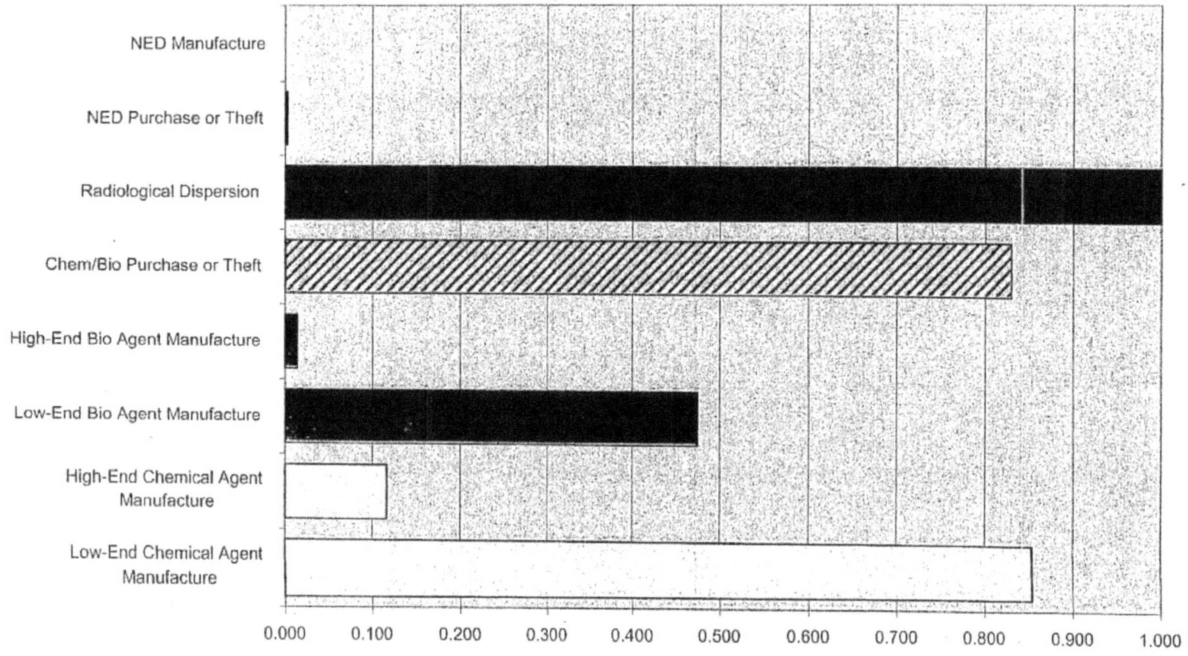

[redacted]

WMD Threat Chart

(more area covered = more threat)

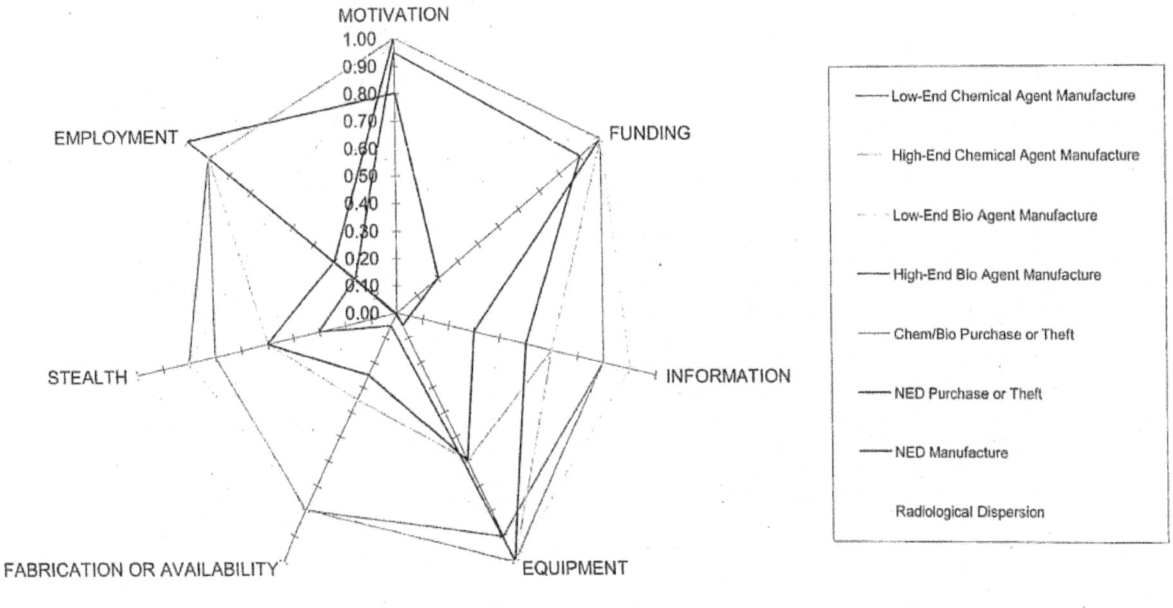

[redacted]

WMD Threat Chart

(more area covered = more threat)

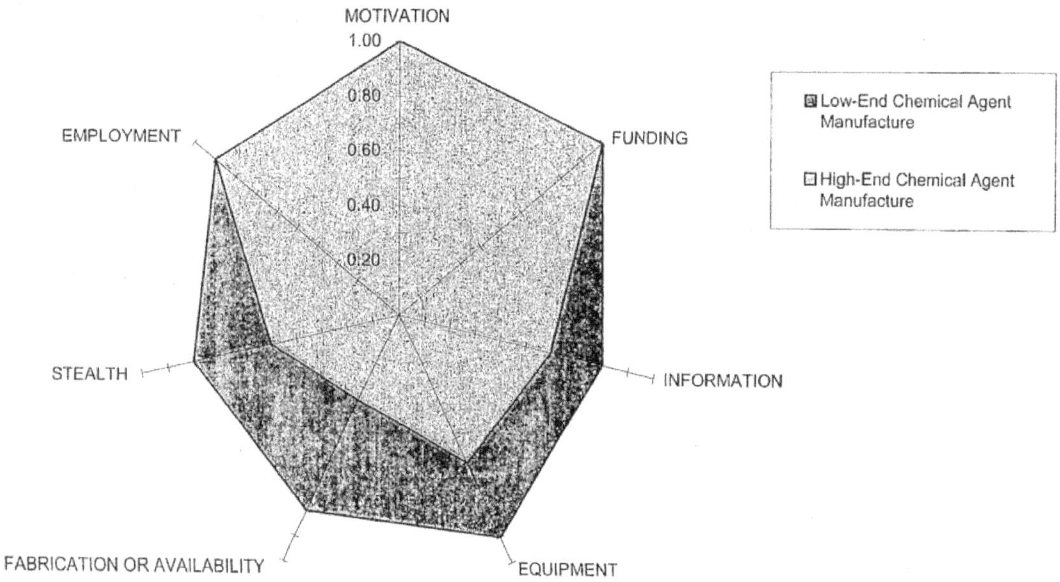

[redacted]

[redacted]

WMD Threat Chart

(more area covered = more threat)

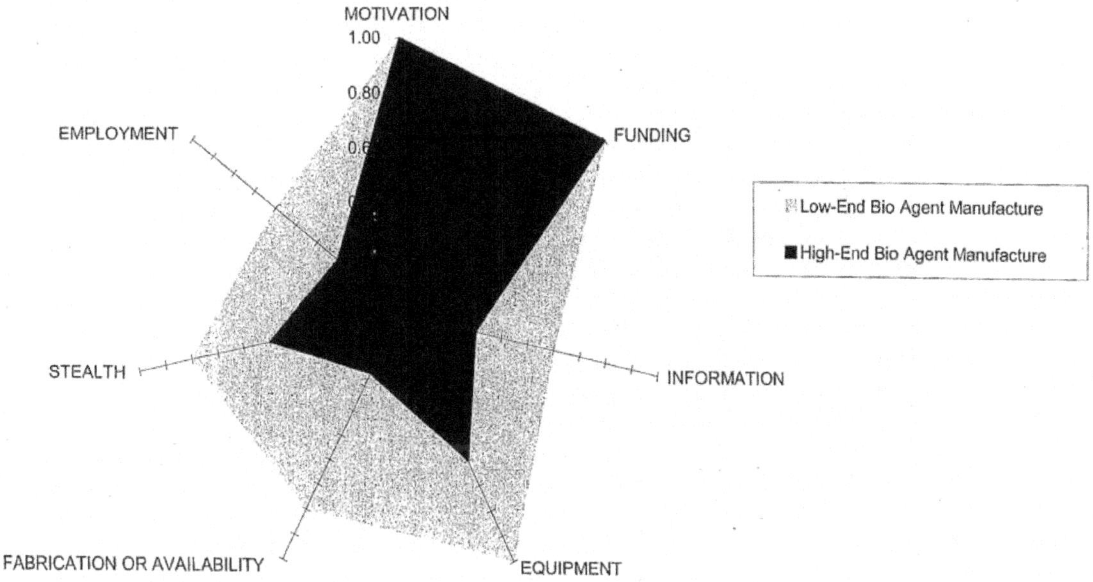

[redacted]

WMD Threat Chart

(more area covered = more threat)

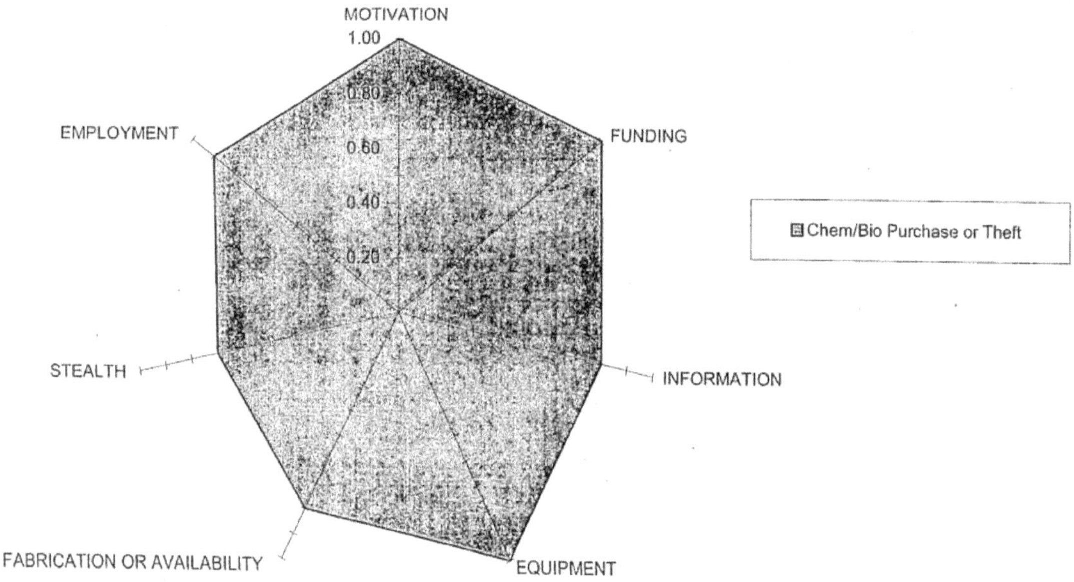

[redacted]

WMD Threat Chart

(more area covered = more threat)

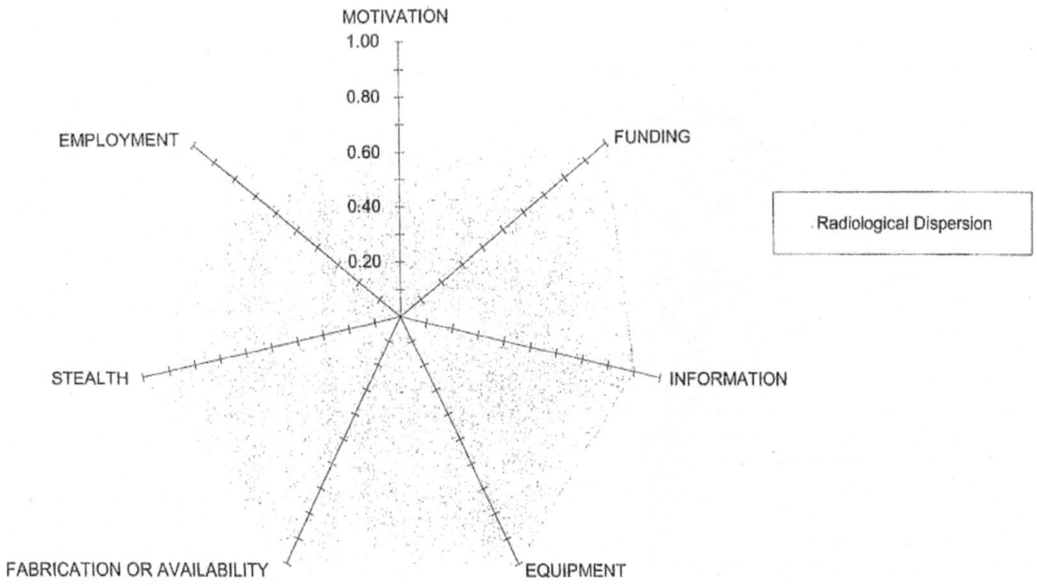

[redacted]

[redacted]

WMD Threat Chart

(more area covered = more threat)

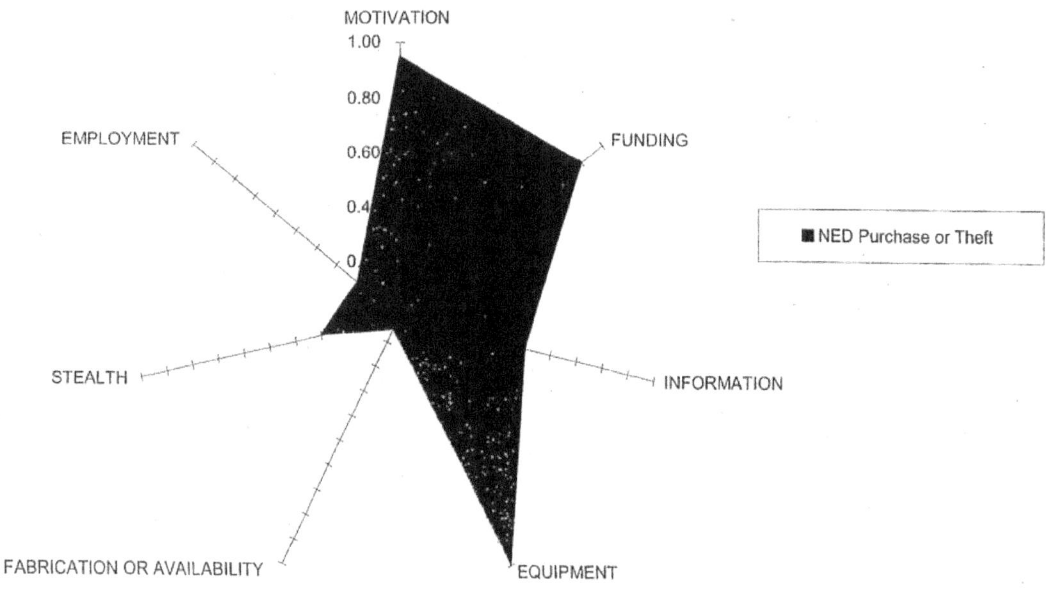

[redacted]

[redacted]

WMD Threat Chart
(more area covered = more threat)

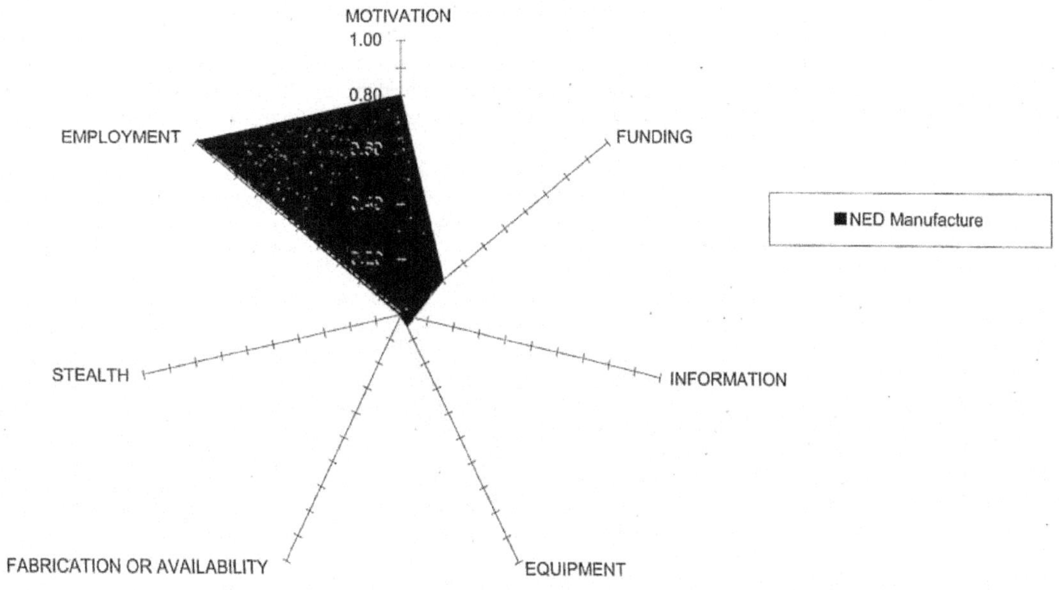

[redacted]

Conclusions

In the tables above, one expert has attempted to quantify the relative difficulties associated with the acquisition and employment of various classes of WMD agents and weapons in an attempt to predict the relative likelihood of future use by Osama bin and his associates. However, such attempts at prediction are fraught with many difficulties. One of the greatest difficulties we face as we attempt to assess the risk of future chem/bio terrorism, is simply the fact that there is so little specificity as to what is meant by the very term "chem/bio". At one end of the spectrum there are chemical and biological agents that are so incredibly difficult to manufacture, and to weaponize, that they have thwarted even the all-out efforts of the military-industrial complexes of the largest nations. No one would be willing to suggest that a terrorist will solve the problems that have stumped nations.

If we consider these "high-end" agents, therefore, we would be tempted to conclude that the terrorist's probability of success must be vanishingly small. Consider, for example, the following statement from a recent report titled "COMBATTING TERRORISM: Observations on the Threat of Chemical and Biological Terrorism" (Unites States General Accounting Office, 20 October 1999, page 1):

> "in most cases terrorists would have to overcome significant technical and operational challenges to successfully make and release chemical or biological agents of sufficient quality and quantity to kill or injure large numbers of people without substantial assistance from a state sponsor".

However, there are two problems with statements such as these:

1. What is one to conclude from it? For example, what does "most cases" mean? Does it mean that 99% of all attempts will fail (that would be comforting) or that 51% of all attempts will fail (not so comforting)? Are the few cases where they can succeed sufficient to warrant alarm? (What about a 5% chance of killing hundreds? Or a 2% chance of killing thousands?) Are incidents with small numbers of casualties of no concern? How many casualties does it take for us to get concerned? (Ten? Fifty? A thousand? What if these agents were used to kill only a few people, such as an aircraft's flight crew, with catastrophic secondary consequences?) Are we willing to allow a large number of incidents with a few casualties each? (Is one incident a month acceptable if each incident only kills ten?)

2. It discounts the fact that the adversary may not even need to manufacture the agent in the first place. Instead, such agents might be stolen from military stocks, sold by disgruntled insiders, or supplied by a state sponsor. For example, there is compelling evidence to suggest that state sponsorship can and will play a role in future terrorism and, specifically, that we cannot rule out that the support provided might include assistance in acquiring and employing WMD agents or weapons. Although much of this evidence

is highly classified, enough of it exists in the open to allow us to question the relevance of any assessment that downplays the possibility.

At the other end of the spectrum, there are several reasons to believe that chem/bio agents might not be so hard to obtain after all:

1. Some agents are very simple to manufacture. For example, some blistering agents can be mixed up in buckets and boiled to effect. In addition, some infectious disease agents can simply be obtained in the form of bodily fluids from infected patients. One expert, *with first-hand experience using the agent*, has said of cholera that all one needs for its manufacture is a sick patient: "you put Gatorade in one end and agent comes out the other end". Furthermore, such agents can be spread using techniques like those employed by the Rajneesh cult in Oregon. Their experiments with the body fluids of sick patients, using several different agents, were quite frightening and remain largely unknown.

2. Some agents could be acquired directly, without a need to manufacture them "from scratch". For example, commercial chemicals such as phosgene (carbonyl chloride or CG) could be purchased through front companies, stolen, or dispersed in place by parking a truck bomb next to a chemical tanker truck, or a chemical factory, in an attempt to create a Bhopal-like disaster. For reference, note that millions of tons of phosgene alone are manufactured every year for legitimate use in the production of foamed plastics, insecticides, dyes, etc.

If we consider these "low-end" agents and options, then we would be tempted to conclude that the probability of success must be very high. Yet we tend to forget that the adversary may not be aware of how easy these options are. The adversary may not even have heard of these agents and will waste their time chasing after some other agent that they have heard of, however more difficult that may be. We tend to take for granted what we know (how easy these options are and the fact that they would really work), yet the fact that we are vulnerable in these areas does not necessarily equate to the existence of a legitimate threat.

The difficulty with expert opinions

Another complicating factor in any assessment is that much of our expertise in these areas comes from those individuals who were associated with our former military programs. These individuals have vivid knowledge of the many obstacles involved and, therefore, have a natural tendency to scoff at the suggestion that a few rag-tag terrorists could do in a garage what they had struggled so hard to do with the resources of the entire nation behind them. Yet the opinions of these experts must always be taken in context. We must never forget that they had set out to do far more than the terrorist needs to do. For our national chem/bio programs we sought many characteristics in our agents which the terrorist may not seek in his/hers. These included factors such as high purity, low signature (e.g., low odor), batch-to-batch consistency, low manufacturing costs, very long storage life, non-corrosive compatibility with storage containers and weapons cases, extreme levels of persistence or volatility (depending on the application), uniform and optimal particle size, optimal dispersion characteristics, near-perfect safety in all phases of handling and employment, high morbidity, high mortality, etc.

In contrast to this, the adversary need not perfect the agent, nor the delivery system. In fact, some very simple modes of employment would pose significant challenges. A bag of impure sarin (like the agent employed by the Aum Shinrikyo cult on the Tokyo subway system) that was opened on an aircraft (instead of in a subway) could have catastrophic secondary consequences (the crash of the aircraft). Furthermore, the agent might easily bypass our enormous investment in metal and explosives detection systems (which have greatly improved aviation safety) and re-open the skies to a rash of new terrorist attacks.

The bottom line

The discussion of chem/bio terrorism has been muddied by extensive media attention. When the experts are consulted, we can all agree that many chemical and biological agents are more difficult to manufacture and to employ than the media articles might imply. In fact, much more difficult. However, by way of an analogy, it is equally true that a nuclear explosive device would be difficult to manufacture. In fact, extremely difficult. Yet low-end explosive devices, in the form of fertilizer bombs, pose a very real and significant threat to public safety. Therefore, we can see that the validity of any statements about the difficulty of attaining the perfect weapon should not preclude us from having a very real set of concerns, because the low-end capabilities pose far fewer challenges to the adversary and can still provide attractive options for that adversary.

In the discussion above, we have mentioned the availability of commercial chemicals (such as phosgene). As an analogy, we might argue that these commercial chemicals are to chem/bio terrorism what the truck bomb (using commercial fertilizers and fuels) is to explosive threats. Certainly the truck-delivered fertilizer bomb is at the very low end of the spectrum of explosive threats when compared to high-end nuclear explosives. And we would all agree that the high-end explosive threats (nuclear explosives) would, "in most cases", pose "significant technical and operational challenges" (quotes from the GAO report). Yet the explosive threat, in the form of low-end devices (fertilizer bombs) is very real, very threatening, and the focus of much attention. ***Likewise, the low-end chemical and biological threat is very real, is very threatening, and should be the focus of much attention even if many of the high-end agents are unattainable in practice.***

Even the low-end chemical and biological agents pose some significant challenges to any inexperienced adversary. Yet this fact is insufficient alone to argue that the threat is low. Continuing the analogy started above, note that even the low-end fertilizer bomb would pose some significant challenges to a novice. For example, the would-be truck bomber must somehow acquire knowledge of what types of fertilizers and fuels will work, fuel-to-fertilizer ratios, how to effectively mix the ingredients (and keep them mixed during storage and delivery), how to use boosters to detonate low explosives, how to acquire detonators, how to install and wire detonators, etc. It is likely that far fewer than 0.01% of individuals interviewed at random would have the know-how to succeed. Unfortunately, the existence of these difficulties does not mean that the truck-bomb threat is low.

Given the indisputable fact that terrorists have a known desire to acquire and use chem/bio agents, the access to low-end agents (such as phosgene or easy-to-make chemicals), coupled with the possibility of thefts of hard-to-make agents or of state-supplied agents, should be sufficient cause for concern, just as the low-end capabilities in the field of explosive threats (fertilizer bombs), coupled with the reality of explosives that are stolen and supplied by state sponsors, are a concern as well. To what extent we expand our response beyond the low-end agents, in an attempt to thwart the high-end threats as well as the low-end threats, should be the only subject still open for debate at this late date.

The future

One could argue that we are positioned today with respect to chem/bio terrorism where we were positioned in 1970 with respect to truck bombs: Only a select few could make an effective chem/bio attack work today. However, the idea appeals to many terrorists, the idea and the know-how are beginning to spread, and we are likely to see increasing numbers of attempted use in the future. The main difference in the analogy with the truck-bomb, is that this evolution from desire to capability is likely to take longer for chem/bio terrorism than it took for truck bombings, and we may be able to delay it even further by acting now (prevention, surveillance, vulnerability reductions, etc.) rather than waiting for the problem to become significant (as we did with the truck-bomb threat).

Response Options

There exists a wide range of options with which America can enhance its preparedness for future terrorism by bin Laden and others. The following pages contain a broad list of these options. Ideally, we should be working continuously to implement, or to be prepared to implement, any and all of the options listed.

Intelligence and law enforcement options

Intelligence and law enforcement operations

- Surveillance of terrorist group members, operatives, supporters, and all known and affiliated facilities such as front companies, banks and other financial institutions, training bases and camps, residences, mosques, refugee centers, charities and other NGOs, etc.
- Surveillance of potential sponsors and suppliers to include nations, facilities, companies, and individuals who might be sources of weapons, ammunition, WMD agents, WMD weapons, precursors, components, development tools, or know-how
- Disruption activities such as arrests, deportations, detainment, searches, asset-seizures, asset "freezing", sabotage, disinformation, computer attacks, communications disruptions, blocked access to bank accounts, cutting connections between cells, severing links to political supporters, etc.
- Enhanced cooperation among nations in sharing intelligence and law enforcement information

Human intelligence

- Rewards should be offered for a variety of forms of assistance including, but not limited to, tips that lead to the arrest and conviction of wanted criminals
- Defectors should be encouraged by a variety of rewards (monetary, immunity, protection, etc.)
- Penetration by "walk-ins" or "volunteers", either directly (via seminaries in Pakistan, for example) or indirectly (through related groups and causes such as the guerilla groups fighting in Kashmir or in the Caucasus)
- Recruitment of existing terrorists or other insiders (such as clerics or employees in suspect Islamic charities) using both rewards (e.g., money) and threats (e.g., imprisonment) as leverage
- Aggressive (but non-violent) interrogations of suspects already in custody

- Recruitment from among former insiders: For example, the large number of Muslim militants already in custody in various parts of the world provides a potentially-pliable pool of ex-terrorists for whom "amnesty" and early release programs might be used to feed informers back into the parent organization

There are a variety of reasons why Al Qaeda should be relatively easy to penetrate

- They actively recruit, which means that they actively come looking for new people: Contrast this with groups that have been based on close family ties and one can see the advantage here
- They seek zealous Muslims, yet neither zealotry nor religion is difficult to falsify
  [As an aside, it is interesting to note that many devout Muslims believe that uttering a certain phrase will actually transform a person into a Muslim on the spot. The basic phrase (which has variations) is: "There is one God, only one God, and Mohammed was his prophet". Some Muslims believe that the phrase must be uttered with conviction. However, many Muslims, including some clerics with a long religious schooling, believe that even if a person is tricked into uttering the phrase, he/she becomes a Muslim instantaneously, regardless of his/her protestations.]
- Their numbers are very large, which may imply that the screening of recruits is cursory: For example, there is no evidence that they employ violent initiation rites (forcing the initiate to commit a murder, for example) as has been used by other groups
- Every member and every cell is a potential entry portal into the group, so the large and far-flung network of members and supporters provides a wide variety of options for penetration
- They recruit from many nations (including America, Europe, Asia), which means that nationality is no obstacle to admittance
- They support a wide variety of causes (e.g., Kashmiri rebels, Chechen rebels, Philippine guerillas, etc.), which means that a variety of motives are available for use by the would-be recruit
- They use their facilities to train fighters for this wide variety of causes, which means that their facilities can be penetrated by moles who join these remote fights (as opposed to having to join al Qaeda directly)

Legal proceedings

Continued collection of evidence by law enforcement agencies is necessary in order to:

- Provide justification for arrest
- Bolster public support for other acts (such as military strikes)
- Pressure other nations to cooperate in the fight against terrorism
- Undercut the plausibility of denials by sponsor states
- Enhance the likelihood of conviction in the event of a trial

Options for reducing our vulnerability

Hardening of likely targets

- Move likely targets (such as embassies) away from crowded urban areas into suburbs
- Provide large clear zones through which all visitors would be channeled along controlled access roads and through effective checkpoints
- Provide standoff barriers (fences) that enforce physical separation and enhance blast shielding
- Provide improved threat detection (e.g., bomb detection)
- Provide improved threat warning systems (e.g., duress alarms)
- Provide effective access-denial procedures
- Enhance physical shielding of walls, windows, etc.
- Improve security force training and equipment
- Improve medical response

Military options

- Continuous military planning and forward placement of intelligence and military assets in order to facilitate military options of all kinds (including personnel seizure, preemptive strikes, and retaliatory strikes directed against the terrorists, their infrastructure, or their state sponsors)
- Visible military deployments and movements that might act as a direct deterrent to the terrorist and/or motivate restraint by sponsor states
- Covert military operations (disruption, sabotage, etc.)
- Overt military operations (raids, snatches, disruption, preemption, retaliation, etc.)
- Targeting of individuals (as serendipitous byproducts of military action or by unconstrained partner nations)

Targeting bin Laden

Of all the options listed above, that which is both the most direct and the most controversial would be to target bin Laden himself. This option has legal and moral implications which are beyond the scope of this study. Suffice it to say, however, that such an option always exits, even if the targeting is ostensibly of leadership quarters, command centers, or other infrastructure. Furthermore, the task can always be carried out by an ally, especially if that ally suffers from looser constraints than do U.S. military and law enforcement agencies.

Given that the option exists, it is worthwhile to examine the pros and cons, since it is by no means obvious that this is an attractive option. Many of these pros and cons have already been presented above, in the sections that deal with the 20 August 1998 cruise missile strikes. Many of those arguments, which apply to the use of force in general, also apply specifically to the use of force with the intent of eliminating Osama bin Laden. Rather than repeat all of those arguments here, we will simply provide a reminder here that bin Laden may be as big a problem dead as he is alive.

Some of the advantages of targeting bin Laden

- It would send a message of resolve
- It would serve justice
- It may act as a deterrent
- He may not be replaceable, therefore dealing a serious blow to his organization and followers

Some of the disadvantages of targeting bin Laden

- He may be easily and rapidly replaced by another leader with equivalent leadership skills (and perhaps even by someone who is more strident or more reckless than bin Laden himself)
- It may only make him a martyr
- It may inflame further violence

Diplomatic options

International diplomacy is probably the single most effective tool at our disposal. It can be used in two ways. First, it can be used to pressure other nations (friend and foe alike) into actions that benefit us or that harm bin Laden and his allies. Secondly, it can be used to minimize the levels of mistrust and anger with which America is viewed in much of the world. Unfortunately, we seem to have concentrated on the former and neglected the latter.

The current problem with America's image in the world is two-fold. First, out present position as undisputed world leader and preeminent military power makes much of the world uncomfortable, fearing the potential for unchecked unilateral use of our strength. Unfortunately, many of our actions seem only to exacerbate these fears. For example, we have taken many steps to limit nuclear proliferation and yet we continue to maintain an enormous nuclear stockpile for ourselves and have recently refused to ratify the CTBT. This is a combination which only fuels suspicions and distrust. While there is little that we can or would do to diminish our position of strength, we can do much to minimize the legitimate fears that we will use this position of strength to force our will on the rest of the world. To that end, we must bend over backward to build coalitions before we act, to encourage debate and discussion in international forums (such as the UN), to consult with allies and others, and to justify our actions to the world (which was a shortcoming in our behavior following the cruise missile strikes).

The second problem with America's image is that we are often perceived as discriminatory. For example, we punish Islamic Pakistan for testing nuclear explosives and yet we turn a blind eye to Israel's not-so-secret capabilities. We punish Afghanistan for harboring bin Laden while taking a much softer approach to cases involving criminals hiding in other nations (e.g., the French case of Ira Einhorn or the Israeli case of Samuel Scheinbein). We refuse to recognize the Taliban as the rulers of Afghanistan, while propping up undemocratic regimes in other nations around the world. These acts seem to many in the Islamic world like just more examples of American cultural arrogance. We must begin to work harder to emphasize our ties with Islamic nations, our support for Islamic causes, and even our own Muslim minority. During the Kosovo crisis, for example, we could have done far more than we did to publicize the fact that we were fighting with and for Muslim peoples. Although these types of efforts will only bear fruit slowly, in the long run they are certain to simplify our efforts in fighting Islamic terrorism and in diminishing support for Muslim militancy.

Diplomacy: Arm twisting

Pressure on nations which provide sponsorship or haven to terrorists can take many forms:

- Air embargoes
- Financial embargoes
- Asset seizures
- Military threats or attacks
- International condemnation (by the UN and other bodies)
- Tangible incentives (such as aid dollars)
- Political incentives (such as international recognition)

In addition to pressuring sponsor states, we must continually pressure our allies and other nations to participate in, or at least to support, a variety of measures which include public condemnation of terrorism and of state sponsors, disruption operations, arrests, seizures, and active military measures.

Diplomacy: Image building

Bin Laden's real genius is that he is able to tap into a bottomless reservoir of ethnic and religious discontent, patch over the differences among different races, nationalities, personalities, and branches of Islam; and then funnel this seething cauldron of discontent against the U.S. However, the greater of the two factors here is the seething cauldron of discontent, not the organizational skills of bin Laden. Ultimately, the greatest payoff will come from addressing this discontent (as opposed to addressing bin Laden). To this end we must have:

- Greater sensitivity and attention to Muslim concerns in the world

[redacted]

- More consultations and partnerships with Muslim nations over issues which affect Muslim interests
- Increased partnerships and foreign aid for Muslim nations to strengthen both our image and our leverage in these nations
- Reduced support for non-democratic Muslim governments (which are seen as puppets of an America that cares not for the rights of Muslim peoples)
- Greater sensitivity and attention to the American image as the "world's policeman" (the polite view) or as a world bully (the less polite view which is shared by many in developing countries)
- Greater attention to the opinions of small players in international affairs, especially Arab and other Muslim players (e.g., expanded UN coordination and consultation)
- Greater emphasis on consensus-building prior to international acts (especially prior to military action)

Miscellaneous options

Unlike some other terrorists, bin Laden very much seeks the limelight. He craves attention and is puffed up by media moguls clamoring for the next "exclusive" interview. To a large extent, therefore, the media make or break his reputation and, indirectly, affect his level of support, numbers of recruits, and more. Every effort should be made to limit his ability to manipulate the media to his advantage and to deflate the imagery which draws so much support to him.

Media Manipulation

- Image deflation: Provide the media with unflattering or embarrassing details of bin Laden's life, family, health, or habits
- Depersonalization: Take steps to minimize references to individuals like bin Laden in ways that bolster their self-image and their image in the eyes of others
  Example: Eliminate all future use of bin Laden's name in press conferences, press releases, etc. Focus instead, as much as possible, on references to al Qaeda, to "the al Qaeda leadership", etc. as a means of depersonalizing the battle
- Disinformation

Options for the sponsor state

Clearly the sponsor state has many options which elude other nations. They can always arrest, try, expel, or assassinate a troublesome resident (or, to be more precise, they would have fewer difficulties implementing any of these options than would any other nation). That is why the U.S. and its allies have tried so hard to persuade the Taliban to act on our behalf. A wide range of carrots (official recognition, the Afghan UN seat, etc.) and sticks (military threats, etc.) have been employed to this end.

Any state harboring bin Laden could take the following overt actions

[redacted]

- Arrest and hold him without trial
- Arrest and try him (in a real trial or in a "show" trial meant to exonerate him)
- Place him in "protective" custody (a form of detention that might be made palatable to his supporters)
- Extradition: Arrest and extradite him to a country with a legal criminal complaint
- Exile/Expulsion: Expel him to a pre-arranged destination or to a destination of his choice

However, overt acts are likely to draw criticism from bin Laden supporters (both internal and external)

The Taliban have apparently been deeply divided over their decision to host bin Laden. On the one hand, bin Laden is a hero in Afghanistan, but his presence there has also been costly. Unfortunately, bin Laden really is, with justification, revered as a war hero among many Afghanis for his role in helping to expel the Soviets during the 1980s. This means that if the Taliban were to cooperate at all, it must be in ways that they can deny or rationalize to his supporters. Therefore, most of the overt options listed above are unlikely choices.

It is difficult to think of an analogy with which to help Americans to understand the Taliban's problem with bin Laden. To come up with an analogy, we would need to identify an individual who is revered as a great patriot and a war hero among a significant conservative segment of the American population, yet someone toward whom there is also a large segment of the American population who are indifferent. Perhaps the best analogy we could come up with would be to compare bin Laden with Oliver North. Right or wrong, both Osama bin Laden and Oliver North are viewed as war heroes by a significant number of conservatives within their own countries. Therefore, although neither is universally loved, each has a strong and vocal domestic constituency. Given this, it would be "political suicide" for the Taliban to turn bin Laden over to America for trial, just as it would be for the U.S. to turn over Oliver North for a war crimes trial in Vietnam. This does not mean, however, that all is lost. There remain a large number of covert options with which a sponsor state can effectively deal with a renegade citizen. The advantage of taking action secrecy is that the nation might hope to avoid criticism from bin Laden's supporters.

Any state harboring bin Laden could take the following covert actions:

- Arrange secretly for him to move out of his own free will
- Secretly expel him
- Seize him and deliver him secretly to another country
- Arrange secretly for another nation to learn of his whereabouts (after which he could be apprehended or killed)
- Arrange secretly for him to be seized by another nation: Such a snatch could be loudly decried for domestic consumption
- Arrange secretly for him to be assassinated by his enemies (e.g., rivals within his own group)

- Secretly kill or incapacitate him: For example, it could be arranged for him to appear to die from an "illness" (biological assassination)
- Secretly imprison him, claiming that he has "disappeared"
- Limit his access to the media so that he ceases to get media attention
- Restrict his movements, communications, and visitors in order to diminish the level of attention which he attracts
- Restrict his movements, communications, and visitors in order to diminish his capability for carrying out any further activities which draw criticism and international pressure

The Big Picture

Up to this point, many of our observations, conclusions, and recommendations have addressed specifically the threat posed by Osama bin Laden, his organization and followers, and the events in 1998 that surrounded his rise to notoriety. In this final section, we will look at the big picture and ask what broader lessons we can learn from all this.

Terrorism is not dead (although it has shifted from Marxist-oriented to religious-oriented)

State sponsorship of terrorism is not over (although it has shifted from Soviet-dominated to third-world-dominated)

Terrorism can be unpredictable and future threats may evolve from unexpected sources

- Today's ally may be tomorrow's enemy: The Afghan resistance turned to bite the hand that fed them
- Bin Laden was initially dismissed by some as a "Gucci terrorist" with a fat wallet and a big mouth

Terrorism is a global phenomenon

- Modern threat groups think globally: For example, both Aum Shinrikyo and bin Laden had followers worldwide
- Threat groups can reach out to strike at a broad range of targets in unexpected places (as happened in Africa)

Our problems with terrorism are exacerbated by our position and image in the world

- Islamic frustrations run deep and wide and serve as a deep well to feed future anti-Western terrorism
- America's current image in the world is dangerously tarnished and will feed future anti-Americanism
- Our most effective counter-terrorist tools may be in the realm of international relations (i.e., repairing our image as a world bully) as opposed to enhancing intelligence, law enforcement, and military powers and capabilities

Religion is a powerful motivational factor in modern terrorism

- Bin Laden taps a bottomless reservoir of ethnic and religious discontent and funnels it against the U.S.
- Religiously-motivated terrorists will kill indiscriminately

Religion is a protective shield which complicates counter-terrorism

- Mosques and religious leaders spread the fiery rhetoric
- Religious organizations (such as charities, scholarship organizations, and refugee centers) are used to finance terrorism

[redacted]

- These organizations also provide a steady supply of would-be terrorists by identifying key individuals and sending them abroad for training
- These organizations can also act as "holding pens" by providing a ready supply of trained operatives who can be called upon to provide local manpower in support of terrorist operations

Killing is an explicit goal of many modern terrorists

- The deaths of innocents do not deter terrorists
- Bin Laden seeks to target all Americans everywhere
- Body counts are the goal of modern terrorists (as opposed to other attention-getting schemes)
- Weapons of Mass Destruction appeal to modern terrorists

Modern terrorism is not easily countered

- Bin Laden has been involved in terrorism for many years and has been linked to many acts and yet has survived repeated attempts to have him killed or detained
- Acts linked to bin Laden and his cohorts demonstrate that terrorists are not easily deterred
- The risk of death does not significantly deter terrorism (as evidenced by suicide bombings)
- The risk of apprehension does not significantly deter terrorism (as evidenced by the heavy pressure under which the Nairobi cell of al Qaeda operated in the months prior to the East African embassy bombings)
- Despite repeated attacks over a period of many years, the truck bomb remains a very potent weapon and remains difficult to defend against

Despite repeated warnings over a period of many months, the Nairobi bombing was not prevented

- Raw intelligence, which looks damning in hindsight, can be very difficult to authenticate at the time
- Even with good intelligence, it can be difficult to predict exact targets and timing
- Even with good intelligence, it is not always possible to prevent an attack
- Even with good intelligence, it is not easy to quickly enact changes that might mitigate the effects of a possible attack

Although the African embassy bombings represent a failure of sorts, we do NOT find negligence to have been a contributing factor

Although we may have underestimated the local threat in East Africa, we were more the victims of resource constraints than of poor intelligence or of a poor threat response

[redacted]

- Our underestimate of the threat in East Africa teaches us that we can never be complacent
- However, our overall capabilities are strong
- Furthermore, we have a record of successes that we can be proud of

The terrorist can always seek out the weakest targets

- Although that may NOT have been the motivating factor behind the choice of the African embassy targets, the bombers certainly benefited from the fact that Nairobi was considered only a medium threat environment

WMD terrorism

- Current terrorist interest in WMD agents and weapons suggests a trend toward new terrorist capabilities in the future
- However, the timing of any evolution towards new methods and capabilities is highly uncertain
- Furthermore, the current effectiveness and availability of explosive devices make it likely that the vehicle bomb will remain a dominant tool for some time yet
- In addition, the apparent inability of al Qaeda to acquire and employ WMD agents or weapons (even after years of trying and with significant resources at their disposal), suggests that the threat of WMD terrorism may be smaller at the present time than we currently seem to imagine
- Nonetheless, the obstacles standing in the way of WMD acquisition and employment are not insurmountable and some forms of WMD employment must be considered quite plausible in the future

The future

- The "war" against terrorism will never be "won": terrorism will always be a world problem
- Terrorists will win some
- We are seeing increasing attention domestically to terrorism as a threat to national security
- We are seeing increasing recognition of terrorism as a global problem (as opposed to strictly being a Western problem)
- We are seeing increasing cooperation among nations to combat terrorism

[redacted]

Enclosure 2

Document # 2

FOIA F# 2006-00279

Laden

tudy

ce Survey

[redacted]

"In today's wars, there are no morals"

Osama bin Laden, May 1998

Dr. Gary W. Richter
Sandia National Laboratories
(925) 294-3298
richter@sandia.gov

This version: 12/06/1999 9:25 AM

[redacted]

[redacted]

Outline

Early History

The African Bombings
- Events Prior
- The Bombings
- Events After

Retaliation
- The Afghan Camps
- The Afghan Attack
- Al Shifa
- The Al Shifa Attack
- Attack Analysis

Recent History

Summary
- Al Qaeda & Islamic Jihad
- Economic Assets
- Incidents
- Global Reach
- Philosophy

Quotes

Interest in WMDs

Analysis
- Lessons Learned
- Findings & Recommendations
- Solutions
- Conclusions
- The Bottom Line

Afghan supporters of bin Laden take to the streets of Kandahar following the cruise missile strikes: 8,000 demonstrated vowed to defend Osama bin Laden

[redacted]

[redacted]

Who is Osama bin Laden?

Usama bin Laden

Usamah Bin-Muhammad Bin-Laden

Shaykh Usamah Bin-Laden

Abu Abdallah

Mujahid Shaykh

Hajj

al Qaqa

The Director

Is he a "Gucci terrorist" with a big mouth and a fat wallet or a potent enemy?

[redacted]

[redacted]

A Short History

1957	Born in Saudi Arabia into a rich family
1979	Traveled to Afghanistan to help the mujahideen fight the Soviet invasion
1980s	Worked during the war on financing, recruiting, construction, and (perhaps) in battle
1989	The Soviet withdrawal from Afghanistan was completed
	Returned to Saudi Arabia
1991	Left Saudi Arabia and moved to Sudan
1991-96	Lived in exile in Sudan, brought over Arab Afghans, built training camps, etc.
26 Feb 93	The World Trade Center was bombed in New York City by Arab Afghans
1993	Worked against UN peacekeepers in Somalia
1994	Was stripped of his Saudi citizenship
	Saudi Arabia froze his Saudi financial assets
1995	From Sudan, his followers began to spread out across the Islamic world
1996	A U.S. investigation began into bin Laden and al Qaeda
	The U.S. Embassy in Sudan was closed and relocated to the U.S. Embassy in Kenya
	Sudan expelled bin Laden, who then moved back to Afghanistan
23 Aug 96	Bin Laden signed and issued a Declaration of Jihad entitled "Message from Usamah Bin-Muhammad Bin-Laden to His Muslim Brothers in the Whole World and Especially in the Arabian Peninsula: Declaration of Jihad Against the Americans Occupying the Land of the Two Holy Mosques; Expel the Heretics from the Arabian Peninsula"
7 Aug 98	Bomb attacks against embassies in Kenya and Tanzania
20 Aug 98	Cruise missile attacks in Sudan and Afghanistan

[redacted]

[redacted]

Early History

1930 Sometime around this year, bin Laden's father, Mohammed Awad bin Laden moved to Saudi Arabia from Hadramout in South Yemen (PBS Online, citing a document provided by a source close to bin Laden)

1930-70 The elder bin Laden eventually developed a close relationship with King Faisal and benefited from a decree that all construction projects should go to bin Laden's construction group (PBS Online, citing a document provided by a source close to bin Laden)

In fact, the elder bin Laden was eventually appointed for a period as the minister of public works (PBS Online, citing a document provided by a source close to bin Laden)

Because their company was responsible for major extensions to the mosques in Mecca and Medina, and rebuilt the Al-Aqsa mosque in 1969 after a fire, the family like to take credit for building all three holy mosques (PBS Online, citing a document provided by a source close to bin Laden)

Bin Laden's father used to host hundreds of pilgrims from all over the world during Hajj Season, including senior Islamic scholars and leaders of Muslim movements: This habit, continued after his death, was used to make contacts and build relationships (PBS Online, citing a document provided by a source close to bin Laden)

1957 Osama bin Mohammed bin Laden was born in Riyadh (Other reports give his birth year as 1956 or 1958)

Bin Laden was the 17th of 52 (or 53) children of Saudi construction magnate Muhammad Awad bin Laden (one of 20 sons)

[redacted]

[redacted]

Early History

Another source says he was seventh of 50 children (PBS Online, citing a document provided by a source close to bin Laden)

His father owned the Bin Laden Group, the largest construction company in Saudi Arabia, worth over $5 billion

Osama eventually ended up controlling a fortune of $250-500 million

His mother (variously reported as Palestinian or from a remote part of Saudi Arabia) was the tenth and least favorite wife of the elder bin Laden: Osama is their only child

Osama was raised in Al Madina, Al Munawwara, and Hijaz

One report says that the bin Laden boys went to school at Victoria College in Alexandria (PBS Online, citing a report from a French source)

As a teenager, Osama bin Laden reportedly worked on restoring the Islamic holy sites at Mecca and Medina

~1970 Bin Laden's father died (PBS Online, citing a document provided by a source close to bin Laden)

[redacted]

[redacted]

Early History

Another report claims that bin Laden's father died in 1968, leaving 54 sons and daughters (PBS Online, citing a report from a French source)

1973 Bin Laden graduated from secondary school in Jiddah

Bin Laden began his interactions with Islamic groups

~1974 Bin Laden was married, at the age of 17, to a Syrian girl (PBS Online, citing a document provided by a source close to bin Laden)

1973-75 Bin Laden was a frequent visitor to Beirut where he caroused in the bars and was known as a heavy drinker embroiled in frequent fights

1975 Civil war broke out in Lebanon

1979 Bin Laden graduated from King Abdul Aziz University in Jiddah with a degree in civil Engineering

Other reports say that he studied management and economics

PBS Online, citing a document provided by a source close to bin Laden, reports that bin Laden got his degree in public administration from King Abdul-Aziz university in 1981

[redacted]

[redacted]

The Soviet War in Afghanistan

24 Dec 1979* The Soviets invaded Afghanistan

*Washington Post and PBS gives invasion date as Dec26, PBS gives date as Dec 26, MSNBC gives invasion date of 11 January 1979

Soviet Troops Invade Afghanistan

Dec 1979 Bin Laden traveled to Pakistan to help the mujahideen fight the Soviet invasion

"When the invasion of Afghanistan started, I was enraged and went there at once – I arrived within days..." (Osama bin Laden, 12/6/93)

[redacted]

[redacted]

The Soviet War in Afghanistan

Jan 1980 After his first exploratory visit to Pakistan, bin Laden returned to Saudi Arabia and started lobbying to support the mujahedeen: he collected a huge amount of money and material as donations and eventually returned to Pakistan (PBS Online, citing a document provided by a source close to bin Laden)

1980-82 Bin Laden went on collecting money and going to Pakistan once or twice a year until 1982 (PBS Online, citing a document provided by a source close to bin Laden)

1982 Bin Laden decided to enter Afghanistan and brought with him construction machinery which he put at the disposal of the mujahedeen (PBS Online, citing a document provided by a source close to bin Laden)

[redacted]

[redacted]

The Soviet War in Afghanistan

During the 1980s Afghan war against the Soviet Union, bin Laden financed construction, recruitment, and training to support the war effort

The State Department credits bin Laden with playing "a significant role in financing, recruiting, transporting, and training Arab nationals. Bin Laden imported bulldozers and other heavy equipment to cut roads, tunnels, hospitals and storage depots through Afghanistan's mountainous terrain to move and shelter fighters and supplies."

He was most closely allied with the most fundamentalist of the Afghan resistance leaders, particularly Gulbuddin Hekmatyar, who was the head of the group called the Islamic Party

He founded the Islamic Salvation Foundation in Saudi Arabia through which he helped to finance the Afghan mujahideen (and which would later extend funding to radical Islamic groups around the world)

He blasted massive tunnels into the Zazi mountains of Bakhtiar province for guerrilla hospitals and arms depots

He also cut enormous lengths of roads to support the Afghan guerrillas

He established, with Sheikh Dr. Abdullah Azzam, the office for mujahideen services in Peshawar, Pakistan: This services office, the MAK (Maktab al-Khidamat), established recruitment centers around the world and organized and funded paramilitary training camps in Afghanistan and Pakistan

Together with Sheikh Azzam, he also established the Sidda camp for the training of Arab mujahideen

[redacted]

[redacted]

The Soviet War in Afghanistan

The number of foreign volunteers for the war eventually grew to 20,000 (JIR, 10/98, p. 24)

Bin Laden financed housing for volunteers in Peshawar, Pakistan and bankrolled the Ma'sadat Al-Ansar military training camp in Afghanistan, which trained local and international volunteers (JIR, 10/98, p. 24)

He established the "Ma sadat Al Ansar" base for Arab mujahideen in Afghanistan

Toward the end of the war, bin Laden established a new organization, known as al-Qaida, the Islamic Salvation Foundation (a.k.a. The Base): According the CIA, al-Qaida remains a "formidable" operation "consisting of mujaheddin of many nationalities who had previously fought with bin Laden"

Ties to the U.S. intelligence community

Although both the U.S. and bin Laden deny that bin Laden was a major recipient of CIA assistance during the war, he undoubtedly benefited from it

For example, there is videotape footage of his fighters using U.S. Stinger missiles in the 1980s

It has also been reported that up until 1988, bin Laden worked for Saudi intelligence services under emir Faycal ben Turki, organizing and financing the logistics of Arab Afghan militants passing through Jeddah on their way to Peshawar, Pakistan

Other reports claim that bin Laden was recruited and funded by the CIA, that from about the mid 1980s on, he worked in close association with U.S. agents, and that he had become deeply disillusioned with the U.S. and its policies by the time the Soviets had been forced to withdraw from Afghanistan (JIRP, 10/98, p. 8)

[redacted]

[redacted]

The Soviet War in Afghanistan

1984	Bin Laden established a guesthouse in Peshawar (Baitul'ansar) that was intended to be the first station for Arab mujahedeen before they went to Afghanistan to fight or to start training (PBS Online, citing a document provided by a source close to bin Laden)
	About this same time, the Jihad Service Bureau was formed by Abdullah Azzam in Peshawar: the bureau's publications were important in attracting more Saudis and Arabs to Afghanistan (PBS Online, citing a document provided by a source close to bin Laden)
	At this time bin Laden did not have his own command or training camps but used to send newcomers to one of the Afghan factions (PBS Online, citing a document provided by a source close to bin Laden)
1986	Bin Laden decided to have his own camps inside Afghanistan (PBS Online, citing a document provided by a source close to bin Laden)
1986-1988	Bin Laden built more than six camps in Afghanistan (PBS Online, citing a document provided by a source close to bin Laden)
1986	Bin Laden participated in the battles of Jalalabad with the Arab Mujahideen
	Bin Laden and a few dozen Arabs reportedly fought off a Soviet attack on Jaji, near the Pakistani border
	This was reportedly his first battle "face to face" with the Soviet Army with pure Arab personnel (PBS Online, citing a document provided by a source close to bin Laden)

[redacted]

[redacted]

The Soviet War in Afghanistan

1987	Bin Laden reportedly led an offensive against Soviet troops in the battle of Shaban
1988	Bin Laden realized that his system of documentation was backward and that he was unable to answer the questions of some families whose loved ones were missing in Afghanistan so he decided to organize better and arranged for better documentation and tracking of all visitors and mujahedeen (PBS Online, citing a document provided by a source close to bin Laden)
	It was at this time that the whole bin Laden complex was named Al-Qa'edah, which means "The Base" (PBS Online, citing a document provided by a source close to bin Laden)
1989-1994	Bin Laden spent more time in Afghanistan than in Saudi Arabia (PBS Online, citing a document provided by a source close to bin Laden)
1989	Bin Laden again participated in the battles of Jalalabad
1989	Bin Laden was interviewed by Issam Daraz, a Muslim journalist
	Video and photographs shot by Daraz clearly show his fighters armed with Stinger missiles
15 Feb 1989	The Soviet withdrawal from Afghanistan was completed
1989	Bin Laden returned to Saudi Arabia

[redacted]

[redacted]

Lessons from the Afghan War

Bin Laden has said that during the Soviet Unions' war with Afghanistan, he had learned the value of tunneling to limit the advantages of air power:

"We dug a good number of huge tunnels and built in them some storage places and in some others we built a hospital. So our experience in this Jihad was great."

(OBL in a 1997 television interview)

"Most of what we benefited from was that the myth of the superpower was destroyed..."

(Osama bin Laden)

"He is an ordinary person who is very religious. He believes in the rule of Islam and where possible the establishment of an Islamic state The time that he spent in Afghanistan [during the war] led him to believe that this might be achieved through military means"

President Omar Hassan al-Bashir of Sudan (NYT, 4/13/99)

[redacted]

[redacted]

The Arab Afghans

During the 1980s bin Laden became the leader of the "Afghan Arabs" with 12,000 to 20,000 followers

The Arab Afghans would later be implicated in numerous terrorist incidents and would join groups such as Hamas, Egypt's Islamic Group, Algeria's Islamic Salvation Front, and the Moro Liberation Front in the Philippines

The Arab Afghans would also end up in many civil wars, fighting for the Islamic cause in Bosnia, Chechnya, Kashmir, and Tajikistan

According to Egypt's Al-Ahram Center for Political and Strategic Studies, the majority of the Arab Afghans have a university education

"They're modern and they use modern methods"

(Al-Ahram Center for Political and Strategic Studies)

[redacted]

[redacted]

Egypt

6 Oct 1981 Egyptian President Anwar Sadat was assassinated by Egypt's Jihad group (a.k.a. Egyptian Islamic Jihad, a.k.a. al-Jihad)

Scene of the Sadat assassination

The assassin was Khaled al-Islambouli, a fundamentalist army lieutenant

Khaled's older brother, Mohammed Shawky al-Islambouli, is a leader of Islamic Group and is a former "Arab Afghan"

Mohammed was later suspected of a having a role in an assassination attempt on Egyptian President Mubarak, for which he was sentenced to death in absentia by an Egyptian court in Dec 1992

The Jihad group's leader is a medical doctor named Ayman al-Zahwahri

Al-Zahwari was eventually convicted of participating in the Sadat assassination

Al-Zahwahri was also an "Arab Afghan" and is believed to be a close friend of bin Laden

As of 1998, al-Zahwahri was thought to be in Afghanistan: A visitor who encountered bin Laden in Afghanistan in May 1998 claimed that he was accompanied by al-Zahwahri

In 1998, with bin Laden and others, al-Zahwahri would help found the International Islamic Front, also known as the World Islamic Front for Jihad Against Jews and Crusaders

[redacted]

[redacted]

Egypt

1983 Mohammed Shawky al-Islambouli, the brother of Sadat's assassin, made his way to Peshawar, Pakistan

He reportedly had close ties to Iran and funneled Iranian money to the Egyptian fundamentalist radicals in Afghanistan

His group eventually split from the mainstream Egyptian faction of Islamic fundamentalists, known as the "Dawa and Sharia" (The Call and Islamic Law), which had been involved with the "Arab Afghans" and had received direct support from U.S., British, French, and Israeli intelligence agencies during the Afghan war

Dec 1992 Mohammed Shawky al-Islambouli, a leader of Egypt's Islamic Group, a former "Arab Afghan", and the brother of Sadat's assassin, was sentenced to death in absentia by Egypt for plotting to overthrow Egyptian President Mubarak and assassinate Egyptian leaders

1993 In separate incidents, the group Egyptian Islamic Jihad used car bombs to attempt to assassinate the then Egyptian Prime Minister Atef Sikdi and then Interior Minister Hassan al-Alfi

Egyptian Islamic Jihad has claimed responsibility for these attempted assassinations

[redacted]

[redacted]

Egypt

June 1995

Egyptian radicals based in Sudan attempted to assassinate Egyptian President Hosni Mubarak in Addis Ababa, Ethiopia

A group known as the Islamic Group (Al-Gama'at al-Islamiyya), is believed to have been responsible for this attempted assassination

Mustafa Hamza, a leader of the Islamic Group, is suspected of having played a leading role in the assassination attempt

Hamza, who also goes by the alias Abu Hazem, had earlier served time for the assassination of Anwar Sadat

Hamza is one of the "Arab Afghans" who participated in the Afghan war

Sheik Omar Abdel Rahman, currently in jail for the 1993 WTC bombing, is the group's spiritual leader

Bin Laden is suspected of having financed this assassination attempt

Dec 1995

Egyptian security officials uncovered a conspiracy by the Islamic Jihad group to assassinate President Hosni Mubarak

An informant's tip claimed that bin Laden helped fund the plot

Early 1997

21 Islamic militants suspected of belonging to the outlawed Islamic Group were arrested for planning to blow up a military target in Alexandria by launching rockets from a boat (and a 22nd suspect was arrested later) (JTWR, 4/7/99)

[redacted]

[redacted]

Egypt

18 Sept 1997 There was a shooting and fire bombing of a tourist bus outside the Egyptian Museum in Cairo's Tahrir Square

9 German tourists and the bus driver were killed and 26 more are injured

Later, two brothers, Saber Abu el-Ulla and Mahmoud Abu el-Ulla, pled guilty while chanting and smiling

The two perpetrators professed support for the Egyptian al-Jihad group although they were not linked to any established group

The scene of a related bus attack that killed 18 in April 1996

One of the perpetrators was an escaped mental hospital inmate who had previously killed four foreign nationals in an attack at a restaurant in the Semiramis Intercontinental Hotel in Cairo in October 1993

The Islamic Group hailed the "mujahideen" brothers and warned tourists not to travel to Egypt

Bin Laden was later linked to this bombing

On 30 Oct 1997 two men were sentenced to death for these killings

[redacted]

[redacted]

Egypt

17 Nov 1997 The Egyptian organization known as the Islamic Group claimed credit for the attack on foreign tourists which took place in the Valley of the Kings near Luxor, Egypt

In this attack, 58 tourists and 4 Egyptians were killed and 26 were wounded

The six perpetrators were killed in a shootout with police during their escape effort

The Islamic Group claimed that it intended to take hostages in the attack in exchange for the release of Shayk Umar Abd al-Rahman, who was serving a life prison term in the US

This claim was belied by eyewitness accounts that the perpetrators slowly and systematically executed those trapped inside the temple

The Islamic Group is an organization that formed an alliance with al-Qaida during The Afghan war to coordinate paramilitary training of recruits for that war and is still closely allied with al-Qaida and bin Laden

Bin Laden may have planned this attack

Switzerland's federal police chief, Urs von Daeniken, said on 13 May 1999 that Egypt believed that Mustafa Hamza, a leader of the Islamic Group, had ordered the attack from Sudan with funding from bin Laden (JTWR, 5/13/99)

[redacted]

Egypt

Dec 1997 Gamaa Al Islamiya said "The Gamaa Al Islamiya has decided to stop targeting the tourism industry and foreign tourists" (JDW, 2/24/99, p. 22)

Public hostility after the Luxor attack had reportedly left Egypt's militant groups in a state of disarray (JDW, 2/24/99, p. 22)

The group said that its own investigation showed that young members had acted on their own (JDW, 2/24/99, p. 22)

However, not all members of the groups leading Shura council agreed with the decision to stop targeting tourists: The organizations leadership in Afghanistan, led by Rifiee Ahmed Taha, refused to condemn the Luxor attack (JDW, 2/24/99, p. 22)

The Al Jihad group was also faced with dwindling popular support and has evidently decided to focus more on US, Israeli, and UK targets to improve its image and attract new funds, members, and sympathizers: The group hopes to capitalize on growing Arab anger with the US and UK policy against Iraq and what they see as a double standard with regard to treatment of Israel when it violates UN Security Council resolutions (JDW, 2/24/99, p. 22-23)

A Jihad statement published 31 March said that a cease-fire with the US and Israel represented "a step back in the face of a new Christian crusade which aims to uproot Islam and give Israel the upper hand" (JTWR, 3/31/99)

[redacted]

Egypt

Unfortunately, the Gamaa's alleged new desire for peace has springboarded some new, extremely violent young emirs into positions of power (such as Mahmoud Farshuti, based in Qena, who is suspected of involvement in the Luxor attack, the murder of nine Christians and four Muslims in the southern district of Nega Hammadi, and the murder of nine police officers at fake roadblocks in Abu Qurqas and Malawi) (JDW, 2/24/99, p. 23)

22 Aug 1998	The Egyptian group Jamma Islamiyya, one of the groups which was part of the umbrella group of Islamic militant organizations founded by bin Laden, called on Moslems around the world "to stand alongside the peoples of Sudan and Afghanistan, to besiege American embassies in Moslem countries and to force their leaders to close them and expel American diplomats who are spying on us" (SGIU, 10/23/98)
Sept 1998	Mutassar al-Zayat, lawyer for the Egyptian group Jamma Islamiyya, said that the group had cut ties with bin Laden in July, after deciding to examine a truce in its war against the Egyptian government (SGIU, 10/23/98)
1 Feb 1999	A military court in Egypt began the trial of 107 alleged members of the Islamic Jihad organization; 62 in absentia (JTWR, 2/2/99)
25 Mar 1999	The Islamic Group issued a statement that it was responding to a call by its spiritual leader, Sheikh Omar Abdel-Rahman (who is in prison in the US), to campaign peacefully (JTWR, 4/26/99)

[redacted]

Egypt

Wk of 12 Apr 99	Seven more Islamic militants belonging to Al-Jihad were extradited to Egypt from three unnamed Arab countries (JTWR, 4/20/99)
18 Apr 1999	A military court trying 107 Islamic militants sentenced 9 to death in absentia, some of whom allegedly have close links with bin Laden (JTWR, 4/19/99)
	11 others were sentenced to life with hard labor, including Ahmed Ibrahim al-Naggar, who was extradited from Albania in the summer of 1998 (JTWR, 4/19/99)
	Al-Jihad leader Ayman al Zawahri, who was believed to be in Afghanistan with bin Laden, was among the defendants (JTWR, 4/19/99)
26 Apr 1999	A lawyer for the Islamic Group claimed that Egyptian authorities had released more than 1,000 members of the group (JTWR, 4/26/99)
27 May 1999	It was reported that Egyptian authorities had arrested 23 suspected Islamic militants believed to belong to the Taleat Fatah group, a militant Islamic group that has carried out attacks in Egypt (JTWR, 5/27/99)]
17 Jun 1999	A military court sentenced 20 Islamic militants to prison terms for being linked to an alleged plot to assassinate President Hosni Mubarak (JTWR, 6/17/99)
6 Sept 1999	A knife-wielding Islamic militant was shot dead by Egyptian President Hosni Mubarak's bodyguards after he slightly wounded the president in Port Said (JTWR, 9/7/99)

Pakistan

7 Feb 1995 The FBI found Ramzi Yousef living in a guesthouse called the Su Casa house in Islamabad, one of many guesthouses that bin Laden had set up for his fighters (PBS Online)

19 Nov 1995 Arab Afghans bombed the Egyptian Embassy in Islamabad, Pakistan.

17 people were killed

The bombing followed Pakistan's extradition of several Arab Afghans

The Egyptian Islamic Jihad group claimed responsibility, saying that the bombing was in retaliation for Pakistan's extradition of its members to Cairo

Scene of the Egyptian Embassy bombing in Pakistan

23 Mar 1997 Yasser Arafat attended a summit meeting of the Organization of the Islamic Conference (OIC)

A plot by Islamists to kill Arafat on this day was revealed by an Algerian informer working for Pakistan's Inter Services Intelligence (ISI)

[redacted]

Pakistan

27 Mar 1998 Pakistan's Inter Services Intelligence (ISI) raided the big Pabi refugee camp near Jallozai, 40km east of Peshawar

The Pabi camp is one of the leading bases of Arab Afghans in the Peshawar region

March 1998 Threats faxed by bin Laden from Kandahar, Afghanistan caused the United States to erect barricades around its embassy in Pakistan (SGIU, 4/16/98)

Nov 1998 The Pakistani militant group Lakshar-e-Taiba, some of whose members were killed in the August 1998 U.S. cruise missile attacks, organized a religious gathering of 50,000 youths near Lahore, Pakistan's second-largest city (WP, 3/7/99)

One large banner said "Soon the flames of holy war will engulf the United States of America" (WP, 3/7/99)

1999 In 1999 a high-ranking Pakistani security official said that "In the shape of [Harkat Ansar] and a few other militant religious groups, Osama has a formidable human asset in Pakistan" (WP, 3/7/99)

[redacted]

Pakistan

23 Aug 1999	Over 4,000 Islamic activists marched in Lahore, Pakistan to protest U.S. actions against bin Laden (JIR, 10/99, p. 5) Members of the group Jamiat-Ulema-Islami shouted anti-U.S. slogans and waved posters that read "Down with America", "Osama is a Muslim World Hero", and "We Will Protect Osama with Our Blood" (JIR, 10/99, p. 5)
2 Nov 1999	Michael Sheehan, the U.S. State Department's Coordinator for Counterterrorism, told a Senate Foreign Relations subcommittee that Pakistan was supporting the training of militant groups in Afghanistan as well as providing "material support" to Kashmiri militants (JTWR, 11/5/99)
3 Nov 1999	A conference began in Muridke, Pakistan of the Lashkar-e-Tayyaba militant Islamic group at which militants praised holy wars and condemned India and the United States (NYT, 11/4/99) The meeting was attended by 300,000 followers from Sudan, Afghanistan, Egypt, and Saudi Arabia (NYT, 11/4/99)
12 Nov 1999	Seven rockets were fired at U.S. and UN targets in Islamabad, Pakistan

[redacted]

The Philippines

Oct 1998	Bin Laden reportedly had three business in the Philippines (SGIU, 10/13/98)
	According to one report, one of bin Laden's wives is a Filipino and bin Laden occasionally visits the Philippines (SGIU, 10/13/98)
	However, Moslem rebel leaders deny this and claim that it is bin Laden's brother-in-law (one of whose wives is Filipino) who frequently visits Mindanao financing mosques and charitable organizations (which Filipino authorities claim to be a front for financing local and international Moslem extremists) (SGIU, 10/13/98)
Dec 1998	Bin Laden was reportedly known to be the chief financial backer of the Abu Sayyaf Group, which has waged a campaign to create an independent Muslim state in the southern Philippines (JIRP, Dec 1998, p. 6)
25 Dec 1998	Security forces foiled an attempt to smuggle a large shipment of arms and ammunition into Mindanao (SGIU, 1/13/99)
	The supplies were reportedly provided by a foreign country sympathetic to Moslems seeking an independent Islamic state in the southern Philippines (SGIU, 1/13/99)
8 Jan 1999	Deutsche Presse Agentur cited MILF Chairman for Western Mindanao, Ustadz Shariff Julabbi, as acknowledging that MILF received funding from sympathizers in Australia, Germany, and unnamed Arab countries (SGIU, 1/13/99)

[redacted]

[redacted]

The Philippines

10 Jan 1999 — Al Haj Murad, the Vice Chairman for Military Affairs of the Moro Islamic Liberation Front (MILF), reportedly told Businessworld Philippines that MILF was receiving help from "civic organizations" in Moslem countries (SGIU, 1/13/99)

12 Jan 1999 — Deutsche Presse Agentur reported that the Philippine Moslem rebel groups Abu Sayyaf and the Moro Islamic Liberation Front (MILF) were expecting a multi-million dollar shipment of arms and ammunition from Middle Eastern Islamic fundamentalist groups (SGIU, 1/13/99)

They quoted a rebel source as saying that most of the funding for the arms came from Afghanistan (SGIU, 1/13/99)

9 Feb 1999 — MILF rebels admitted that they had received financial aid from bin Laden for a decade (FYEO, 2/15/99)

However, they claim to have refused the payments starting in 1998 because they found them too costly politically (FYEO, 2/15/99)

It is also alleged that militants from Pakistan and Saudi Arabia have provided military training to the MILF (FYEO online "strategypage")

11 Feb 1999 — Salamat Hashim, leader of the Moro Islamic Liberation Front (MILF) told Reuters in an interview that bin Laden had supplied some funds to people in his area prior to 1984 to support the construction of mosques and Islamic schools on Mindanao Island, but had not given any aid in the form of weapons (JTWR, 2/11/99)

[redacted]

The Philippines

21 Feb 1999 Philippine government sources charged that the Moro Islamic Liberation Front, MILF, was waiting for a massive arms shipment, allegedly purchased with funds provided by bin Laden (SGIU, 2/24/99))

MILF, which is fighting for a separate Islamic state in Mindanao, formed as a splinter group of the Moro National Liberation Front (MNLF) (SGIU, 2/24/99)

Agence France Presse reported on 22 February that rebel sources claimed that a cache of 3,000 high-powered weapons would be delivered aboard a foreign vessel via Indonesia (SGIU, 2/24/99)

On 24 February the Radio Republic of Indonesia reported that the Tanjungperak Port Authority in Tanjungperak, Indonesia was monitoring the planned of arrival of MV Alkeen Perdaba, which was believed to be carrying 3,000 anti-tank rockets from Afghanistan to Muslim Moros in the Philippines (SGIU, 2/24/99)

However, MILF vice-chairman for military affairs, Mohammad Murad, insisted that MILF was not expecting any arms shipment and that bin Laden stopped sending financial aid to the MILF after he became "very much involved in the Afghan war" (SGIU, 2/24/99)

[redacted]

Saudi Arabia

Late 1989 — After the Soviet withdrawal from Afghanistan, bin Laden went to Saudi Arabia on a trip and, while there, was banned from travel because of his intentions to start a new "front" of jihad in South Yemen (PBS Online, citing a document provided by a source close to bin Laden)

He was also instructed officially to keep a low profile and not to give public talks (PBS Online, citing a document provided by a source close to bin Laden)

2 Aug 1990 — Iraq invaded Kuwait

Bin Laden "immediately" forwarded a letter to the King suggesting in detail how to protect the country and volunteering to bring all the Arab mujahedeen to defend the country (PBS Online, citing a document provided by a source close to bin Laden)

A Saudi prince has said that he "marched into several princes' offices with maps and flowcharts to demonstrate how the kingdom could defend itself without foreign forces" (JIRP, 10/98, p. 8)

"While he was expecting some call to mobilize his men and equipment he heard the news which transferred [transformed] his life completely. The Americans are coming." (Quote from a document provided by a source close to bin Laden, PBS Online)

[redacted]

[redacted]

Saudi Arabia

7 Aug 1990 U.S. troops began to arrive in Saudi Arabia in the buildup that preceded the Gulf War

To bin Laden, the deployment of American troops in the land of Mecca and Medina smacked of the Crusades (NYT, 4/13/99)

Bin Laden had reportedly offered to defend Arabia after the invasion of Kuwait but was rejected by the Saudis

Another source has contradicted this: former chief of the CIA's Near East operations has said that "One of the stories put out by bin Laden is that he went to King Fahd and promised that he would raise holy warriors who would protect Saudi Arabia [from Iraq]. His violent opposition to the Saudi royal family began when King Fahd denied or rejected that offer." (NYT, 4/13/99)

1990-91 Bin Laden started lobbying through religious scholars and Muslim activists and succeeded in getting a fatwah from one of the senior scholars that training and readiness was a religious duty (PBS Online, citing a document provided by a source close to bin Laden)

Bin Laden circulated the fatwah and convinced as many as 4000 men to have training in Afghanistan (PBS Online, citing a document provided by a source close to bin Laden)

The Saudis, unhappy with bin Laden's activities summoned him for questioning and limited his movement to Jeddah only (PBS Online, citing a document provided by a source close to bin Laden)

[redacted]

[redacted]

Saudi Arabia

1991	Because of concerns about the financing of terrorism, King Fahd summoned leaders of the kingdom's wealthiest families to urge them to be more careful in their charitable donations (NYT, 8/14/96)
April 1991	Bin Laden left Saudi Arabia after being confined to Jiddah for his opposition to the Saudi alliance with the United States (PBS Online)
	Sources close to bin Laden claim that he went to Afghanistan, where the Saudis, with Pakistani help, tried "more than once to kidnap or kill him" (PBS Online, citing a document provided by a source close to bin Laden)
	By late 1991 he left Afghanistan in disguise in a private jet (PBS Online, citing a document provided by a source close to bin Laden)
Nov 1991	Saudi intelligence officers caught bin Laden smuggling weapons from Yemen (NYT, 4/13/99)
	Following this, Saudi officials withdrew his passport (NYT, 4/13/99)
1992	At Egypt's request, the Saudis severed aid to the Afghan border camps in Pakistan and helped to persuade the Pakistani government to close many of the camps (NYT, 8/14/96)
1993	Because of concerns about the financing of terrorism, the Saudis issued a royal decree banning the collection of money in the kingdom for charitable causes without official permission (NYT, 8/14/96)

[redacted]

[redacted]

Saudi Arabia

16 May 1993 — Saudi authorities issued an arrest warrant for bin Laden both because of his support for fundamentalist groups and because of his ties with upstart religious circles that tried to establish an independent human rights organization in Saudi Arabia at the beginning of May (PBS Online, citing a report from a French source)

1992-1995 — On at least two occasions, members of al Qaeda transported weapons and explosives from Khartoum, Sudan to the coastal city of Port Sudan for shipment to the Saudi Arabian peninsula

1994 — Because of concerns about the financing of terrorism, King Fahd set up a Supreme Council of Islamic Affairs, headed by his brother Prince Sultan, the Defense Minister, to centralize and supervise aid requests from Islamic groups (NYT, 8/14/96)

Although the Saudi government stopped financing militant Islamic groups, individual Saudis were still helping them without the knowledge or consent of the government (NYT, 8/14/96)

9 Apr 1994 — Saudi authorities stripped bin Laden of his Saudi citizenship and moved to freeze his assets in Saudi Arabia because of his support for Muslim fundamentalist movements (NYT 4/10/94; PBS Online)

Saudi authorities considered bin Laden responsible for an attack against the Saudi ambassador to Pakistan and a failed attempt to hijack a Saudi aircraft flying between Karachi and Jeddah

[redacted]

[redacted]

Saudi Arabia

Sep 1994	The Saudi government clamped down on the country's Muslim scholars, dismissing many from their posts The Saudi government also banned the distribution of certain materials At this time, bin Laden has said, "I decided to myself… that I would start saying what was right and denouncing what was wrong" (Interview with Al Quds Al Arabi in Nov 1996 in a cave near Kandahar, Afghanistan)
1995	Bin Laden began sending scathing attacks on the royal family of Saudi Arabia from Khartoum, Sudan According to President Bashir of Sudan: "Bin Laden took a chance and started doing some political activities" (NYT, 4/13/99)
3 Aug 1995	Bin Laden issued a communiqué called "an Open Letter to King Fahd" calling for a campaign of guerilla attacks to drive U.S. forces out of the Saudi Kingdom (PBS Online, "Osama bin Laden v. the U.S.: Edicts and Statements")

[redacted]

[redacted]

Saudi Arabia

13 Nov 1995 A car bomb exploded outside the Riyadh headquarters of the Office of the Program Manager/Saudi Arabian National Guard (OPM/SANG) where there was a training school run by Americans

7 persons were killed (5 US service personnel and 2 Indians) and 42 injured

Three of four men accused in this bombing were members of the "Afghan Arabs" [they had fought against the Soviets in Afghanistan] who admitted receiving pamphlets from bin Laden

One of these men had fought for the Muslim-led government in Bosnia

They said that they had been influenced by faxes sent by bin Laden's Advice and Reformation Committee

Publicly, bin Laden has denied involvement but praised the attack: "What they did is a great job and a big honor that I missed participating in."

Bin Laden reportedly took credit for the bombing in telephone conversations

U.S. officials have said that they have evidence linking bin Laden to the bombing (NYT, 10/18/98)

In his May 1998 interview with ABC News, bin Laden referred to the four men executed for the bombing as "shahids" or martyrs

[redacted]

Saudi Arabia

Jan 1996 Hassan al Srihi (a.k.a. Hassan al Sarai, aka Abu Abdulrahman al Madani), a suspect in the Nov 1995 bombing in Riyadh was extradited from Pakistan to Saudi Arabia

Al Srihi had traveled to Peshawar in 1978 for military training and served as a Saudi Mujahideen during the Afghan War

He had belonged to the al Ansar battalion financed and sponsored by bin Laden

31 May 1996 Four Saudis who confessed to the Nov 1995 bombing in Riyadh were beheaded in Saudi Arabia (NYT, 4/13/99)

Before their execution, they were coerced into a public confession in which they claim to have read bin Laden communiqués (PBS Online)

Spring 1996 President Clinton signed a top secret order that authorized the CIA to use any and all means to destroy bin Laden's network (PBS Online)

[redacted]

Saudi Arabia

25 Jun 1996

The bombing at the Khobar Towers military barracks in Dharan, Saudi Arabia killed 19 and injured hundreds

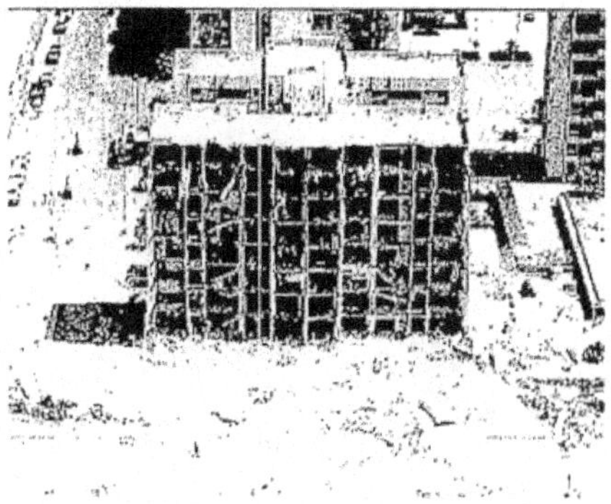

Telephone intercepts and other intelligence later indicated that bin Laden was involved in the attack

Bin Laden reportedly took credit for the bombing in telephone conversations

Publicly, bin Laden has denied involvement but praised the attack

Some U.S. officials suspect bin Laden was involved in financing the bombing

Other reports say that U.S. officials have learned enough to regard bin Laden as a prime suspect (NYT, 10/8/98)

A Saudi national named Hani al-Sayegh was later arrested by Canadian authorities (March 1997) and deported to the US for allegedly participating in the Khobar Towers bombing as a member of Saudi Hizballah

Al-Sayegh reneged on his plea-bargain agreement and was turned over to immigration authorities because there was insufficient evidence to prosecute him

[redacted]

[redacted]

Khobar Towers after the bombing

[redacted]

Saudi Arabia

10 July 1996 The British newspaper The Independent quoted bin Laden as saying:

"What happened in Riyadh and [Dhahran] when 24 Americans were killed in two bombings is clear evidence of the huge anger of Saudi people against America." (PBS Online, "Osama bin Laden v. the U.S.: Edicts and Statements")

23 Aug 1996 Bin Laden declared war against the United States, saying

"the situation in Saudi Arabia is like a great volcano about to erupt" (NYT, 4/13/99)

Aug 1996 The London-based Arabic-language newspaper al-Quds al-Arabi published a 12-page statement by bin Laden in which he called for a holy war "against the Americans who are occupying the land of the two shrines [Saudi Arabia]"

He referred to American forces in the Gulf as a "crusader" army

Al Qaeda is believed to have had plans to kidnap U.S. military personnel in the Gulf

Aug 1996 A secret grand jury investigation against bin Laden began in New York (PBS Online)

[redacted]

Saudi Arabia

Oct-Nov 1996 The 15th issue of the Nida'ul Islam magazine (Australia) carried an interview with bin Laden

Regarding attacks against Americans in Saudi Arabia: "So the people became aware that their main problems were caused by the American occupiers and their puppets in the Saudi regime..."

"...all that has been proved is our joy at the killing of the American soldiers in Riyadh and Khobar, and these are the sentiments of every Muslim."

Feb 1997 Bin laden was interviewed by an Arabic language newspaper in London and said:

"We had thought that the Riyadh and Al Khobar blasts were a sufficient signal to sensible U.S. decision-makers to avert a real battle between the Islamic nation and U.S. forces, but it seems they did not understand the signal"

Late Mar 1997 Bin Laden was interviewed in eastern Afghanistan by CNN's Peter Arnett

In his televised special that aired on 11 May 1997, Arnett refers to a videotape provided to CNN by members of the "Saudi opposition" which documents their video surveillance of U.S. troops inside Saudi Arabia and also shows how easily they can enter areas where U.S. civilians live (CNN)

[redacted]

[redacted]

Saudi Arabia

June 1998 Saudi Prince Turki al-Faisal, the chief of Saudi intelligence, led a small Saudi delegation to Taliban headquarters in Kandahar, Afghanistan to seek either bin Laden's ouster from Afghanistan or his custody for trial in Saudi Arabia (LAT, "Bin Laden slipped past Saudis' grip")

According to Prince al-Faisal, Taliban leader Mullah Omar agreed to surrender bin Laden to the Saudis in a deal that was to have been carefully orchestrated (LAT, "Bin Laden slipped past Saudis' grip")

Unfortunately, the negotiations ended amid a flurry of recriminations after the East African embassy bombings (LAT, "Bin Laden slipped past Saudis' grip")

The Taliban's representative in New York, Abdul Hakeem Mujahid, said that there was never an agreement to turn over bin Laden; that the Taliban's understanding was that the Saudis wanted bin Laden confined in Afghanistan (LAT, "Bin Laden slipped past Saudis' grip")

Summer 1998 Two representatives of wealthy Saudis visited bin Laden and paid him not to conduct operations in Saudi Arabia

"Allah willing, the next victory will be in Saudi Arabia, and it will make the Americans forget the horrors of Vietnam and Beirut."

(Osama bin Laden, 28 May 1998)

[redacted]

[redacted]

Iran

Before moving to Sudan, bin Laden stayed for several months in Afghanistan, and then in Iran

It was reportedly Iranian diplomats who first introduced bin Laden to Sudanese government officials

Mamdouh Mahmud Salim, a top bin Laden aide detained in Germany on 16 Sep 1998, had met with Iranian officials in Tehran and Khartoum to arrange for bin Laden militants to receive explosives training in Lebanon from Hezbollah

Court papers claim that the government of Iran had entered into a formal three-way "working agreement" with bin Laden and the National Islamic Front of Sudan to "work together against the United States, Israel, and the West"

1983	Mohammed Shawky al-Islambouli, the brother of Sadat's assassin, made his way to Peshawar, Pakistan
	He reportedly had close ties to Iran and funneled Iranian money to the Egyptian fundamentalist radicals in Afghanistan
June 1994	A Shia holy place in Iran was bombed (ECON, 10/9/99, p. 26)
	Ramzi Yousef, who was convicted in the bombing of the World Trade Center, has been linked to this bombing (ECON, 10/9/99, p. 26)

[redacted]

[redacted]

Iran

21-22 Jun 1996	Several extremist movements staged a "parallel" conclave in Tehran
	Officials suspect that this meeting was a terrorist planning conference (NYT, 8/14/96)
	Present were Ahmed Jibril, leader of the PFLP-GC, Imad Mugnieh, head of "strategic security" for Lebanon's Hezbollah, Ahmed Salem, a leader of Egypt's Islamic Jihad, and Mohamed Ali, "right-hand man" of bin Laden
June 1996	Intelligence officials believe that bin Laden attended a "terrorism summit" that they believe took place in Tehran
Early 1997	Bin Laden attended a meeting in Tehran with Iranian intelligence officials to plot recruiting, logistical and intelligence strategy
Jul 1997	Bin Laden is believed to have been working with Hezbollah and its patron Iran

[redacted]

[redacted]

Bangladesh

Feb 1998	There were reports that bin Laden attended an Islamic gathering near the capital Dhaka (JTWR, 1/29/99)
	Bin Laden's visit was uncovered following the arrest in January 1999 of 44 people in a foiled plot to kill a Bangladeshi poet in Dhaka on 18 January 1999 (JTWR, 1/29/99)
	Bangladeshi newspapers have said that bin Laden visited Bangladesh in recent years (WP, 2/19/99)
23 Feb 1998	Sheik Abdul Salaam Mohamed, the chief of Bangladesh's Jihad, was among those who signed the communiqué issued by the International Islamic Front in Afghanistan on this date
Late Oct 1998	Police in Bangladesh seized leaflets promoting bin Laden's cause and arrested six people (SGIU, 12/1/98)
Early Nov 1998	Prior to the reading of the verdict in the trial of the accused assassins of Bangladesh's Prime Minister, the police in Bangladesh obtained information that bin Laden's group was planning a terrorist action at the time of the verdict (SGIU, 12/1/98)

[redacted]

[redacted]

Bangladesh

1999 Bangladesh security officials said that bin Laden has financed at least one Muslim militant group in Bangladesh (WP, 2/19/99)

The group, known as Harkat-ul-Jihad, sought to transplant to Bangladesh the extreme brand of Islam that the Taliban militia has enforced in most of Afghanistan (WP, 2/19/99)

Harkat-ul-Jihad, had apparently been formed by 1995 at an Islamic seminary in Chittagong (WP, 2/19/99)

The groups founders were Abdul Hye and another cleric known as Sheik Farid (WP, 2/19/99)

The group recruited seminary students, trained them to use light arms, and sent them to fight alongside the Taliban in Afghanistan (WP, 2/19/99)

The small-arms training took place at two small camps in southeastern Bangladesh (WP, 2/19/99)

In its monthly magazine (Wake Up, Freedom Fighter), Harkat has published excerpts of bin Laden's media interviews as well as the group's appeals to Bangladeshis to join "holy wars" in Afghanistan and Kashmir (WP, 2/19/99)

[redacted]

[redacted]

Bangladesh

Jan 1999 — 44 people were arrested in a foiled plot to kill a Bangladeshi poet (70 year old Shamshur Rahman) in Dhaka on 18 January (JTWR, 1/29/99; WP, 2/19/99)

The men admitted to being members of a group called the Harakat ul-Jihad, which is allegedly linked to the Taliban in Afghanistan (JTWR, 1/29/99)

Some of the men confessed to receiving funds from bin Laden to train Islamic militants to bring about a Taliban-style Islamic revolution in Bangladesh (JTWR, 1/29/99)

Some of the suspects have told police that one of the fugitives, Abdul Hye, a Muslim cleric from Chittagong, received funds directly from bin Laden (WP, 2/19/99)

Other suspects have said that one of the men who was arrested, a South African of Indian descent named Ahmed Sidiq Ahmed, was a "personal friend" of bin Laden (WP, 2/19/99)

A Bangladeshi newspaper said that bin Laden funneled $1 million to the group through four bank accounts in Dhaka (WP, 2/19/99)

8 Mar 1999 — A rally of about 15,000 Muslims in the capital Dhaka expressed support for bin Laden, denounced the Saudi Arabian monarchy (which forced bin Laden into exile), and praised the Taliban regime in Afghanistan (JTWR, 3/12/99)

[redacted]

[redacted]

Miscellaneous Connections

In recent years, bin Laden has reportedly been seen in Iran, Malaysia, the Philippines, Yemen, and Switzerland

In addition, his followers and supporters have been active in many countries:

Austria

On 21 April 1999 Austrian police in Vienna arrested and questioned Adel Assayed Abdul Kudus, an Islamic activist who had been a member of Egyptian Jihad's consultative council (Majlis Shura): Egypt charges that he headed a branch of Jihad in Austria and sentenced him to death in absentia in April 1999 (IPIN, 5/13/99, p. 8)

China

Moslem guerillas trained by bin Laden have been reported in the Xinjiang region of China

Senior Chinese Communist Party officials claimed that Muslim terrorists trained in Afghanistan were infiltrating China's Muslim-majority Xinjiang Province were up to 20 training bases were set up by "minority splittists"

In October 1998 Moslem militants trained by the Taliban and, allegedly, by bin Laden had recently begun to appear in the Xinjiang region (SGIU, 10/13/99)

On 20 Apr 1999 an Amnesty International report claimed that 200 Uighurs were sentenced to death in the past two years as the Chinese struggled to suppress anti-Chinese sentiment among Muslim Uighers in the northwestern province of Xinjiang (JTWR, 4/21/99)

[redacted]

[redacted]

Miscellaneous Connections

Azerbaijan

1995

Mahmud Sayyid Jaballah, a leader of Egypt's Jihad, was asked to find new recruits in Baku Azerbaijan: He managed to quickly set up a fundamentalist network with branches in Afghanistan, Bosnia, Albania, and the United Kingdom (IPIN, 6/24/99, p. 8)

Sept 1998

The CIA broke up a bin Laden ring that had been planning an attack on the U.S. embassy in Baku, Azerbaijan

Among those taken into custody was Ahmad Salama Mabrouk, a member of the Egyptian militant group Al-Jihad (SGIU, 4/20/99)

On 19 April 1999 the London-based newspaper Al-Hayat quoted Ahmad Salama Mabrouk from jail as saying that bin Laden's umbrella group (the International Islamic Front for Fighting Jews and Crusaders) not only possessed biological and chemical weapons, but was planning about 100 operations against U.S. and Israeli interests around the world (SGIU, 4/20/99)

The report also said that details of these planned attacks were found on a computer program which was confiscated by the CIA in September 1998 at the time Mabrouk was taken into custody in Azerbaijan (SGIU, 4/20/99)

[redacted]

[redacted]

Miscellaneous Connections

Eritrea

Bin Laden has reportedly trained members of the Eritrean Islamic Jihad, which has attacked civilians using anti-tank mines to destroy several passenger buses (JIR, 10/98, p. 25)

Ethiopia

Bin Laden has reportedly trained members of the Oromo Islamic Front, a separatist group

Bin Laden has been accused of masterminding the unsuccessful attack on the life of Hosni Mubarak in Addis Ababa in 1995

Gulf States

Sheik Ali Salman, a former student in Qom (Iran), a top ideologist for Shi'ites in the Gulf, and one of the leaders of a high political command speaking for Islamic fundamentalists in six Gulf countries, has cultivated close relations with bin Laden

In late 1998 U.S. intelligence agents monitored conversations between bin Laden in Afghanistan in Afghanistan and some of his supporters during which a plot was discussed to attack one or more U.S. targets in the Gulf region

In response to this, "new measures" were introduced in December 1998 around U.S. facilities in several countries, including Saudi Arabia, Kuwait, and Bahrain

[redacted]

[redacted]

Miscellaneous Connections

Indonesia

Bin Laden has been trying to recruit among the Moslems in Indonesia, who have vowed to oust President Habibe

Iraq

According to the 4 November 1998 indictment against bin Laden, "al Qaeda reached an understanding with the Government of Iraq that al Qaeda would not work against that government and that on particular projects, specifically including weapons development, al Qaeda would work cooperatively with the Government of Iraq" (USIA, 11/4/98)

Jordan

In December 1994 bin Laden's brother-in-law, Mohammed J. A. Khalifah, was detained by authorities in San Francisco because he was wanted by Jordan, who had sentenced him to death in absentia for conspiring to commit terrorist acts as part of an organization established "to fight Jews and Americans" (NYT, 8/14/96)

The Jordanian indictment said he had agreed to finance the organization, whose activities included bombing movie theaters in Jordan (NYT, 8/14/96)

[redacted]

Miscellaneous Connections

Kosovo

Bin Laden has supported Muslim fighters in Kosovo (according to a senior U.S. official)

Lebanon

Al Qaeda terrorists allegedly received explosives training in Lebanon from Hezbollah

Bin Laden and his associates allegedly plotted with Hezbollah to strike U.S. military forces in Saudi Arabia, Yemen, and in the Horn of Africa

Libya

In early 1998 in Jalalabad, Pakistan, Said Sayyed Salameh, who was considered on of bin Laden's closest associates, was asked by bin Laden to become involved in bin Laden's financial activities in several African countries and, particularly, to hand money to the leaders of fundamentalist factions in Libya and Egypt

Miscellaneous Connections

Malaysia

Bin Laden has followers, and some of his money, in Malaysia (SGIU, 10/13/98)

According to the U.S. case against Mamdouh Mahmud Salim – a founder, financial manager, and weapons procurer for al Qaeda – as early as 1990 Salim met with members of al Qaeda in Malaysia to "engage in financial transactions for the benefit of al Qaeda and its affiliated groups" (SGIU, 10/13/98)

He evidently maintains contacts and possibly banking operations in Malaysia and has used Malaysia as a transshipment point for arms, money and personnel to the Philippine Muslim extremist groups Abu Sayyaf and the Salafiyah Fighters (SGIU, 1/13/99)

Tajikistan

Bin Laden has supported Tajik Muslim rebels and has dispatched guerillas with Harkat Ansar to fight the Tajik government

Bin Laden has admitted sending Islamic fighters to Tajikistan (JIR, 10/98, p. 25)

Miscellaneous Connections

Uzbekistan

16 Feb 1999 Car bombings in Tashkent, Uzbekistan killed 15 people and injured more than 100 (JTWR, 2/25/99)

Uzbek authorities have linked the bombings to Islamic extremists who are suspected of getting help from abroad (JTWR, 2/25/99)

Nearly all of the 22 men accused of the six car-bomb attacks that killed 16 persons received their training in Chechnya: The men, members of an Islamic group called Hizb-e Takhrir, were trained by the Chechen military at a special camp to carry out a holy war (JTWR, 6/10/99)

Prosecutors claimed that about 150 Uzbeks had been trained in camps in Chechnya (JTWR, 6/10/99)

5 Apr 1999 Reuters reported that Uzbek Interior Minister Zakirdzhon Almatov, in a bid to curb the growing threat of Islamic fundamentalism, urged young men who studied "non-traditional" Islam abroad to give themselves up (JTWR, 4/6/99)

Uzbekistan has accused Tajikistan, Afghanistan, Pakistan, and Chechnya of allowing young Uzbeks to train on their territory before returning to Uzbekistan in armed fundamentalist opposition (JTWR, 4/6/99)

[redacted]

Russia/Chechnya/Caucasus

Bin Laden formed alliances with Muslim rebels who fought for independence from Russia in 1994-96

In interviews, bin Laden has admitted sending Islamic fighters to Chechnya (JIR, 10/98, p. 25)

Many Chechens made their way to the border region between Pakistan and Afghanistan, where they trained for months in guerilla warfare tactics, learning how to use different weapons, lay mines, and plan ambushes (JIR, Mar 1999, p. 14-15)

Volunteers from many Islamic countries, including a Mujahideen battalion from Afghanistan, also served in Chechnya (JIR, Mar 1999, p.17)

Many believed that liberation of Chechnya from Russia was only the first step in the general liberation of the Muslim peoples of the Caucasus (JIR, Mar 1999, p.17)

Chechen Guerillas

[redacted]

[redacted]

Russia/Chechnya/Caucasus

2-3 Aug 1999 Fighting broke out along the Dagestan border with Chechnya (FYEOX, 8/11/99)

7 Aug 1999 After rising unrest in the region, a Muslim rebel offensive was unleashed in Dagestan by Chechen leader Shamil Basayev on the first anniversary of the bomb attacks against American embassies in East Africa (IPIN, 8/26/99, p. 1)

10 Aug 1999 Islamic guerillas supported by Chechen warlords declared Russia's Dagestan province an independent state (NYT, 8/10/99)

Russians target Islamic militants in Dagestan (JIR, 10/99, p.9)

Russia claimed that the rebels were members of the militant Sunni Wahhabi sect of Muslims (NYT, 8/11/99; FYEOX, 8/11/99)

Many Arabs, Africans, Tajiks, Uzbeks, and Russians were reported to be with the rebels (FYEOX, 8/11/99)

The rebels were actively backed by Afghanistan's Taliban, Bin Laden's al Qaeda organization, several Wahabite groups in Saudi Arabia, and Pakistani and Egyptian extremist movements (IPIN, 8/26/99, p. 1)

[redacted]

[redacted]

Russia/Chechnya/Caucasus

Chechen guerilla leaders said that they intend to drive Russian forces out of the area as they did in Chechnya after their 1994-96 war for independence (NYT, 8/10/99)

Chechen guerilla leaders also demand that Dagestan and Chechnya be merged into a single Islamic state (FYEOX, 8/11/99)

The leaders of the rebels are reported to be Chechen warlord Shamil Basayev (who was prime minister of Chechnya from January to July 1998 and who led a daring raid in southern Russia in June 1995 in which he took 1,000 people hostage) and a Jordanian known as Khottab (FYEOX, 8/11/99; JIR, 10/99, p. 9)

Khottab is a Wahabite leader who joined Chechen rebels in 1994, fought against the Russians during the Chechen war, and is reportedly the organizer of military training camps in Chechnya (FYEOX, 8/11/99; JIR, 10/99, p. 9)

Khattab joined the first batch of Jordanian "Afghans" to fight in Afghanistan in a brigade formed by the Palestinian Abdallah Azzam and financed by the World Islamic League (IPIN, 8/26/99, p. 8)

Khattab led the "Jordanian Afghans" in the 1980s, a 400-man unit that fought with the mujahideen in Afghanistan (IPIN, 8/26/99, p. 1)

Khattab joined Basayev's separatist fighters in Chechnya in 1994 (IPIN, 8/26/99, p. 8)

[redacted]

[redacted]

Russia/Chechnya/Caucasus

Khattab has been linked in intelligence reports to bin Laden (NYT, 9/20/99)

Khattab was being assisted in the Caucasus by Pakistani mujahideen under the command of Safir Ahmed, who had met in late June with bin Laden in Jalalabad (IPIN, 8/26/99, p. 1)

Chechen rebels were also getting material backing from Ayman Zawahri, head of Egypt's Jihad, and a very close ally of bin Laden (IPIN, 8/26/99, p. 1)

Shamil Basayev said that he had never met bin Laden (NYT, 9/20/99)

Basayev said that Khattab had known bin Laden during the time when he fought in Afghanistan, but in a later message an intermediary said that this was incorrect, the result of a transcription error in Basayev's written reply to questions about bin Laden (NYT, 9/20/99)

By 31 August 1999 there were reports of up to 300 mercenaries from Saudi Arabia, Algeria, and Libya stationed in the Iskhan preserve in Chechnya near the Dagestan border (JTWR, 8/31/99)

"We will fight until the full victory of Islam in the world"

Chechen leader Shamil; Basayev (NYT, 8/11/99)

"There is no force on Earth capable of stopping the Muslim fighters other than the Almighty, who guides them on the road of sacred war"

Chechen leader Shamil; Basayev (WP, 8/12/99)

[redacted]

[redacted]

Russia: The September Bombings

In September 1999 there was a series of bomb attacks in Russian cities which Russia blamed on Islamic militants associated with the fighting in Dagestan and Chechnya: (JIR, 10/99, p. 2)

31 Aug 1999	A bomb in a shopping mall near the Kremlin killed 1 and injured over 40
4 Sept 1999	A bomb in a building housing Russian servicemen and their families in Buinaksk, Dagestan killed 64
9 Sept 1999	A bomb in an apartment block of the Pechatniki suburb of Moscow killed 94
13 Sept 1999	A bomb attack at Block 3, Number 6 Kashirskoyoe Highway in southern Moscow killed 118
16 Sept 1999	A truck bomb outside a nine-block apartment building in Volgodonsk in southern Russian killed 18

Some of those involved in these bombings allegedly traveled from an Islamic seminary in Tatarstan (which the Russians claim to be a recruitment source for Islamic separatists) to a terrorist training center in the Chechen mountains run by Commander Kahttab to be prepared for combat against the Russians (JIR, 10/99, p. 2)

There was evidence that bin Laden, while not the instigator of the urban bombing campaign, had offered financial support to its perpetrators (ECON, 10/9/99, p. 25)

Furthermore, fighters under the influence of bin Laden were active in Chechnya and Dagestan, although their presence was probably not the main reason why the war was raging there (ECON, 10/9/99, p. 25)

[redacted]

[redacted]

Russia/Chechnya/Caucasus

12 Sept 1999 — Russian Prime Minister Vladimir Putin said that Russia had information that bin Laden's followers were involved in the fighting in Dagestan and Chechnya (JIR, 10/99, p. 56)

That same day, Mahrez Amduni, a terrorist on Interpol's list of most wanted criminals and a leading associate of bin Laden, was captured in Turkey carrying a Bosnian passport (FYEOX, 9/24/99; IPIN, 9/23/99, p. 7) after a tip-off from the CIA and an investigation that shed light on a widespread drive to recruit Arab fundamentalists for service in the Caucasus (IPIN, 9/23/99, p. 7)

15 Oct 1999 — Russia Interior Minister Vladimir Rushailo said that police had seized 515 metric tons of explosives, 4,000 detonating devices and 7,000 firearms between 15 September and 2 October during a nation-wide anti-terrorism sweep (JTWR, 10/15/99)

20 Oct 1999 — AP reported that Russia's Federal Security Service (FSB) suspects that an Egyptian man named Said el-Maban traveled to Chechnya in December 1998 and paid Chechen warlords $200,000 to carry out the two apartment building bombings in Moscow in September 1999 that killed more than 200 people (JTWR, 10/20/99)

"The difference between us and the Russians is that they like to live and we like to die. We will win, but with huge losses."

Representative of Chechnya (ECON, 10/30/99, p. 55)

[redacted]

[redacted]

The United Kingdom

Bin Laden has been linked by U.S. government officials to Saudi opposition groups located in London (NYT, 8/14/96)

Some of the history of his ties to Muslim, militants in the UK are documented here:

1995 Mahmud Sayyid Jaballah, a leader of Egypt's Jihad, was asked to find new recruits in Baku Azerbaijan (IPIN, 6/24/99, p. 8)

He managed to quickly set up a fundamentalist network with branches in Afghanistan, Bosnia, Albania, and the United Kingdom (IPIN, 6/24/99, p. 8)

The head of the Egyptian Jihad, Ayman Zawahri, is believed to have asked Mahmud Sayyid Jaballah to collect funds for the movement and to serve as liaison with units in Britain (IPIN, 6/24/99, p. 8)

The Egyptian, Jordanian, and Yemeni intelligence agencies all view Kamal al Habawi, who was president of the U.K. branch of the Islamic League as of April 1999, as a veteran figure in the jihad in Afghanistan, Bosnia, and Chechnya (IPIN, 4/8/99, p. 8)

[redacted]

The United Kingdom

28 Sept 1998 Five Islamic militants were arrested in London: Hani Mohamed al Sibai, Ibrahim al Aidarous, Ussama Hassan Ahmed, Sayyed Abdul Maksud, and Sayyed Ajami Mohalhal (IPIN, 5/13/99, p. 8)

Bin Laden's right-hand man, sheikh Khaled al Fawaz, was also arrested (IPIN, 5/27/99, p. 6)

Khalid al-Fawwaz once served as bin Laden's press spokesman

An informer identified Khalid al-Fawwaz as the UK head of al Qaeda (JTWR, 9/8/99)

The spokesman for the Advice and Reformation Committee in London, Khaled al-Fauwaz, was a friend of bin Laden who has said that he was "proud" to be his friend and described the charges of supporting terrorism as "rubbish" (NYT, 8/14/96)

Some of these individuals had been associated with The Islamic Observation Center in London (IPIN, 5/13/99, p. 8)

The Islamic Observatory in London spreads the ideas of fundamentalists close to bin Laden (IPIN, 2/11/99, p. 6)

The leader of the Islamic Observation Center, Tewfik al Sirri, was sought by Egypt as of early 1999 (IPIN, 2/11/99, p. 6) and was among those put on trial in absentia (JIR, Mar 1999, p. 7)

Al-Sirri called on the Egyptian people and the army to overthrow President Hosni Mubarak: "If the head of state is a non-believer, it is our duty to remove him" (JIR, Mar 1999, p. 7)

[redacted]

The United Kingdom

19 Jan 1999 The London Evening Standard reported that bin Laden was planning to kidnap a high-profile US national through his London connections (JTWR, 1/19/99)

US intelligence sources said that the US was on high alert the week before, expecting bin Laden to attempt a kidnapping or assassination in the UK (JTWR, 1/19/99)

Documents seized at the home of Khalid Al-Fawaz, bin Laden's alleged connection in London, showed fax numbers in ten US cities, where orders were allegedly sent to murder US citizens (JTWR, 1/19/99)

Also, two US post office box numbers had been rented by bin Laden operatives in Denver and Kansas City (JTWR, 1/19/99)

21-22 May 1999 There was a gathering of Islamic movements in London at the Friend's House center (IPIN, 5/27/99, p. 6)

At the gathering, sheikh Omar Bakri Muhammad warned that if London extradited the six Islamic militants arrested on 28 Sept 1998, then "British terrorism would be matched by fundamentalist terrorism" (IPIN, 5/27/99, p. 6)

Bakri also indicated privately that he was summoning soldiers who had deserted from certain Moslem armies, especially those in Iraq and Iran, to join him in preparing a "Caliphate state" to "stamp out Western insolence" (IPIN, 5/27/99, p. 6)

[redacted]

[redacted]

The United Kingdom

20 Jan 1999 Abu Hamza, the leader of the Supporters of Shariah, a London-based Islamic fundamentalist group, denied having links with a group of five Muslim UK nationals who were arrested in Yemen on terrorism charges on 24 December (JTWR, 1/21/99)

However, he warned UK citizens against foreign travel because he said the UK government is involved in the "oppression of Muslims" (JTWR, 1/21/99)

Hamza, aka Abu Hamza al-Masri, is an Egyptian-born Afghan war veteran who lost both hands and an eye while fighting with the mujahideen against the Soviets (JTWR, 1/21/99; JTWR, 1/26/99)

25 Feb 1999 The London-based Arabic newspaper Al Hayat reported that UK Islamic militant Abu Hamza Al Masri had threatened to blow up Western military and civilian aircraft in mid-air in an attempt to end the West's monopoly on global aviation (JTWR, 2/26/99)

Abu Hamza told the newspaper that the full extent of his plot would be revealed on 26 February at a conference in London sponsored by his group, the Supporters of Shari (JTWR, 2/26/99)

The plot reportedly involved attaching "flying mines" to balloons that would be released into the air to disrupt aircraft flights (JTWR, 2/26/99)

[redacted]

The United Kingdom

15 Mar 1999 A police spokeswoman in London said that three men were being held after a series of raids by anti-terrorist detectives (JTWR, 3/16/99)

The Supporters of Sharia organization said that Abu Hamza Al-Masri had been arrested (JTWR, 3/16/99)

Hamza, an Afghan war veteran, has openly preached from his base at the North London Central Mosque that Muslims worldwide should fight for a more Islamic way of life and was accused of being linked to a recent kidnapping of Western tourists in Yemen (JWR, 3/16/99)

[redacted]

India & Kashmir

Bin Laden has trained Muslim separatist guerillas fighting Indian security forces in India's portion of the disputed Kashmir region

A Moslem terrorist captured in Hyderabad said that he had been trained in Afghanistan by bin Laden

India claims that bin Laden has moved as many as 500 trained guerillas to fight in Kashmir

Other sources say that more than 700 "elite Islamic mercenaries" recruited by bin Laden have crossed the border from Pakistan into Kashmir

Kashmiri guerillas

July 1995 — Six westerners were kidnapped in Kashmir by affiliates of the Harakat ul-Ansar (HUA)

Other sources say that five were kidnapped: Norwegian Hans Christian Ostro was beheaded and the other four (2 Americans, 1 Brit, and 1 German) are missing and believed dead (JIR, 8/99, p.32)

In October 1997 the Pakistan-based Kashmiri group HUA was designated as a foreign terrorist organization by the US

Following this designation, bin Laden praised the HUA

[redacted]

[redacted]

India & Kashmir

1st wk Oct 1998 Sayed Abu Nasir and six others slipped into India from Bangladesh (NYT, 1/22/99; SGIU, 1/27/99)

After their arrival in India, these men spent time in both Madras and Calcutta, examining the U.S. consulates for vulnerable areas in preparation for an attempt to bomb these consulates (NYT, 1/22/99)

4 Oct 1998 An article in the London Sunday Times stated that bin Laden had declared a jihad in Kashmir, had ordered Afghan and Arab militants to gather in Kashmir for a concentrated offensive against Indian troops, and that trained Afghan mujahideen guerillas had reached Srinagar

10 Oct 1998 At a news conference in Delhi, Jayaram Jayalalitha, the leader of the regional All-India Anna Dravida Munnetra Khazagham, warned that some 200 Afghan-trained supporters of bin Laden were "roaming" in Tamil Nadu and other southern Indian states (SGIU, 10/13/98)

She claimed that bin Laden's agents might have been responsible for bombings in the city of Coimbatore earlier in the year and that suspicions that bin Laden may be active in India were reinforced following the recent arrest of a Moslem suspect in Hyderabad who reportedly confessed that he had received six months of training in Afghanistan (SGIU, 10/13/99)

Oct 1999 Moslem militants trained by the Taliban and, allegedly, by bin Laden had recently begun to appear in disputed Kashmir (SGIU, 10/13/99)

[redacted]

[redacted]

India & Kashmir

7 Jan 1999* Indian police arrested Sayed Abu Nasir on suspicion of involvement in a plan to bomb the U.S. Embassy in New Delhi and the U.S. consulates in Madras and Calcutta (FYEO, 2/1/99, p. 466-3)

Nasir, a 27 year old Bangladeshi man, was arrested at the New Delhi train station with two kilograms of the explosive RDX and was allegedly plotting to blow up the U.S. Embassy in New Delhi and two American consulates elsewhere in India (NYT, 1/22/99; WP, 2/17/99)

Police have said that Nasir confessed to spying on Indian military operations, as well as to planning attacks on U.S. consulates that were foiled by his arrest (NYT, 1/22/99)

According to police, Nasir contended that he had met bin Laden once several years earlier while Nasir was in training at a camp in Afghanistan and he was working with an Islamic fundamentalist terrorist group on bombing the consulates (NYT, 1/22/99)

Three others were arrested in West Bengal in the case and six additional suspects from Egypt, Myanmar, and Sudan were at large as of January 1999 (NYT, 1/22/99)

Indian police said he was part of a nine-member team backed by bin Laden (FYEO, 2/1/99, p. 466-3)

Other reports said that Indian authorities believed that Nasir was part of a seven-member cell funded by bin Laden (WP, 2/17/99)

*SGIU on 1/27/99 said that Nasir was arrested "last week" although two other sources give 7 Jan

[redacted]

[redacted]

India & Kashmir

17 Jan 1999 Police in India arrested four people suspected of plotting to bomb the US Embassy in New Delhi and the US consulates in Madras and Calcutta (JTWR, 1/20/99)

Police said that the attacks were to have taken place before 26 January (JTWR, 1/20/99)

19 Jan 1999 A team of U.S. counterterrorism experts arrived in India to investigate charges that Sayed Abu Nasir and others had planned to bomb U.S. consulates in India and that bin Laden may have been involved as well (NYT, 1/22/99)

30 Aug 1999 Harkat-ul Ansar leader Mohammad Akbar Bhatt was arrested along with an aide in New Delhi and police seized military explosives intended to disrupt upcoming general elections (JTWR, 9/3/99)

[redacted]

Harakat-ul-Ansar (HUA)/Harakat ul-Mujahideen (HUM)

Origins

- Was originally named the Harakat-ul-Ansar (HUA) (JIR, Jan 1999, p. 40)
- Was formed in 1993 (JIR, Jan 1999, p. 40)
- Another source claims that the Harkat Ansar was formed in the 1980s to join Islamic guerillas in their fight against the Soviet Union (WP, 3/7/99)
- Was known as the Harakat-ul-Ansar (HUA) until being declared a terrorist organization at the end of 1997, after which it renamed itself the Harakat ul-Mujahideen or Harkat-ul-Jehed-e-Islami (JIR, Jan 1999, p. 40; JIR, 8/99, p.32)
- Is led by Fazl Rahman Khalil and his deputy Farook Kashmiri (JIR, Jan 1999, p. 40)

Activities

- After the end of the Afghan-Soviet war in 1989, Harkat sent a large number of Muslim militants from Pakistan across the unrecognized border dividing the disputed Himalayan territory of Kashmir in order to fight security forces in Indian-controlled areas (WP, 3/7/99)
- Has become a frontrunner in the militant fighting in Kashmir (JIR, Jan 1999, p. 40)
- Is also believed to have kidnapped and murdered five Westerners in Kashmir in 1995 (USNWR, 7/19/99)

[redacted]

Harakat-ul-Ansar (HUA)/Harakat ul-Mujahideen (HUM)

Strength

- In 1999 senior Pakistani intelligence officials estimated that Harkat commanded at least 500 well trained militants (WP, 3/7/99)
- Other sources say that its strength is about 350, led by Maulvi Siddique, and that its main areas of influence and operation are the Kashmir Valley, Poonch, Doda, and Rajauri (JIR, 8/99, p. 32)
- As of mid 1999, the HUA had about 350 troops led by Maulvi Siddique and was closely tied to bin Laden (FYEOX, 8/26/99)

Links to bin Laden and Afghanistan

- Harkat, as well as other militant Pakistani groups, was using bin Laden's camps to provide military training to its members (WP, 3/7/99)
- Was handed the newly captured training camps at Khost (in eastern Afghanistan) by the Taliban in the autumn of 1996 (JIR, Jan 1999, p. 40)
- Has close contacts with Taliban leaders and with bin Laden (JIR, Jan 1999, p. 40)
- The group is closely associated with the Afghan Taliban and with militant training camps run by bin Laden (JIR, 8/99, p. 32)
- As of 1999, the group had an office in Kabul situated in the Shahr-e-Nao quarter of the city which was run in early 1999 by a Punjabi party official named Abdul Jabbar (JIR, 10/99, p. 33)
- In 1999 a high-ranking Pakistani security official said that "In the shape of [Harkat Ansar] and a few other militant religious groups, Osama has a formidable human asset in Pakistan" (WP, 3/7/99)

[redacted]

[redacted]

India & Kashmir

Indian troops after re-claiming territory in Kashmir that had been taken by Islamic rebels in 1999 (JIR, 10/99)

[redacted]

[redacted]

Uganda

1990s	Members of the Lord's Resistance Army, a group that terrorizes civilians, have been armed by Sudan and trained at camps financed by bin Laden on Sudanese territory (JIR, 10/98, p. 24)
1998	Ugandan press reports claimed that Ugandan security forces had thwarted a plan to bomb the U.S. embassy in Kampala in coordination with the other East African bombings on August 7
17-18 Sept 1998	Eight Ugandans and ten Somalis were arrested in Uganda on suspicion of planning an attack on the U.S. Embassy in Kampala using a one-ton bomb in a dump truck
	Others were also arrested, after these suspects told police of other operatives in Uganda
	Police seized a large quantity of explosives and the dump truck that was to be used in the attack
	Many of the suspects had taken training at camps in Sudan
	Some of the suspects apparently had ties to bin Laden

Because news of this bombing plot was buried in the massive reporting that covered events surrounding the August bombings in Nairobi and Dar es Salaam, it went unnoticed by many observers

This is just one of the success stories that have been overshadowed by the Nairobi and Dar es Salaam bombings

[redacted]

[redacted]

Uganda

24 Sept 1998

Ugandan Minister of State for Security, Muruli Mukasa, said that 18 suspects were being held in Kampala

The suspects included Ugandans and Somalis, including a Ugandan sheikh or Islamic cleric said to have been recently trained in Sudan under bin Laden's sponsorship

Some of these suspects had confessed to having links with bin Laden and that a planned attack on the US Embassy in Kampala had been foiled

The aborted Kampala bomb would have gone off at the same time as the bombs in Nairobi and Dar es Salaam on 7 August 1998

In addition to the US Embassy, the aborted Kampala bombing also targeted the Bank of Uganda, the Post Office, and a downtown market

Mukasa said that alert security forces had detected the explosives in time

According to a report in the Washington Post on 25 Sept 1998, US government sources claimed that the CIA had alerted Ugandan authorities to the Kampala bombing plot

17 May 1999

The US Embassy in Kampala said that the US had suspended its Peace Corps program in Uganda over growing concerns for the safety of its 43 volunteers (JTWR, 5/18/99)

[redacted]

[redacted]

The Taliban Connection

Mullah Mohammed Omar, a one-eyed village cleric, founded the Islamic Taliban movement in 1994

Taliban Fighters

The Taliban first offered bin Laden sanctuary in 1996, knowing that he would be able to support their movement with money and arms

Bin Laden, both on his own and as a conduit for other wealthy Muslims, provided millions of dollars for the Taliban's attempted conquest of Afghanistan

Bin Laden funded hundreds of Koranic schools in Afghanistan and Pakistan

Bin Laden also built a new house for Mullah Omar

Bin Laden's supporters claim that he and his own private army of 300 Arab and Sudanese commandos joined in a Taliban assault at Bagram airbase, north of Kabul in 1998

Bin Laden became "a houseguest the Taliban like having around" (TIME magazine)

However, Taliban leader Mullah Omar has chafed at the audacity of bin Laden on more than one occasion

[redacted]

[redacted]

The Taliban Connection

Taliban leader Mullah Omar was reportedly "furious" with bin Laden after the February 1998 press conference where bin Laden announced his jihad against America and after the cruise missile attacks Omar stated that there cannot be two different governments in Afghanistan

By late 1998 at least two members of the Shura council in Afghanistan, Mullah Muhammed Hassan (Taliban Foreign Minister) and Mullah Mohammed Rabbani (head of the Shura council), were known to harbor feelings of near-enmity toward bin Laden

Furthermore, anti-bin Laden sentiment was said to be widespread throughout the Taliban movement as a whole

However, Taliban leader Mullah Omar (known as the Amir-ul-Momineen or Commander of the Faithful) supported bin Laden and held a great deal of political power

So long as the Taliban continued to support bin Laden, they had little chance of achieving the official UN recognition that they were desperate to achieve

However, bin Laden is seen as a war hero to many in Afghanistan, which complicates the ability of the Taliban to deal harshly with him

[redacted]

[redacted]

Afghanistan

1992 A young Palestinian from Jordan named Mohammed Saddiq Odeh joined al Qaida in Afghanistan

1994 Haroun Fazil, a native of the Comoros Islands, received paramilitary training from bin Laden in Afghanistan

Early 1996 Bin Laden started making contacts with his old friends in Afghanistan to prepare for a move there (PBS Online, citing a document provided by a source close to bin Laden)

May 1996 Bin Laden was expelled from Sudan and moved to Afghanistan

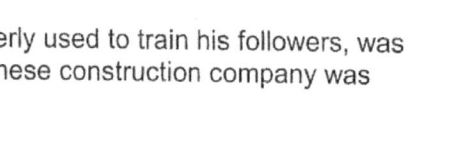

His farm at Jebel Kadr, in eastern Sudan, formerly used to train his followers, was given to a UN agricultural project and his Sudanese construction company was auctioned off

However, bin Laden retained some businesses in Sudan and retained strong ties with the Sudanese leadership

[redacted]

[redacted]

Afghanistan

May 1996	Bin Laden was expelled from Sudan and moved to Afghanistan
	The area he arrived in was under the control of Yunis Khalis, a warlord who later joined the Taliban (PBS Online, citing a document provided by a source close to bin Laden)
	Bin Laden lived outside Jalalabad, then moved to a new location outside of Kandahar
	He established at least two sets of terrorist training camps, the largest near the provincial capital of Khost
	The Khost camp hosted members of the Egyptian Islamic Jihad (including their leader Ayman el-Zawahri) and members of the Islamic Group (which assassinated Sadat in 1981)
1996	Mohamed Rashed Daoud Al-'Owhali met with bin Laden and asked him for a "mission"
21 May 1996	The Tanzanian passenger ferry Bukoba sank in Lake Victoria, killing more than 500 people (Washington Post says more than 800 drowned)
	Bin Laden's top military aid at the time, Abu Ubaidah al Banshiri, drowned in this accident (and was replaced by Abu Hafs al Masry)
	Wadih el Hage and his housemate, Haroun Fazil, visited the accident scene to search for the body of Banshiri

[redacted]

[redacted]

Afghanistan

12 Jun 1996 Bin Laden was interviewed in Afghanistan by Robert Fisk of The Independent Newspaper of London

He stated of American troops in Saudi Arabia that "their military presence is an insult for the Saudi people"

He also stated that: "Resistance against America will spread in many, many places in Muslim countries."

Aug 1996 Bin Laden exhorted his followers to strike against U.S. forces in Saudi Arabia: "Efforts should be pooled to kill him [the American soldier], fight him, destroy him, lie in wait for him"

23 Aug 1996 From the Hindu Kush mountains of Afghanistan, bin Laden signed and issued a Declaration of Jihad entitled "Message from Usamah Bin-Muhammad Bin-Laden to His Muslim Brothers in the Whole World and Especially in the Arabian Peninsula: Declaration of Jihad Against the Americans Occupying the Land of the Two Holy Mosques; Expel the Heretics from the Arabian Peninsula"

This 60-page fatwa, which he called the "Ladenese Epistle", formally constituted a declaration of war against the United States

It reads, in part: "Muslims burn with anger at America. For its own good, America should leave [Saudi Arabia]" (PBS Online)

[redacted]

[redacted]

Afghanistan

Oct-Nov 1996 The October/November issue of Nida'ul Islam magazine quotes bin Laden as giving several examples of "America and Israel killing the weaker men, women and children in the Muslim world and elsewhere" (PBS Online, Osama bin Laden v. the U.S.: Edicts and Statements"):

Bin Laden listed the "Qana massacre in Lebanon", the "death of more than 600,000 Iraqi children because of the shortage of food and medicine" (resulting from UN Sanctions), the "withholding of arms from the Muslims of Bosnia-Herzegovina leaving them prey to the Christian Serbians", and the "dropping of the H-bombs" (in Japan)

Nov 1996 Gwynne Roberts conducted an interview of bin Laden for the British documentary program Dispatches (Reuters, 2/20/97; PBS Online)

Nov 1996 An Arab source claimed that bin Laden was in London, where his organization Al Nassiha wal Islah was located, under the protection of British intelligence

1997 Islamic extremists, including large numbers of Egyptians, Algerians, Palestinians, and Saudis, continued to use Afghanistan as a training ground

The Taliban and other combatants in the Afghan civil war facilitated the operation of training and indoctrination facilities for non-Afghans in the territories they controlled

Several Afghani factions also provided logistic support, free passage, and sometimes passports, to members of various terrorist organizations

These individuals were involved in fighting in Bosnia and Herzegovina, Chechnya, Tajikistan, Kashmir, the Philippines, and the Middle East

[redacted]

[redacted]

Afghanistan

1997 — Mohammed Saddiq Odeh was sent on a mission to Somalia for bin Laden by Wadih el Hage

Early 1997 — Bin Laden relocated from Jalalabad to the Taliban's capital of Qandahar and established a new base of operations

Late Mar 1997 — In his first-ever television interview, bin Laden was interviewed in eastern Afghanistan by CNN's Peter Arnett:

"We declared jihad against the U.S. government because the U.S. government is unjust, criminal, and tyrannical."

"[The collapse of the Soviet Union] made the U.S. more haughty and arrogant and it has started to look at itself as a Master of this world..."

"Wherever we look, we find the U.S. as the leader of terrorism and crime in the world."

"The U.S. does not consider it a terrorist act to throw atomic bombs at nations thousands of miles away... These bombs were thrown at entire nations, including women, children, and elderly people..."

"The U.S. does not consider it terrorism when hundreds of thousands of our sons and brothers in Iraq died for lack of food or medicine..."

On his future plans: "You'll see them and hear about them in the media, God willing."

[redacted]

Afghanistan

26 Mar 1997 — Pakistani commandos attacked a village near Peshawar where a number of Arab mujahideen reside: At least 6 mujahideen were killed

Apr 1997 — Pakistani commandos entered Afghanistan to capture or kill bin Laden

The Taliban intercepted and disarmed the Pakistani soldiers

4 Apr 1997 — Bin Laden moved with his family to his Kandahar camp near Khost

Mid May 1997 — The Saudi intelligence service made available to the CIA and to British intelligence (MI6) an individual from the bin Laden finance department

Along with him was an assistant to bin Laden named "Jallud" who may have cooperated with the Saudi government after being arrested in May

Another individual, named Sidi Tayib, had advised the American intelligence service about the scope of the distribution of money to various Arab communities who cooperated with bin Laden in the United States, especially in Brooklyn, New Jersey, and Jersey City

(The three items above are from the British newspaper The Daily Telegraph, as quoted by Haroun Fazul in a letter recovered from the personal computer of Wadih El Hage; see PBS Online, "The Letter from El Hage's Computer")

Sidi Tayeb, an Algerian, was a former deputy of bin Laden who defected in Nairobi and took refuge in the U.S. (IPIN, 11/4/99, p.6)

[redacted]

Afghanistan

July 1997 According to Islamic sources, a US-backed multinational mercenary force was formed to abduct or kill bin Laden (Mideast Mirror, 7/14/97; PBS Online)

A source said that the force was composed of 1000 non-US mercenaries (Mideast Mirror, 7/14/97; PBS Online)

Witnesses claimed to see 11 black Land Cruisers crossing into the Afghan city of Khost along with 2 helicopters (Mideast Mirror, 7/14/97; PBS Online)

Aug 1997 Nairobi police and American FBI agents visited the Nairobi home of Wadih El Hage with a search warrant (PBS Online, "A Portrait of Wadih El Hage, Accused Terrorist")

Although El Hage was not present, they collected all the papers in the house and took El Hage's personal computer (PBS Online, "A Portrait of Wadih El Hage, Accused Terrorist")

Sept 1997 Wadih el Hage, bin Laden's former personal secretary, moved from Nairobi to Arlinton, TX

Shortly after his move, el Hage was questioned by the FBI and allegedly lied about his search for the body of Ubaidah al Banshiri, who drowned at Lake Victoria in May 1996

(The FBI had videotape of el Hague and Haroun Fazil at the scene of the Lake Victoria ferry disaster)

[redacted]

[redacted]

Afghanistan

1997 Saudi Arabian intelligence arranged the defection of Mohamed bin Moisalih, who had been bin Laden's chief treasurer

Bin Moisalih left Afghanistan for Peshawar, Pakistan where a business jet flew him to Saudi Arabia

He has provided detailed information on the banking channels used by bin Laden

1998 Bin Laden's supporters claim that he and his own private army of 300 Arab and Sudanese commandos joined in a Taliban assault at Bagram airbase, north of Kabul

Jan 1998 Bin Laden hosted a terrorist conference in Afghanistan

Meetings were held with leading members of his network to prepare for a new wave of terrorism (NYT, 9/6/98)

Jan 1998 According to bin Laden (28 May 1998), during the month of Ramadan (which ran from 30 Dec 1997 to 8 Feb 1998), the Saudi Arabian government captured a number of anti-aircraft missiles("SAM and Stinger missiles")

However, bin Laden said that "what the Saudi Arabian government captured is much less than what was not captured"

[redacted]

[redacted]

Afghanistan

Feb 1998 Osama bin Laden played a leading role in the formation of the International Islamic Front, also known as the World Islamic Front for Jihad Against Jews and Crusaders

Some reports say that the movement was actually created some years ago, but had remained dormant until the publication of a communiqué on Feb 23

The group includes the Egyptian Al-Jihad (aka Egyptian Islamic Jihad) Movement, the Egyptian Armed Islamic Group (aka al-Gama'a al-Islamiya), the Association of Pakistani Religious Scholars, the Al-Ansar Movement in Kashmir, the Jihad Movement in Bangladesh, and the Afghan military wing of the Advice and Reform Organization (headed by bin Laden)

The group's Consultative Council is headed by bin Laden and its military wing is headed by Ayman al-Zawahri (the head of the Egyptian Islamic Jihad)

Refai Ahmed Taha's Jamaa Islamiya and Ayman al Zawahiri's Egyptian Jihad were reconciled after having split apart in 1993

The agreement signed between these two Egyptian fundamentalist movements provides for operational coordination with financial and logistical backing from Pakistani movements, Mir Hamze's Harakat al Ansar and Qazi Hussein Ahmed's Jamaa

[redacted]

[redacted]

Afghanistan

On 22 Feb 1998 bin Laden issued an edict announcing the new coalition of extremist groups and states:

"For over seven years the United States has been occupying the lands of Islam in the holiest of places, the Arabian Peninsula, plundering its riches, dictating to its rulers, humiliating its people, terrorizing its neighbors, and turning its bases in the peninsula into a spearhead through which to fight the neighboring Muslim peoples."

"We – with God's help – call on every Muslim who believes in God and wishes to be rewarded to comply with God's order to kill the Americans and plunder their money wherever and whenever they find it"

"The ruling to kill the Americans and their allies – civilians and military – is an individual duty for every Muslim who can do it in any country in which it is possible to do it"

[redacted]

[redacted]

Afghanistan

23 Feb 1998 The International Islamic Front published a communiqué in Afghanistan

Among those signing this communiqué were:

1. Sheik Refai Ahmed Taha (aka Abu Yasser), the spiritual leader of Egypt's Jamaa Islamiya (Al-Gama'a Al-Islamiya)
2. Ayman al Zawahiri, the head of Egypt's Jihad
3. Mir Hamze, the secretary of the Pakistani Ulemas' Association (Jamia-ul-Ulema-e-Pakistan)
4. Fazal al Rahman Khali, the leader of Pakistan's Harakat al Anser
5. Sheik Abdul Salaam Mohamed, the chief of Bangladesh's Jihad movement

In the Arabic-language London newspaper Al-Quds al'-Arabi, bin Laden, together with al-Zawahiri and Rifa'i Taha, issue a fatwa to "kill Americans everywhere"

The fatwa states that: "We - with God's help - call on every Muslim who believes in God and wishes to be rewarded to comply with God's order to kill the Americans and plunder their money wherever and whenever they find it"

This was apparently the first time that bin Laden said that even American civilians could be killed

Bin Laden: "To kill Americans and their allies, both civil and military, is an individual duty of every Muslim who is able, in any country where this is possible", until American armies "shattered and broken-winged, depart from all the lands of Islam" (NYT, 4/13/99)

[redacted]

[redacted]

Afghanistan

May 1998 — Soon after calling the press conference where bin Laden launched his "International Islamic Jihad" against the USA, bin Laden was summoned before a "furious" Taliban leader, Mullah Omar, and called to account

Early 1998 — President Clinton decided to pursue a two-track effort to apprehend bin Laden

Preparations for a commando extrication team would be authorized for possible insertion into Afghanistan

Meanwhile, the Administration tried to get the Taliban to cooperate in forcing the surrender of bin Laden to the US

American military and counter-terrorist teams were secretly sent to Peshawar, in the event that the commando operation was to be launched or a hand-over of bin Laden was facilitated by the Taliban

A small CIA-FBI team at Pakistan's border with Afghanistan collected intelligence on bin Laden

Meanwhile, contingency plans were being developed back in the U.S. for a possible commando raid to snatch him from Afghanistan

Pakistani press carried reports of U.S. commandos and intelligence personnel "staking out" bin Laden from Peshawar (on the Afghan-Pakistan border) and rumors abounded throughout the press and media about the US counter-terrorist force

[redacted]

Afghanistan

mid Apr 1998 — UN Ambassador Bill Richardson led the first high-level U.S. delegation to Afghanistan since the early 1970s

One item high on the agenda was asking Taliban officials to suppress bin Laden's threats against the United states

Although he showed the Taliban some of the evidence revealing bin Laden's direct hand in international terrorism, Richardson failed to persuade the Taliban to hand over bin Laden

Early May 1998 — Bin Laden caused to be published in the newspaper Al-Quds al-'Arabi a fatwah issued by the "Ulema Union of Afghanistan" which termed the United States Army the "enemies of Islam"

May 1998 — A visitor who encountered bin Laden claimed that he was accompanied by Aiman al-Zawahiri, the head of the Islamic Jihad Group of Egypt and by two sons of Sheik Omar Abdel Rahman, the blind Egyptian preacher in jail for his role in the World Trade Center bombing

The two sons, Omar and Assin, are said to work with bin Laden and were also seen with him at a press conference

May 1998 — According to the Grand Jury indictment, bin Laden held a press conference in Khost, Afghanistan (also attended by Muhammed Atef and Mohamed Rashed Daoud Al-'Owhali) where he repeated his intention to kill Americans

[redacted]

Afghanistan

26 May 1998 The International Islamic Front for Jihad Against Jews and Crusaders called a news conference in Peshawar, Pakistan to announce the formation of the coalition

In the press conference, bin Laden implied that some type of terrorist attack could be mounted in the next few weeks

On 28 May bin Laden referred to this as a "great meeting" that was "attended by 150 scholars in Pakistan"

According to bin Laden (28 May), "the goal of the meeting was to work toward liberating the Holy Land" and "great joint fatwas were passed"

28 May 1998 Bin Laden granted an interview with John Miller of ABC News:

Bin Laden sees "Jihad" as necessary to raise the Muslim world above the world of the heretics

He argues that terrorism is justified by the degraded moral standards of his enemies

He maintains that the US is responsible for the most reprehensible acts of terrorism, such as the bombings of Hiroshima and Nagasaki and the bombings in Iraq

When asked if he was worried that the US would put a price on his head for his capture, bin Laden replied "Praise be to Allah. It does not worry us what the Americans think. What worries us is pleasing Allah."

[redacted]

[redacted]

Quotes from the 28 May 1998 ABC News Interview

"We have seen in the last decade the decline of the American government and the weakness of the American soldier... This was proven in Beirut when the Marines fled after two explosions. It also proves they can run in less than 24 hours, and this was also repeated in Somalia."

"American history does not distinguish between civilians and military, and not even women and children. They are the ones who used the bombs against Nagasaki. Can these bombs distinguish between infants and military?"

"Also, by testimony of relief workers in Iraq, the American led sanctions resulted in the death of over 1 million Iraqi children. All of this was done in the name of American interests. We believe that the biggest thieves in the world and the terrorists are the Americans. The only way for us to fend off these assaults is to use similar means. We do not differentiate between those dressed in military uniforms and civilians; they are all targets."

"America will see many youths who will follow Ramzi Yousef."

"We predict a black day for America and the end of the United States as united states, and will be separate states, and will retreat from our land and collect the bodies of its sons back to America."

"The prophet said, 'A woman entered hell because of a cat. She did not feed it and blocked it from finding food on its own.' She is going to hell for blocking cat to death, but what say to those who agreed and gave reason for the hundreds of thousands of troops to blockade millions of Muslims in Iraq?"

"You will leave when the youth send you the wooden boxes and the coffins, and you will carry in it the bodies of American troops and civilians. This is when you will leave."

"The Muslim masses are moving towards liberating the Muslim worlds."

[redacted]

[redacted]

Quotes from the 28 May 1998 ABC News Interview

"After leaving Afghanistan they [Muslim youths] headed for Somalia and prepared for a long battle, thinking that the Americans were like the Russians... The youth were surprised at the low morale of the American soldiers and realized more than before that the American soldiers are paper tigers. After a few blows, they ran in defeat... After a few blows, they forgot about this title [world leader] and left, dragging their corpses and their shameful defeat... this great defeat pleased me very much, the way it pleases all Muslims."

"Allah willing, the next victory will be in Saudi Arabia, and it will make the Americans forget the horrors of Vietnam and Beirut."

"...our primary target are military and those in its employment. Our religion forbids us to kill innocents..."

"So, we tell the American as a people, and we tell the mothers of soldiers, and American mothers in general, if they value their lives and those of their children, find a nationalistic government that will look after their interests and not the interest of the Jews."

"The continuation of the tyranny will bring the fighting to America, like Ramzi Yousef and others."

Referring to the capture of anti-aircraft missiles by Saudi authorities during Ramadan: "Can the American government explain to its people when a SAM missile is launched against a passenger military airplane with 250 soldiers aboard? Can they justify their deaths?... The American government... has no choice but to pull its sons from the Holy Land."

"My word to American journalists is not to ask why we did that, but to ask what had their government done that forced us to defend ourselves?"

"It is our duty to lead people to light."

[redacted]

[redacted]

Albania

1994	Bin Laden set up a network of people in Albania after telling the government that he headed a wealthy Saudi humanitarian agency that wanted to help Albania
1995	Mahmud Sayyid Jaballah, a leader of Egypt's Jihad, was asked to find new recruits in Baku Azerbaijan: He managed to quickly set up a fundamentalist network with branches in Afghanistan, Bosnia, Albania, and the United Kingdom (IPIN, 6/24/99, p. 8)
1997	More than 100,000 blank Albanian passports were stolen during riots in Albania, providing the opportunity for terrorists to acquire false papers
12 Jun 1998	American and Albanian agents broke into the apartment of Ahmed Ibrahjim al Najjar, took him prisoner, and extradited him to Egypt where he was sentenced to life imprisonment at a trial of 107 fundamentalists which began in Feb 1999 (IPIN, 4/22/99, p. 8)
	His extradition to Egypt may have triggered the bomb attacks against the embassies in Nairobi and Dar es Salaam (IPIN, 4/22/99, p. 8)
	Al Najjar was imprisoned until 1984 for his associations with the assassins of Egyptian president Anwar Sadat: Behind bars he became friendly with Egyptian Jihad members like Ayman al Zawahiri and was later (1996) sent to Tirana under the cover of the Islamic Aid Movement (IPIN, 4/22/99, p. 8)

[redacted]

[redacted]

Albania

Jun-Aug 1998 Raids in Tirana, Albania seized material that included plans to bomb the U.S. Embassy in Albania

At least 5 Egyptians were arrested in Albania and deported to Egypt with U.S. help

Several of these were suspected of being bin Laden associates

Some reports refer to four of them as "bin Laden lieutenants"

At least some of these Egyptians were associated with the Islamic Revival Foundation (WP, 8/12/98; PBS Online)

Following the arrests, US agents took custody of a van-load of documents and computer gear (WP, 8/12/98; PBS Online)

One day before the Kenya and Tanzania bombings, Egypt's Jihad group vowed revenge for these deportations

16 Aug 1998 Over 200 U.S. military personnel are sent to Albania to evacuate U.S. dependents and other nonessential personnel and to guard the American residential compound

[redacted]

[redacted]

Albania

Late 1998 According to Albanian intelligence service head Fatos Klosi:

Bin Laden operated a terrorist network out of Albania that had sent units to fight in the Serbian province of Kosovo

Bin Laden sent troops in late 1998 to fight for separatists in Kosovo (SGIU, 12/1/98)

Bin Laden's people penetrated into other parts of Europe using thousands of blank Albanian passports acquired in 1998 while they were involved in the insurgency in Kosovo (SGIU, 12/1/98)

18 Apr 1999 At a trial in Cairo, nine leaders of the Egyptian Jihad, including Ayman al Zawahiri, were sentenced to death in absentia (IPIN, 4/22/99, p.6)

Following the trial, the Egyptian Jihad organization moved and altered some of its branches, particularly those in Albania where their members were infiltrated into humanitarian organizations in Tirana, Shkoder, Mitrovica, Oblic, and Glogavac (IPIN, 4/22/99, p. 6)

July 1999 There were reports that Albania continued to round up and expel people linked to bin Laden (STRATFOR Commentary, "Noose Closing on Bin Laden")

[redacted]

[redacted]

Events Before The African Bombings

1994 Mohammed Saddiq Odeh moved to Mombasa, Kenya

He set up a fish business there to finance his activities and to provide an alibi for trips to Nairobi: conducting business with restaurants in Nairobi allowed them to clandestinely survey the security at the U.S. Embassy

Abu Ubaidah al Banshiri was the bin Laden operative who set up Odeh in the fishing Business

Abu Ubaida was both a landowner and a businessman in Mwanza, Tanzania and is believed to have been one of bin Laden's two most influential military commanders (PBS Online, "FBI Executive Summary")

Wadih El Hage moved from Khartoum to Nairobi, Kenya and set up businesses and other organizations in Kenya

El Hage also met repeatedly with Abu Ubaidah al Banshiri, a military commander of al Qaeda

1994 Ali A. Mohamed, a former Egyptian and American army officer who eventually worked for bin Laden, used his U.S. passport to enter the U.S. Embassy in Nairobi on an apparent surveillance mission (WP, 8/1/99)

[redacted]

Events Before The African Bombings

1995 & 1996	Ali Abul-Saud Mustafa made visits to Tanzania, Kenya, Uganda, Nigeria, and Somalia (JIR, June 1999, p. 3)
	Ali Abul-Saud Mustafa was an Egyptian Islamist who had been charged by bin Laden to gather information about US embassies in Africa (JIR, June 1999, p. 3)
1996	The U.S. Embassy in Sudan was almost totally evacuated after a terrorist threat and relocated to the U.S. Embassy in Nairobi, Kenya
1996	Abdallah Mohammed Fazul falsely obtained a Kenyan identity card using the name Haroon
	Abdallah Mohammed Fazul would allegedly end up leading the Kenyan cell of al-Qaidia
1996	An individual associated with al Qaeda displayed TNT and detonators to Mohamed Sadeek Odeh
Early 1997	Intelligence officials briefed Ambassador Bushnell about the presence in Kenya of the bin Laden group (NYT, 1/9/99)
	However, they told her there was no evidence of a specific threat against the embassy or American interests in Kenya (NYT, 1/9/99)

[redacted]

Events Before The African Bombings

1997 Wadih el Hage, a U.S. citizen who once served as bin Laden's personal secretary in Sudan, and who is suspected of having tried to help bin Laden procure chemical weapons, was living in Nairobi

It is suspected that el Hage was leader of a bin Laden cell operating in Nairobi

El Hage's deputy, Haroun Fazil, lived and worked with el Hage in Nairobi

Fazil, who is from the Comoro Islands, allegedly took part in the Kenyan cell of al-Qaida

The FBI suspects that the explosive material for the Nairobi and Dar es Salaam bombs came from the Middle East , through the Comoros Islands (located about 180 miles east of the African coast)

Fazil was later charged with helping to plan and execute the Nairobi embassy bombing

Fazil allegedly rented the villa (43 Rundu Estates) where the bomb was built

Fazil had warned that the security of bin Laden's East African cell had been compromised and its members put "at 100% danger": "There are many reasons that lead me to believe that the cell members in East Africa are in great danger, which leaves us no choice but to think and work hard to foil the enemy's plans" (from a letter written by Fazil that was discovered in the computer files of Wadih el Hage)

[redacted]

Events Before The African Bombings

Aug 1997 By this time the CIA had identified the cell of bin Laden operatives in Nairobi

Aug 1997 Haroun Fazil, the "media officer" for bin Laden's Nairobi cell, wrote a letter that was later discovered in the computer files of Wadih el Hage (CTSR, vol. 8, no. 1, p. 11)

Aug 1997 Nairobi police and American FBI agents visited the Nairobi home of Wadih El Hage with a search warrant (PBS Online, "A Portrait of Wadih El Hage, Accused Terrorist"; NYT 1/9/99)

Although El Hage was not present, they collected all the papers in the house and took El Hage's personal computer (PBS Online, "A Portrait of Wadih El Hage, Accused Terrorist") on which they later found a letter describing the existence of an "East African cell" of bin Laden's group (NYT, 1/9/99)

The letter also indicated that the group had moved a cache of incriminating files from Mr. Hage's house and hidden them elsewhere, after which American investigators began a "somewhat frantic, concerted effort" to locate the missing files (NYT, 1/9/99)

Aug 1997 Two days after the raid on his house, Wadih El Hage returned to Nairobi from Afghanistan, was questioned by police, and was told to leave the country (which he did in September, returning to the U.S. with his wife) (PBS Online, "A Portrait of Wadih El Hage, Accused Terrorist")

The raid on El Hage's home was a deliberate counter-terrorism disruption operation and forcing him to leave Nairobi was part of an attempt to fracture the al Qaeda cells (PBS Online, "A Portrait of Wadih El Hage, Accused Terrorist")

[redacted]

Events Before The African Bombings

Sept 1997 — As part of the effort to locate incriminating files which were moved from el Hage's home and hidden elsewhere, a search was conducted in Kenya at another location (NYT, 1/9/99)

Summer 1997 — The intelligence service of another country turned over an informant to the CIA (NYT, 1/9/99)

The informant said that the Nairobi branch of the Islamic charity known as the Al Haramain Foundation was plotting terrorist attacks against Americans (NYT, 1/9/99)

The informant eventually warned that the group was plotting to blow up the American Embassy in Nairobi (NYT, 1/9/99)

[Authors note: We will assume here that the informant described above is the same as that described in the next item (see next page), with some confusion in the media over the details of how the informant came to the attention of American authorities. However, it is possible that two separate informants were involved in warning authorities of the activities of the Al Haramain Foundation. Given limited resources, the resolution of this issue did not seem to be of sufficiently high priority as to warrant additional research.]

[redacted]

Events Before The African Bombings

Sept 1997

A tipster walked into the U.S. Embassy in Nairobi and claimed that seven Arabs who worked for a local Islamic charity had connections with a bin Laden terror group

The charity was called the Al Haramain Foundation (PBS Online, "Warnings to The FBI")

By 31 October Kenyan police had arrested nine Arabs connected to the Al Haramain Foundation charity (PBS Online, "Warnings to The FBI")

Police had also seized the group's files (PBS Online, "Warnings to The FBI")

The CIA sent a counterterrorism team to investigate, but they found no evidence of a bomb plot (PBS Online, "Warnings to The FBI")

The counterterrorism team had wanted to question Al Haramain members in jail, but did not because the local station chief did not want to strain his relations with the Kenyans (NYT, 1/9/99)

The nine employees of the charity were later deported (in late 1997) (PBS)

[redacted]

Events Before The African Bombings

Nov 1997 Mustafa Mahmoud Said Ahmed, an Egyptian, walked into the U.S. Embassy in Nairobi and warned that unnamed terrorists planned to car bomb the compound

He claimed that the plan was to detonate a truck bomb in the parking garage of the embassy (PBS Online, "Warnings to The FBI"; NYT, 1/9/99)

He admitted that he had taken part in surveillance of the embassy, including taking photos (PBS Online, "Warnings to The FBI")

He also said that the attack was to involve several vehicles and stun grenades (NYT, 1/9/99)

He was grilled for days, and provided details of the attack, but was believed to have fabricated the tale

A warning was issued that said that Ahmed was probably making up the story, but could be telling the truth or could be approaching the embassy to check its security

In response, extra guards were posted at the front and back of the building and a letter was sent to Madeleine Albright warning that the embassy was vulnerable to car bombs

Ahmed was later arrested in connection with the bombing in Dar es Salaam

[redacted]

[redacted]

Events Before The African Bombings

Early 1998	In Jalalabad, Pakistan, Said Sayyed Salameh was asked by bin Laden to become involved in bin Laden's financial activities in several African countries and, particularly, to hand money to the leaders of fundamentalist factions in Libya and Egypt
Approx Feb 98	Odeh left his rented house in Mombasa and moved to the northeast Kenyan village of Witu, where he employed two or three local men making carved furniture
March 1998	A team from Diplomatic Security and the Foreign Building Office, which handles embassy leases and construction projects, arrived in Nairobi to conduct a security review (NYT, 1/9/99)
March 1998	Threats faxed by bin Laden from Kandahar, Afghanistan caused the United States to erect barricades around its embassy in Pakistan (SGIU, 4/16/98)
April 1998	According to the London-based Arab language newspaper Al-Quds al-Arabi, US Permanent Envoy to the UN Bill Richardson, who was to meet with Taliban officials on 17 April in Kabul, was carrying an offer for the US to recognize the Taliban regime as the official government in Afghanistan in exchange for the Taliban handing over bin Laden (SGIU, 4/16/98)
	The newspaper reported that some factions among the Taliban supported the idea of handing over bin Laden, but that they were a minority (SGIU, 4/16/98)
	The newspaper also reported that bin Laden had been making contacts with Somalia and Yemen as possible places of refuge (SGIU, 4/16/98)

[redacted]

Events Before The African Bombings

Spring 1998 — Initial planning for the US Embassy attacks began (PBS Online, "FBI Executive Summary")

Spring 1998 — U.S. intelligence officials drew up secret plans for a covert raid by American forces to extricate bin Laden from his hideout in Afghanistan (NYT, 9/6/98)

The plans were ultimately shelved by the Director of Central Intelligence (George Tenet) and other senior officials because of the high risks involved (NYT, 9/6/98)

May 1998 — Fazul Abdullah Mohammed rented a villa located at 43 Rundu Estates in Nairobi, Kenya

The villa at 43 Rundu Estates

[redacted]

Events Before The African Bombings

Early June 1998	An Egyptian "Afghan", Said Sayyed Salameh, was arrested at the frontier post at Salom as he tried to sneak into Egypt from Tobruk, Libya Salameh was considered one of bin Laden's closest associates
June 1998	The International Islamic Front, presided over by bin Laden, met in Peshawar, Pakistan (near the border with Afghanistan) The group resolved to hit U.S. interests worldwide in order to "pressure the United States into withdrawing their forces from the Gulf region and lift the embargo on Iraq"
June 1998	Saudi Prince Turki al-Faisal, the chief of Saudi intelligence, led a small Saudi delegation to Taliban headquarters in Kandahar, Afghanistan to seek either bin Laden's ouster from Afghanistan or his custody for trial in Saudi Arabia (LAT, "Bin Laden slipped past Saudis' grip") According to Prince Turki al-Faisal, Taliban leader Mullah Mohammed Omar agreed to surrender bin Laden to the Saudis in a deal that was to have been carefully orchestrated, but the negotiations ended amid a flurry of recriminations after the East African embassy bombings (LAT, "Bin Laden slipped past Saudis' grip") The Taliban's representative in New York, Abdul Hakeem Mujahid, said that there was never an agreement to turn over bin Laden; that the Taliban's understanding was that the Saudis wanted bin Laden confined in Afghanistan (LAT, "Bin Laden slipped past Saudis' grip")

[redacted]

[redacted]

Events Before The African Bombings

June 1998	Mustafa Mohamed Fadhil and another suspect rented a villa in Dar es Salaam which became the "bomb factory" for the Tanzania bombing (NYT, 12/17/98)
	Another report says that Khalfan Khamis Mohammed signed a lease to rent a house in the Ilala District of Dar es Salaam (PBS Online, "FBI Executive Summary")
	Like the house at 43 Rundu estates in Nairobi, this house was away from the city center, surrounded by high walls, and had a large garage to accommodate a truck (PBS Online, "FBI Executive Summary")
	This house is believed to be the location where the Dar es Salaam bomb was constructed and stored (PBS Online, "FBI Executive Summary")
8 June 1998	The grand jury investigating bin Laden since 1996 issued a sealed indicted (PB Online)
Jun & Jul 1998	Suspects in the Tanzanian bombing bought a 1987 Nissan Atlas truck to carry the bomb to the embassy and a white Suzuki Samurai, in which the suspects would flee (NYT, 12/17/98)
	The suspects arranged for welding and other mechanical work to be done on the truck, apparently to equip it to carry the bomb, and bought oxygen and acetylene tanks and two large truck batteries (NYT, 12/17/98)

[redacted]

[redacted]

Events Before The African Bombings

10 Jun 1998 Bin Laden was interviewed on ABC's Nightline:

"We believe that the biggest thieves in the world are Americans and the biggest terrorists on earth are the Americans"

"We do not differentiate between those dressed in military uniforms and civilians. They're all targets in this fatwah."

"You will leave when the bodies of American soldiers and civilians are sent in the wooden boxes and coffins. That is when you will leave."

12 Jun 1998 The State Department issues a Public Announcement: "terrorist financier Osama bin Laden reiterated his threats against the U.S. ... maintain a high level of vigilance..."

14 Jun 1998 U.S. State Department reports that the U.S. is stepping up security at embassies and sites in the Middle East and South Asia after a bin Laden television news interview

12 Jun 1998 American and Albanian agents broke into the apartment of Ahmed Ibrahjim al Najjar: He was arrested and extradited to Egypt where he was sentenced to life imprisonment at a trial of 107 fundamentalists which began in Feb 1999 (IPIN, 4/22/99, p. 8)

His extradition to Egypt may have triggered the bomb attacks against the embassies in Nairobi and Dar es Salaam (IPIN, 4/22/99, p. 8)

Al Najjar was imprisoned until 1984 for his associations with the assassins of Egyptian president Anwar Sadat: Behind bars he became friendly with Egyptian Jihad members like Ayman al Zawahiri and was later (1996) sent to Tirana under the cover of the Islamic Aid Movement (IPIN, 4/22/99, p. 8)

[redacted]

Events Before The African Bombings

Jun-Aug 1998	Raids in Tirana, Albania seized material that included plans to bomb the U.S. Embassy in Albania
	At least 5 Egyptians were arrested in Albania and deported to Egypt with U.S. help
	One day before the Kenya and Tanzania bombings, Egypt's Jihad group vowed revenge for these deportations
July 1998	Planning began for the Kenya and Tanzania bombings under the direction of Ali Saleh, according to the later written confession of Mohammed Sadiq Odeh (PBS Online, "Notes on The Interrogation of One Suspect")
	Ali Saleh was a member of the Egyptian Islamic Jihad (PBS Online, "Notes on The Interrogation of One Suspect")
Date unknown	A local bank in Dar es Salaam received a large sum of money from abroad for payment to suspects before the 7 August bombings
July 1998	Mohamed Rashed Daoud Al-'Owhali and an individual known as Azzam filmed a videotape to celebrate their anticipated martyrdom in a bombing operation
	On the tape they claim credit in the name of a fictitious organization, the "Army for the Liberation of Islamic Holy Places"

[redacted]

Events Before The African Bombings

Late Jul-early Aug 1998	Osama bin Laden was charged in a sealed indictment with inciting violence against U.S. citizens
	The federal grand jury indicted bin Laden for the 1994 plot to assassinate President Clinton
	It also linked bin Laden with plots to kill Egyptian President Mubarak, efforts in 1994 to bomb a U.S.-bound jet, and the Khobar Towers bombing in 1996
	The grand jury had been established over a year ago to examine the activities of Islamic groups after the Khobar Towers bombing
	The indictment would allow authorities to arrest bin Laden and would persuade foreign governments to deny him protection
31 July 1998	On or about this date Mohamed Al-'Owhali traveled from Lahore, Pakistan to Nairobi (USIA, "Criminal Complaint Against Kenya Bombing Suspect Al-'Owhali")
1 Aug 1998	Fazul led Owhali to the US Embassy to look it over
1 Aug 1998	An al Qaeda member advised Mohamed Sadeek Odeh that all members of al Qaeda had to leave Kenya by 6 August 1998,.the day before the bombings (USIA, "U.S. Court Document Links Bombing Suspect to Bin Laden Organization")

[redacted]

[redacted]

Events Before The African Bombings

2 Aug 1998 Mohamed Sadeek Odeh and other members of al Qaeda traveled from Mombasa to Nairobi for a meeting with other members of al Qaeda (USIA, "U.S. Court Document Links Bombing Suspect to Bin Laden Organization")

Odeh, who was allegedly using a false passport, stayed with the other al Qaeda members at the Hilltop Hotel (USIA, "U.S. Court Document Links Bombing Suspect to Bin Laden Organization")

2 Aug 1998 Mohamed Sadeek Odeh, Fazul Abdullah Mohammed and other members of al Qaeda met at the Hilltop Hotel in Nairobi

Fazul ran the meeting and warned those not planning to die in the blasts on 7 August to be out of town by 6 August

Scenes from the Hilltop Hotel, including (far right) one of the rooms used by the conspirators (photos by author)

[redacted]

[redacted]

Events Before The African Bombings

2-6 Aug 1998	Mohamed Sadeek Odeh and other members of al Qaeda stayed at the Hilltop Hotel
1st wk Aug 1998	Fazul Abdullah Mohammed, Mohamed Rashed Daoud, Azzam, and other members of al Qaeda met at 43 Rundu Estates in Nairobi
	During these meetings they made final preparations for the Nairobi bombing
3 Aug 1998	Four foreigners involved in the bombings checked into a Nairobi hotel
Aug 1998	The Nairobi bomb was assembled under the guidance of Mohammed Saddiq Odeh, a Palestinian engineer of Jordanian nationality
3 Aug 1998	A private security guard working near the U.S. Embassy in Nairobi, Kenya saw a man with two bodyguards taking video pictures of the embassy from all sides
	The cameraman hid the video camera and departed when observed
	This incident was reported to the embassy guards
Date unknown	Prior to the two bombings, bin Laden's teams had also called in phony bomb threats in order to observe security measures

[redacted]

[redacted]

Events Before The African Bombings

4 Aug 1998	The U.S. has charged that Fazul Abdullah Mohammed, Mohamed Rashed Daoud al-'Owhali, Azzam, and other members of al Qaeda reconnoitered the Nairobi embassy on or about this date (see 3 Aug) (USIA, "Criminal Complaint Against Kenya Bombing Suspect Al-'Owhali")
	Another report says that Saleh and al-Owhali conducted a reconnaissance of the embassy on this date and decided to locate the truck as close as possible to the rear of the building, instead of attempting to drive it into the Embassy's underground garage or place it in front of the building (PBS Online, "FBI Executive Summary")
	Haroun Fazil is also accused of scoping out the embassy in the days before the attack
5 Aug 1998	Abdul Rahman is said to have made the final connection between the bomb and the detonation device in the garage at 43 Rundu Estates (PBS Online, "FBI Executive Summary")
5 Aug 1998	Mohamed Sadeek Odeh shaved his beard and obtained new clothing in preparation for travel outside of Kenya to Afghanistan to meet with Osama bin Laden
5 Aug 1998	Mohamed Sadeek Odeh walked along Moi Avenue in Nairobi in the vicinity of the U.S. Embassy
5 Aug 1998	One of the conspirators in the Tanzanian bombing telephoned a counterpart in Nairobi (NYT, 12/17/98)

[redacted]

Events Before The African Bombings

6 Aug 1998 The Egyptian Jihad, associated with the bin Laden camps in Afghanistan, sent the U.S. a warning that they would soon deliver a message to Americans

"which we hope they read with care, because we will write it, with God's help, in a language they will understand"

They vowed revenge against the U.S. for its role in the recent deportation of several Egyptians from Albania to Egypt

6 Aug 1998 Mohammed Saddiq Odeh flew out of Nairobi for Pakistan under an assumed name on Pakistani International Airways flight 746 after ensuring that final preparations were in place for the Nairobi bombing

Prior to leaving Kenya, Odeh was allegedly told by other al Qaeda members that members of al Qaeda who were located in Afghanistan were in the process of relocating to avoid retaliation (USIA, "U.S. Court Document Links Bombing Suspect to Bin Laden Organization")

At least two of the suspects in the Dar es Salaam bombing left Dar es Salam for Karachi on this same day

[redacted]

Events Before The African Bombings

Aug 1998 — The tanker truck working for the U.S. Embassy in Dar es Salaam was at the Tommy Spades Manufacturing Company for repairs shortly before Aug 7

(Because the water supply in Tanzania is unreliable, the U.S. Embassy would routinely supply water from wells on the embassy grounds to nearby embassies and homes)

It was originally suspected that the Dar es Salaam bomb may have been constructed at the Tommy Spades plant and welded to the chassis of this water truck, although it was later determined that the bomb was located in a second vehicle that had pulled up behind the water truck immediately before the explosion

7 Aug 1998 — Abdallah Mohammed Fazul had arranged for his father-in-law, Fazul Badroudin, to fly from Nairobi, where he had been hospitalized, back to Moroni (Comoros Islands) on the day of the bombings

[redacted]

[redacted]

The African Embassy Bombings

On 7 August 1998 the U.S. embassies in Nairobi, Kenya and Dar es Salaam, Tanzania were bombed nearly simultaneously using two large bombs composed of TNT

August 7 was the anniversary of the date in 1990 when U.S. troops began to arrive in Saudi Arabia in the buildup preceding the Gulf War

Both structures withstood collapse from the bombings but were rendered unusable (RARB)

U.S. Embassy, Dar es Salaam, 1998

Scene near the U.S. Embassy in Tanzania, August 1998

Scene near the U.S. Embassy in Kenya, August 1998

Scene near the U.S. Embassy in Nairobi

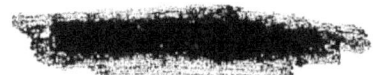

[redacted]

[redacted]

The African Embassy Bombings

Money for the bombings has been traced back through accounts at a Saudi-backed bank in Dar es Salaam and through Islamic charities in Nairobi

Bombing suspect Mohamed Saddiq Odeh allegedly stated that bin Laden was involved in the bombings

After the African embassy bombings, informants revealed that bin Laden planned assaults on other U.S. embassies in Africa, Asia, and the Middle East

The Hilltop Hotel was quickly identified as a haunt of the bombing suspects

[redacted]

[redacted]

The Nairobi Embassy

The embassy was closely bordered on two sides by very busy Nairobi streets

The embassy was surrounded by a 2.6 meter high steel picket vertical bar fence (RARB)

The embassy also had an outer perimeter beyond the fence consisting of a line of steel bollards at a distance of 5-18 meters from the outer walls (RARB)

Nairobi had been designated a "medium" threat post (RARB)

The U.S. embassy shortly after the bombing, seen from the side opposite of the detonation

[redacted]

[redacted]

Nairobi Bombing Event Sequence

(Times approximate)

9:30 AM

Two trucks left the villa at 43 Rundu Estates and drove toward the U.S. Embassy

Fazul Abdullah Mohammed drove a white Datsun pickup truck which led the way to the US Embassy

Azzam drove a battered Toyota cargo truck containing the bomb and was accompanied by Mohamed Rashed Daoud al-'Owhali,

Al-'Owhali possessed a handgun, four stun-grenades, and keys to the padlocks on the bomb truck

The stun grenades were taken in order to draw people inside the embassy toward the windows where they would be more vulnerable to the blast

Another report says that Al-Owhali's role was to "scare away" people in the vicinity of the Embassy compound to reduce the number of Kenyan casualties (PBS Online, "FBI Executive Summary")

Al-Owhali was also to manually detonate the bomb in the event that the detonation device malfunctioned (PBS Online, "FBI Executive Summary")

10:30 AM

The local-hire contract guards at the rear of the embassy saw a truck pull into the uncontrolled exit lane of the rear parking lot just as they closed the fence gate and the drop bar after a mail van had exited the embassy's garage (RARB)

[redacted]

[redacted]

Nairobi Bombing Event Sequence

(Times approximate)

The truck proceeded to the embassy's rear access control area but was blocked by an automobile coming out of the underground garage of the Co-op Bank (RARB)

When one of the truck occupants demanded that the guards open the gate, the guards refused (RARB)

Mohamed Rashed Daoud al-'Owhali (the truck passenger) exited from the bomb truck as it approached the rear of the Embassy building

He had forgotten his pistol and was left with only the stun grenades (PBS Online, "FBI Executive Summary"): He brandished a stun grenade, thew the stun grenade in the direction of a security guard, and fled on foot (even though the operation was supposed to have been a suicide mission from which al-'Owhali did not expect to survive)

Azzam (the driver) fired a handgun at the windows of the Embassy building

The guards, who were unarmed, ran for cover and tried to contact the Marine Security Guard at the command post via radio and phone but the radio frequency was occupied and the phone was busy (RARB)

In the several second time lapse between the grenade/gunshots and the bomb blast, many embassy employees went to the windows to observe what was happening: Those who did were either killed or seriously injured (RARB)

Azzam manually detonated the explosive device in the rear parking area, near the ramp to the basement garage

[redacted]

[redacted]

Nairobi Bombing Results

Little structural damage to the embassy (RARB)

However, massive damage to the embassy interior (RARB)

Most embassy casualties were caused by secondary fragmentation (RARB)

The adjacent Ufundi building, a secretarial college, collapsed (USIA, "Criminal Complaint Against Kenya Bombing Suspect Al-'Owhali")

Most Kenyan casualties were from this collapse and from flying glass (RARB)

The empty lot is the former location of the Ufundi building, which collapsed

Casualties (RARB; USIA):	Dead	Seriously Injured	Injured
Americans	12	10	3
Africans	201		
Africans employed by the embassy	32	11	
Total embassy employees	44		
Total	213		~4,000

This building, on the opposite side of the collapsed Ufundi building from the embassy, also suffered serious damage

[redacted]

[redacted]

Nairobi Bombing Results

After the bombing, the Nairobi embassy relocated to a building on the outskirts of town with a carefully-controlled (and heavily guarded) approach

The approach to the Nairobi embassy as of December 1998 (author's photo)

[redacted]

[redacted]

The Nairobi Bombing
DoS Findings & Recommendations

There had been no information or intelligence to warn of the actual attack (RARB)

Although a number of intelligence reports had cited alleged threats, they were largely discounted because of doubts about the sources; because they were imprecise, changing, and non-specific; and because actions taken by intelligence and law enforcement authorities were believed to have dissipated the threat (RARB)

Employees had not been trained on how to respond in the event of a vehicular bomb: Had they been trained to duck and cover when they heard the grenade blast and gunshots, some lives might have been saved (RARB)

Perimeter guards had no dedicated duress or alert alarms with which to raise an alarm (even though guards at embassy residences did have radio duress or panic alarms to use in emergencies) (RARB)

The Kenyan government had denied an embassy request to have more than one radio frequency: If the perimeters guards had had a dedicated frequency to communicate with the Marine Security Guard, an alarm might have been raised (RARB)

The embassy lacked sufficient setback/standoff (RARB)

[redacted]

[redacted]

The Nairobi Bombing
DoS Findings & Recommendations

The embassy had responded to reports of threats in a number of positive ways and, in general, security systems and procedures had been implemented well (RARB):

1. They had increased the number of roving guards
2. They had instituted closer monitoring of the visa line
3. They had instituted additional vehicular and perimeter searches
4. They had advised personnel on security precautions
5. They had advised personnel on the importance of reporting incidents of surveillance
6. The Regional Security Officer (RSO) and the Marine Security Guards (MSGs) had conducted numerous emergency react drills
7. The RSO had asked the Kenyan government to enhance security around the embassy
8. The RSO had met with Kenyan police to discuss their bomb react scenarios
9. They had requested and received a team from Washington to further familiarize the MSGs and local guards with explosive devices
10. The Emergency Action Committee had met frequently to review security
11. The Ambassador cabled Washington on 24 December 1997 to request support for a new chancery, which was denied
12. A security assessment team from Washington visited in March 1998 to review security
13. The Ambassador sent letters to the Secretary of State (April 1998) and to Under Secretary Cohen (May 1998) restating her concerns about security and the need for a new chancery
14. The embassy had tried several times, unsuccessfully, to gain control of the back parking lot from the Co-op Bank
15. Local security guards had performed as trained and had refused the terrorists access to the embassy perimeter

[redacted]

[redacted]

The Nairobi Bombing
DoS Findings & Recommendations

The prevailing view in the embassy and in Washington at that time was that the crime threat was far more serious than the terrorist threat (RARB)

No attention was paid to vehicle bomb attacks in DoS guidance or in the embassy's security systems and procedures (RARB)

Training levels called for in the contract for the embassy's local guards fell well short of specifications, both in quality and frequency (RARB)

Local guards did not participate in embassy emergency drills nor have much interchange with the Marine Security Guard detachment (RARB)

Airlift for support from outside Kenya was hampered by breakdowns and logistical difficulties (RARB)

The Foreign Emergency Support Team , which normally deals with crises like hostage taking, did not have a personnel package appropriate for the situation faced in Nairobi (RARB)

Recommendations:

Better crisis management training and contingency planning for DoS (RARB)

DoS should explore chartering commercial aircraft in emergencies to provide reliable airlift (RARB)

The RARB found a chronic shortage of funding for embassy replacement and a systemic and institutional failure to properly assess threat levels or to prepare for vehicular bombs

[redacted]

[redacted]

The Dar es Salaam Embassy Bombing

Background

The Embassy

The US Embassy in Dar es Salaam consisted of a 3-story Chancery and a 4-story Annex (RARB)

The Chancery had a minimal number of ground-floor windows (RARB)

The Chancery and Annex were surrounded by a wall which provided a 10-12 meter setback (RARB)

Dar es Salaam had been designated a "low" threat post (RARB)

The Bomb

A residence was rented to use as a bomb factory

A truck was purchased and fitted with the bomb

Oxygen and acetylene were purchased for use in the bomb

[redacted]

[redacted]

The Dar es Salaam Embassy Bombing

Event Sequence

7 Aug 1998	A truck laden with explosives drove up Laibon Road to one of the two vehicular gates of the US Embassy located at 36 Laibon Road (RARB)
	The truck was unable to penetrate the perimeter because it was blocked by an embassy water tanker (RARB)
10:35 AM	The embassy water tanker had finished its rounds and pulled up to the embassy gate
10:39 AM	While guards were making a standard security check of the truck, a massive explosion blew it to bits
	The explosive device was detonated at a distance of about 35 feet from the outer wall of the chancery (RARB)
	A man described as "Ahmed the German" detonated the explosive device, which was being carried in a Nissan Atlas truck (NYT, 12/17/98)
Minutes later	An operative driving a Suzuki Samurai photographed the embassy ruins as he left the scene (NYT, 12/17/98)

[redacted]

The Dar es Salaam Embassy Bombing

Casualties (RARB; USIA, "US, Kenya and Tanzania to Cooperate On Finding Embassy Bombers")

- 11 dead
- No American deaths
- 8 of the dead were Foreign Service Nationals and locally contracted employees
- 1 missing and presumed dead
- 85 injured
- 76 of the injured were Foreign Service Nationals and locally contracted employees
- 1 US embassy employee was injured and sent to London for treatment
- No one inside the chancery was killed

DoS Findings

- There had been no information or intelligence to warn of the actual attack (RARB)
- There was no video recording capability for the Closed Circuit Television (used to monitor guard actions) that might have provided information useful to the post-blast investigation (RARB)
- There were no duress alarms at guard stations which could have been used to provide warning (RARB)
- Because the threat in Dar es Salaam had been considered "low", there was no priority attached to providing a greater setback than existed (RARB)
- Foreign Emergency Support Team personnel from Washington were delayed 24 hours in taking off because of slow decision-making and problems with aircraft availability (RARB)
- With the exception of a failure to meet the standard for a 100 foot standoff, security at Dar es Salaam met or exceeded standards: Therefore, it is apparent that the standards themselves were inadequate (RARB)

[redacted]

The African Embassy Bombings

It was originally estimated that the bombs killed 265 (254 in Kenya and 11 in Tanzania) and injured roughly 5,000-5,500 or more

Kenya later revised the number of dead there from 247 to 213, saying that dismembered bodies had been double-counted

More than 4,500 people were injured in Nairobi and at least 85 more in Dar es Salaam

Of the dead, 12 were US government employees and family members and 40 were foreign citizens employed by the US government (32 Kenyan and 8 Tanzanian) (RARB)

Rescuers amid the ruble in Nairobi

Rescuers in Nairobi

[redacted]

The African Embassy Bombs

The bombs were large devices with as much as 2,000 pounds of TNT each

- Statements made by suspects and/or witnesses have mentioned the use of TNT (PBS Online, "FBI Executive Summary"), and
- The FBI Laboratory has confirmed its presence at both sites (PBS Online, "FBI Executive Summary")
- The explosives were acquired from Luanda (PBS Online, "Notes on The Interrogation of One Suspect")
- A senior Kenyan police official has said that they think the TNT was brought into Kenya "a little at a time"

Scene of the Nairobi bombing

Blasting caps and RDX (a plastic explosive) were used to initiate the bombs

- The Dar es Salaam bomb designed by Mohammed Sadiq Odeh used 250 kg of TNT with mechanical detonators and 10 m of RDX cord (PBS Online, "Notes on The Interrogation of One Suspect")

Investigators also found bits of cylindrical tanks that held oxygen and acetylene which are commonly used by Mideast terrorists in the mistaken belief that they enhance the blast

Vehicles:

- The Nairobi bomb was carried in a Toyota cargo truck
- The Dar es Salaam bomb had been welded to the chassis of a 1987 Nissan Atlas refrigeration truck

[redacted]

The Nairobi Conspirators

Mohammed Saddiq Odeh

Mohammed Saddiq Odeh, a.k.a. Mohammad Sadiq Howaida, a.k.a. Abu Moath, a.k.a. Noureldine, a.k.a. Marwan, a.k.a. Hydar, a.k.a. Abdull Bast Awadh

- Born 1 March 1965 in Saudi Arabia (PBS Online, "FBI Executive Summary")
- Educated in Jordan where he was affiliated with the PLO (PBS Online, "Notes on The Interrogation of One Suspect")
- Acquired a diploma in architecture from the Philippines in 1990 (PBS Online, "Notes on The Interrogation of One Suspect")
- A Palestinian engineer from Jordan
- Went to Pakistan in 1990 and on to Afghanistan to participate in the fighting (PBS Online, "Notes on The Interrogation of One Suspect")
- Stayed in Afghanistan for 2 years and 5 months and acquired expertise in explosives (PBS Online, "Notes on The Interrogation of One Suspect")
- Claims to be an expert at handling the U.S. man-portable Stinger surface-to-air missile which was supplied to the Afghan mujahideen in the 1980s
- While in Afghanistan, he came in contact with Osama bin Laden's group and with a Somali, Sheikh Hassan (PBS Online, "Notes on The Interrogation of One Suspect")
- Joined al Qaida in Afghanistan in or about 1992 (USIA, "U.S. Court Document Links Bombing Suspect to Bin Laden Organization")
- Was trained in explosives in al Qaida camps in the early 1990s
- In 1992, on the direction of Saiful Adil of bin Laden's group, he went to Somalia with some Arabs and joined Sheikh Hassan (PBS Online, "Notes on The Interrogation of One Suspect")
- In Somalia, he participated in a number of acts of terrorism, including the killing of some Belgian nationals (PBS Online, "Notes on The Interrogation of One Suspect")

[redacted]

[redacted]

The Nairobi Conspirators

Mohammed Saddiq Odeh

- In 1993 Odeh trained Islamic fighters in Somalia who opposed the UN peacekeeping mission there (USIA, "U.S. Court Document Links Bombing Suspect to Bin Laden Organization"): He later boasted of providing the rifles and rocket launchers that killed 18 US soldiers and wounded 73 in Mogadishu in Oct 1993
- Moved to Kenya in 1994 on the invitation of Mustapha, an ex-Afghan fighter
- In Kenya he married a Kenyan woman of Arab origin and settled down in the small town of Witu where he started trading in furniture (PBS Online, "Notes on The Interrogation of One Suspect") (Wadih el Hage attended Odeh's wedding in 1994)
- In Witu he joined an Arab terrorist group led by an Egyptian, Ali Saleh, who was working for bin Laden (PBS Online, "Notes on The Interrogation of One Suspect")
- Between 1994 and 1997 he visited Somalia a number of times (PBS Online, "Notes on The Interrogation of One Suspect")
- Used al Qaida money to set up a fishing business in Mombassa and had a seven-ton boat to catch fish or to transport the catch of others for sale down the coast
- Had been visited in Kenya by commanders of al Qaidia
- Planned the attack with others at meetings in the Nairobi Hilltop Hotel
- Was instructed in explosives by Fazul, the explosives expert who led the Kenyan cell of al-Qaida
- Allegedly supervised construction of the Nairobi bomb; referred to as the "explosives consultant"
- Also designed the Dar es Salaam bomb: 250 kg of TNT with mechanical detonators and 10 m of RDX cord (PBS Online, "Notes on The Interrogation of One Suspect")
- Was later arrested with a false passport in Pakistan
- Was arrested by the Kenyans on 14 August (PBS Online, "FBI Executive Summary")
- Was rendered to the United States on 28 August (PBS Online, "FBI Executive Summary")
- Claimed the attack was sponsored by bin Laden

[redacted]

[redacted]

The Nairobi Conspirators

Mohammed Rashed Daoud al Owhali, a.k.a. Khalid Salim Saleh bin Rashid, a.k.a. Mohammed Akbar, a.k.a. Abdul Jabbar Ali Abdel-Latif, a.k.a. Latif, a.k.a. Abdel Jabbar al-Baloushi, a.k.a. M'aad, a.k.a. Mohammed al-Qatari, a.k.a. Moath

Born 18 January 1977 in Liverpool, England (PBS Online, "FBI Executive Summary")

Mohammed Rashed Daoud al'Owhali

A Yemeni national; another report says a citizen of Saudi Arabia (PBS Online, "FBI Executive Summary")

Joined al Qaeda in the mid 1990s

In or about 1996 he received training in explosives, hijacking, kidnapping, assassination, and intelligence techniques at a number of camps in Afghanistan including camps that were affiliated with al Qaeda

In or about 1996 he met with bin Laden and asked him for a "mission"

He attended conferences and meetings with bin Laden, including a press conference (USIA, "Criminal Complaint Against Kenya Bombing Suspect Al-"Owhali")

Traveled from Pakistan to Kenya a week before the attack (Washington Post says he arrived in Nairobi in July)

[redacted]

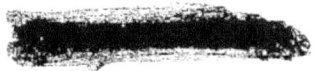

[redacted]

The Nairobi Conspirators

Mohammed Rashed Daoud al Owhali

Cased the embassy with Fazil in the days before the bombing: reconnoitered the embassy on 4 August (USIA, "Criminal Complaint Against Kenya Bombing Suspect Al-"Owhali")

Was allegedly a passenger in the truck that carried the bomb to the Nairobi embassy

Expected to die in the attack

Left the truck to throw a grenade at a guard outside the embassy and fled

Went to the M.P. Shah Hospital in Nairobi for treatment of the wounds he suffered during the Nairobi embassy blast

In a men's room in the hospital he had sought to hide three bullets and the keys to the padlock on the rear door of the bomb truck

Went from the hospital to an apartment building where Kenyan police tracked him two days later

Was contacted by Kenyan officials on 9 August and was subsequently arrested (USIA, "Criminal Complaint Against Kenya Bombing Suspect Al-"Owhali")

He was rendered to the Unites States on 27 August (PBS Online, "FBI Executive Summary")

Admitted to being one of bin Laden's men

[redacted]

[redacted]

The Nairobi Conspirators

Fazul Abdullah Mohammed, a.k.a. Fazhl Abdullah, a.k.a. Haroun (or Harun or Haroon) Fazil (or Fazhl or Fadhul or Faidhul), a.k.a. Fazhl Khan

- A native of the Comoros Islands (just off the East African coast)
- May have been educated abroad in physics
- Fluent in French, Swahili, Arabic, and English (PBS Online, "FBI Executive Summary")
- Good with computers (PBS Online, "FBI Executive Summary")
- Was offered a scholarship to study Islam in Sudan by an Islamic organization called jabha, or "front", a group based in Nairobi which had promoted Muslim scholarships on the Comoros Islands for years
- Trained in the use of explosives in camps in Afghanistan
- Was in Somalia to train followers of the local warlords fighting US troops there
- Received paramilitary training from bin Laden in Afghanistan in 1994
- Moved to Kenya in 1994
- Falsely obtained a Kenyan identity card in 1996 (using the name Haroon)
- Was an active member in al Qaida's Kenya cell
- Played a leading role in planning and executing the Nairobi blast
- Rented the villa where the bomb was built (and where explosives residue was found after the attack)
- Attended meetings at the Hilltop Hotel in Nairobi
- Cased the embassy with Owhali in the days before the bombing
- Drove a white Datsun pickup truck that led the bomb-laden vehicle to the embassy in Nairobi
- Returned to the Comoran capital of Moroni a week after the attack
- Departed Moroni on 22 Aug on a flight to Dubai and disappeared before the FBI arrived
- The FBI raided his family's homes: At his home, investigators found incriminating letters and computer disks tying him to al Qaeda and to Wadih el Hage
- Currently at large with a $2 million reward for his capture

Fazul

[redacted]

[redacted]

The Nairobi Conspirators

Wadih el Hage, a.k.a. Abdus Sabbur, a.k.a. Abd al Sabbur, a.k.a. Norman, a.k.a. Wa'da Norman

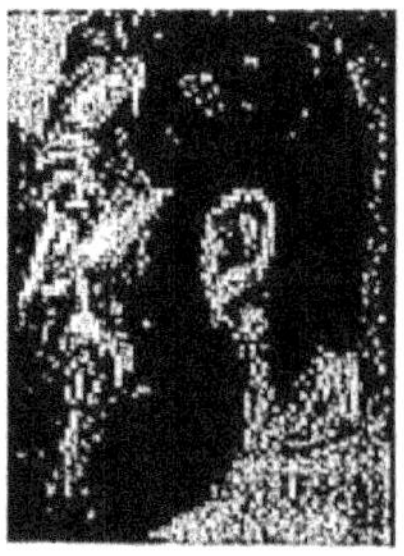

Wadih el Hage

- Born into a Catholic family on 25 July 1960 in Sidon, Lebanon (PBS Online, "A Portrait of Wadih El Hage, Accused Terrorist"; PBS Online, "FBI Executive Summary")
- Grew up in Kuwait and converted to Islam as a teenager (PBS Online, "A Portrait of Wadih El Hage, Accused Terrorist")
- Came to the US in 1978 to attend school at the University of Southwestern Louisiana (USL) in Lafayette (JCSI, Fall 1998, p. 24; PBS Online, "A Portrait of Wadih El Hage, Accused Terrorist")
- At the beginning of the Afghan war against the Soviets, he traveled to Pakistan to enroll in mujahedeen war training programs (PBS Online, "A Portrait of Wadih El Hage, Accused Terrorist")
- By January 1985 he returned to the U.S. and to USL (PBS Online, "A Portrait of Wadih El Hage, Accused Terrorist")
- Educated as an urban planner in the United States
- In 1985 he traveled to Arizona to marry an 18-year-old American Muslim (PBS Online, "A Portrait of Wadih El Hage, Accused Terrorist")
- In May 1986 he graduated from USL and moved permanently to Arizona (PBS Online, "A Portrait of Wadih El Hage, Accused Terrorist")
- He and his wife returned to Pakistan several times over the next few years (PBS Online, "A Portrait of Wadih El Hage, Accused Terrorist")
- Moved to Tucson in 1987, where he became an active member of the Al Kifah office at the Islamic Center (JCSI, Fall 1998, p. 24)

[redacted]

The Nairobi Conspirators

Wadih el Hage

- While in Tucson, El Hage hosted an unidentified visitor who surveilled a black Muslim cleric named Rashid Khalifa who was later murdered in Tucson (JCSI, Fall 1998, p. 25)
- In December 1988 he met with other Islamic fundamentalists, including Mahmud Abuhalima (later convicted in the WTC bombing) and top officials of the Al Kifah Center at a major radical Islamic conference held at the convention center in Oklahoma City (JCSI, Fall 1998, p. 24)
- In 1989 he was granted U.S. citizenship (PBS Online, "A Portrait of Wadih El Hage, Accused Terrorist")
- In December 1989 he met Mahmud Abouhalima at an Islamic conference in Oklahoma City (PBS Online, "A Portrait of Wadih El Hage, Accused Terrorist")
- According to a confession Abouhalima later gave to U.S. Attorneys, Abouhalima contacted El Hage in 1990 to purchase assault weapons to be used against radical Jewish Rabbi Meir Kahane (who was murdered in New York City in November 1990) (PBS Online, "A Portrait of Wadih El Hage, Accused Terrorist")
- In 1990 he hosted a visitor who said he was there to check on Dr. Rashad Khalifa, an unorthodox imam in Tucson: Khalifa was found murdered a few weeks later and prosecutors suspect that El Hage may have been involved in the murder (PBS Online, "A Portrait of Wadih El Hage, Accused Terrorist")
- In 1991 he moved from Tucson to Arlington, TX where he remained very active with Al Kifah and was chosen as the successor to Al Kifah Director Shalabi (JCSI, Fall 1998, p. 26)
- In early 1991 he was called to New York to help direct the Alkifah Refugee Center (PBS Online, "A Portrait of Wadih El Hage, Accused Terrorist")

[redacted]

The Nairobi Conspirators

Wadih el Hage

- On the same day that he arrived in New York, 1 March 1991, the leader of the Alkifah Center, Mustafa Shalabi, disappeared and was later found murdered in what prosecutors believe was a dispute over allocation of the Alkifah Center's resources (PBS Online, "A Portrait of Wadih El Hage, Accused Terrorist")
- He lived in Brooklyn and managed the Alkifah Refugee Center, which recruited Muslim fighters for Afghanistan
- He was friends with many people who were later convicted in the World Trade Center and New York City Landmark bombing cases (PBS Online, "A Portrait of Wadih El Hage, Accused Terrorist")
- Moved to Khartoum, Sudan in late 1992 or early 1993 (JCSI, Fall 1998, p. 26); another source says he moved in early 1992 (PBS Online, "A Portrait of Wadih El Hage, Accused Terrorist")
- Served as bin Laden's secretary while he was living in Sudan until 1994
- Moved to Kenya in 1994 (WP, 8/1/99) and worked as a "sometime gem dealer"
- Attended the wedding of Mohammed Saddiq Odeh in 1994
- In 1995 he set up the Help Africa Foundation in Kenya, which served as a cover group for bin Laden (JCSI, Fall 1998, p. 26)
- In 1995, while still in Kenya, he received a document from Ali A. Mohamed in California about the New York trial of Sheik Omar Abdel Rahman which he was directed to hand-deliver to Osama bin Laden (WP, 8/1/99)
- Played a leading role in the Kenya cell of al Qaida until 1997
- Registered a charity called Help Africa People with the Kenyan government as a branch of a German charity: The registration also mentioned Mercy International Relief Organization, a Nairobi group that worked in Somalia during 1992 and 1993, but the purpose of Hage's charity was always vague

[redacted]

[redacted]

The Nairobi Conspirators

Wadih el Hage

- Hage sometimes mentioned a side business as a gem dealer, although this may not have been true
- Engaged in coded correspondence with other members and associates of al Qaeda during the course of the Nairobi bombing conspiracy
- Had ties to terrorists who had bombed the World Trade Center and killed 18 U.S. soldiers in Somalia
- Searched for the body of bin Laden's drowned military commander (Ubaidah al-Banshiri) at the scene of a ferry disaster on Lake Victoria in May 1996
- Haroun Fazul, a bin Laden associate, moved into El Hage's house in Nairobi and began to work for El Hage (PBS Online, "A Portrait of Wadih El Hage, Accused Terrorist")
- In February 1997, Wadih el Hage sent a coded fax from Kenya to an unnamed co-conspirator in Orlando, saying that he had just returned from a meeting with bin Laden's military commander, Muhammed Atef, in Pakistan (WP, 8/1/99)
- In August 1997 his Nairobi home was raided by police while he was away in Afghanistan (PBS Online, "A Portrait of Wadih El Hage, Accused Terrorist")
- Two days after the raid, El Hage returned from Afghanistan, was questioned by police and told to leave the country (PBS Online, "A Portrait of Wadih El Hage, Accused Terrorist")
- Moved from Nairobi to Arlington, TX in September 1997 (JCSI, Fall 1998, p. 26; PBS Online)
- El Hage attended the Center Street Mosque in Arlington, TX: Moataz Hallack, who was the imam or prayer leader at the mosque, and Khader Ibrahim, a fellow worshiper at the mosque, have both been before the grand jury to answer questions abut their links to el Hage (WP, 8/1/99)
- Odeh admitted that he knew El Hage in Kenya, said that he considered el Hage "a very close friend, like an older brother", and that El Hage had attended his wedding

[redacted]

[redacted]

The Nairobi Conspirators

Wadih el Hage

- Two weeks after the August 1998 East African bombings, El Hage was interviewed by the FBI and denied knowing Odeh (PBS Online, "A Portrait of Wadih El Hage, Accused Terrorist")
- On 15 September 1998 El Hage testified before the grand jury that he did not know Odeh and that he had never heard that al-Banshiri had died (PBS Online, "A Portrait of Wadih El Hage, Accused Terrorist")
- Several days later, El Hage was arrested in Arlington, TX and charged with perjury (PBS Online, "A Portrait of Wadih El Hage, Accused Terrorist")
- Had been useful to bin Laden because of his ability to travel freely around the world with an American passport (PBS Online, "A Portrait of Wadih El Hage, Accused Terrorist")
- Was allegedly at the heart of al Qaeda and traveled around the world on his U.S. passport to meet with operatives, manage communications, move money for bin Laden and to seek chemical weapons (WP, 8/1/99)

wadih el hage

[redacted]

[redacted]

The Nairobi Conspirators

Jihad Mohammed Ali, a.k.a. Azzam, a.k.a. Jihad Mohammed Abdou Ali, a.k.a. Abu Obaida

- Born 19 March 1974 in Saudi Arabia (PBS Online, "FBI Executive Summary")
- Citizen of Saudi Arabia (PBS Online, "FBI Executive Summary")
- Was the driver of the truck
- Likely perished in the explosion

Abdullah Ahmed Abdullah, a.k.a. Mohammed Saleh, a.k.a. Saleh, a.k.a. Abu Mohammed, a.k.a. Abu Marium

- Sudanese
- The "mastermind" of both the Nairobi and Dar es Salaam attacks (PBS Online, "FBI Executive Summary")
- One of the bomb makers
- Fled to Afghanistan

Abdullah

- A Saudi
- One of the bomb makers
- Fled to Afghanistan

Fahad Mohammed Ally, a.k.a. Fahad Mohammed Ally Msalam

- The owner of the pickup truck subsequently used by Harun to lead the bomb delivery vehicle to the Nairobi embassy (PBS Online, "FBI Executive Summary")

Abdul Rahman, a.k.a. Abdul Rahman Al-Muhasar

- Egyptian citizen (PBS Online, "FBI Executive Summary")
- A bomb technician (PBS Online, "FBI Executive Summary")

[redacted]

[redacted]

The Dar es Salaam Conspirators

Mustafa Mohamed Said Ahmed

Was charged with 11 counts of murder in Tanzania

Had been involved in a past incident of surveilling the US Embassy in Nairobi (PBS Online, "FBI Executive Summary")

Rashid Saleh Hemed (a.k.a. Rasheed Saleheh Hemed)

Blasting caps and explosive residue like those used in the bombings were found in his home

Was charged with 11 counts of murder in Tanzania

Mustafa Mohamad Fadhil

One of the Tanzania bombing suspects (WP, 8/1/99)

Khalfan Khamis Mohamed, a.k.a. Elfani Hamis Ahmed

One of the Tanzania bombing suspects (WP, 8/1/99)

Allegedly rented a house in Tanzania to manufacture bombs for the August 1998 US embassy bombings in East Africa (JTWR, 10/8/99)

On 7 October 1999 he was arrested in Cape Town's airport as he was about to be deported for illegally entering South Africa (JTWR, 10/8/99)

He was then flown into New York by FBI agents (JTWR, 10/8/99)

[redacted]

[redacted]

The Dar es Salaam Conspirators

Ahmed Khalfan Ghailani, a.k.a. Abu Khabar, a.k.a. Abu Bakr, a.k.a. K. Ahmed, possibly a.k.a. Ahmed the Tanzanian

Born in Tanzania (PBS Online, "FBI Executive Summary")

Citizen of Tanzania (PBS Online, "FBI Executive Summary")

Purchased the Tanzania bomb delivery vehicle with the assistance of Swedan (PBS Online, "FBI Executive Summary")

Fahid Mohammed Ally Msalam

One of the Tanzania bombing suspects (WP, 8/1/99)

Sheikh Ahmed Salim Swedan, a.k.a. Ahmed Ally, a.k.a. Sheikh Bahamad

Born 9 April 1969 (PBS Online, "FBI Executive Summary")

Citizen of Kenya (PBS Online, "FBI Executive Summary")

One of the Tanzania bombing suspects (WP, 8/1/99)

Hamden Khalif Allah Awad, a.k.a. "Ahmed the German"

Born 13 August 1970 in Egypt (PBS Online, "FBI Executive Summary")

Citizen of Egypt (PBS Online, "FBI Executive Summary")

Was driver of the bomb delivery vehicle and was killed instantly (PBS Online, "FBI Executive Summary")

[redacted]

[redacted]

Who's Who

Khalid al-Fawwaz

- Once served as bin Laden's press spokesman
- Arrested on 28 Sept 1998 in the U.K. (IPIN, 5/27/99, p. 6)
- Was being held on terrorism charges in London as of 4 Dec 1998
- On 8 September 1999 a UK magistrate ordered his extradition to the U.S. on suspicion of conspiring with bin Laden's al Qaeda group to bomb the US embassies in Nairobi and Dar es Salaam (JTWR, 9/8/99)
- An informer identified Khalid al-Fawwaz as the UK head of al Qaeda (JTWR, 9/8/99)
- Described as bin Laden's "right-hand man" (IPIN, 5/27/99, p. 6)
- Set up businesses in Nairobi with bin Laden's military commander (Reuters, 6/17/99)

Sidi Tayyib

- Former aide to bin Laden
- Reportedly cooperating with Saudi, British, and American authorities (according to a report by the Daily Telegraph of London in 1997)

Muhammed Atef (a.k.a. Abu Hafs, a.k.a. Abu Hafs el Masry, a.k.a. Abu Hafs el Masry el Khabir, a.k.a. Taysir, a.k.a. Sheikh Taysir Abdullah)

- Egyptian (PBS Online, "FBI Executive Summary")
- Sat on the Al Qaeda military committee
- Was one of bin Laden's two principal military commanders (along with Banshiri until the death of Banshiri in 1996)
- Had principal responsibility for training Al Qaeda members

[redacted]

[redacted]

Who's Who

Ali A. Muhammed

- Born in Egypt (JCSI, Fall 1998, p. 28)
- He had served as a major in the Egyptian army (WP, 8/1/99)
- Graduated as a captain from a Special Forces Officers School at Fort Bragg in 1981 in a program for visiting military officials from foreign countries (JCSI, Fall 1998, p. 28)
- Moved to the US in 1985 (JCSI, Fall 1998, p. 28) and became a permanent resident (AP, 5/20/99)
- Immigrated to the United States in 1986 (WP, 8/1/99)
- It has been reported that Mohamed entered the United States under a special visa program controlled by the CIA
- He joined the U.S. Army and was assigned to the John F. Kennedy Special Warfare Center at Fort Bragg, N.C. (WP, 8/1/99)
- During 1986-1989 he served in the U.S. Army at the Special Forces base in Fort Bragg, N.C. where he taught soldiers in the U.S. special forces about Muslim culture (AP, 5/20/99)
- He was involved in training and lecturing U.S. soldiers who were being deployed to the Middle East on that regions culture and politics
- While he was in the U.S. Army, he gave tapes and books on military techniques and weapons to a group of men who wanted to help Afghan rebels: some of these materials were later recovered from the apartment of El Sayyid Nosair, the Egyptian immigrant convicted of conspiracy in the killing of Jewish Defense League founder Rabbi Meir Kahane in 1990 (AP, 5/20/99)
- In 1989 he began giving training sessions in guerilla warfare to Islamic militants in New Jersey (including El Sayyid Nossair) (JCSI, Fall 1998, p. 28)

[redacted]

[redacted]

Who's Who

Ali A. Muhammed

- In 1989, while on active duty as a U.S. Special Forces sergeant, Ali Mohamed traveled to New York and provided military training to local Muslims preparing to fight the Soviets in Afghanistan
- However, these visits were reportedly not part of his official duties
- The training included survival techniques, map reading, and how to recognize tanks and other Soviet equipment
- He also gave the militants several U.S. Army manuals that described how to throw grenades and how to make booby-traps with explosives
- For example, when FBI agents raided the New Jersey home of El Sayyid Nosair on 8 November 1990 (following his arrest in the shooting of Rabbi Meir Kahane in New York City), items found in Nosair's possession included sensitive military documents (some of which were classified) that had been supplied by Ali (JCSI, Fall 1998, p. 28)
- He was discharged from the U.S. army in 1989 (WP, 8/1/99) (he was honorably discharged from the Army; AP, 5/20/99) and moved to Santa Clara after which he traveled to Afghanistan and Pakistan where he befriended bin Laden (JCSI, Fall 1998, p. 28)
- Within a year of his discharge, he was training al Qaeda members in Afghanistan and Sudan and travelling the world for bin Laden, delivering messages and conducting financial transactions (WP, 8/1/99)
- Mohammed emerged as a top aide to bin Laden, traveled regularly to and from Pakistan and Afghanistan (JCSI, Fall 1998, p. 28)
- Mohammed helped oversee bin Laden's terrorist bases in Khost and other terrorist camps in Afghanistan (JCSI, Fall 1998, p. 28)
- In 1991 he personally escorted bin Laden from Pakistan to Sudan, where he helped train bin Laden's bodyguards (WP, 8/1/99)

[redacted]

[redacted]

Who's Who

Ali A. Muhammed

- In 1991 he was in charge of bin Laden's move from Afghanistan to the Sudan and helped bin Laden to set up his new home and terrorist base in Khartoum, where 2000 :Arab Afghans" were headquartered (JCSI, Fall 1998, p. 28-29)
- Mohammed stated that he did this because he loved bin Laden and believed in him (AP, 6/6/99)
- One witness in the New York City Landmarks bombing trial, Khalid Ibrahim, said that he had encountered Ali Mohamed (who went by the name Abu Omar) at an Afghan rebel training camp near Khost in Afghanistan in the fall of 1992
- He allegedly provided training to a group of Islamic militants who were later implicated in the 1993 World Trade Center bombing and in a plot to blow up New York City landmarks (AP, 5/20/99)
- In 1993 he was in Somalia and claims to know that bin Laden's operatives were responsible for the killing of 18 U.S. servicemen in a firefight in Mogadishu (WP, 8/1/99)
- Began telling the FBI about bin Laden as early as 1993 (AP, 6/6/99)
- Mohammed had frequent contact with the FBI between 1993 and 1999 and even sought unsuccessfully at one point to work as a translator for the FBI (AP, 6/6/99)
- As early as 1993 he allegedly discussed with other members of Al Qaeda how to attack the U.S. Embassy in Nairobi and Israeli, British, and French targets in Kenya (AP, 5/20/99)
- In 1994 he used his U.S. passport to enter the U.S. Embassy in Nairobi on an apparent surveillance mission (WP, 8/1/99)
- In 1996 he helped move bin Laden back from the Sudan to Afghanistan (JCSI, Fall 1998, p. 29)
- Mohammed continued working for bin Laden in 1997 and 1998 (JCSI, Fall 1998, p. 29)
- He was arrested on 11 September 1998 (AP, 5/20/99) and held in secret in New York (WP, 8/1/99)
- He was added to the list of criminal defendants in May 1999 (WP, 8/1/99)
- Sources claim that Mohamed has become a witness for the prosecution in the bin Laden indictments (PBS Online, "The Suspects & Charges")

[redacted]

[redacted]

Who's Who

Ayman al Zawahiri

Born in June 1951 to a prominent family (IPIN, 3/10/99, p. 8)

Joined the Moslem Brotherhood in high school (IPIN, 3/10/99, p. 8)

Joined Egypt's Jihad in the 1970s (IPIN, 3/10/99, p. 8)

Graduated from Cairo's medical faculty in 1976 (IPIN, 3/10/99, p. 8)

After graduation, he took part in founding the first university unit of Jihad (IPIN, 3/10/99, p. 8)

In 1981 he was sentenced to three years in jail in the trial that followed the Jihad assassination of Anwar Sadat (IPIN, 3/10/99, p. 8)

Traveled to Peshawar, Pakistan in 1985 and gradually emerged as a leader of the Jihad organization (IPIN, 3/10/99, p. 8)

Cultivated links with Osama bin Laden (IPIN, 3/10/99, p. 8)

Set up operations in Sudan in 1992-93 (IPIN, 3/10/99, p. 8)

In 1995, realizing that armed struggle in Egypt had failed, he adopted a more international and anti-American line (IPIN, 3/10/99, p. 8)

In Feb 1998 he joined bin Laden and others in forming the World Islamic Front for the Holy War against Jews and Crusaders (IPIN, 3/10/99, p. 8)

Heads the New Jihad Group and the Vanguards of the Conquest, which both operate under the aegis of Egyptian Islamic Jihad (JIR, Mar 1999, p. 7)

[redacted]

[redacted]

Who's Who

Mamdouh Mahmud Salim (a.k.a. Abu Hajer al Iraqi)

- Born around 1949 (JIR, June 1999, p. 36)
- A Sudanese national of Iraqi descent (JIR, June 1999, p. 36)
- Helped found al Qaeda (JIR, June 1999, p. 36)
- Believed to have been close to bin Laden (JIR, June 1999, p. 36)
- Served as a financial aide to bin Laden (WP, 8/1/99)
- Reportedly sat on al Qaeda's advisory council and helped to approve military operations (JIR, June 1999, p. 36)
- Was an advocate of Islamic solidarity who lectured al Qaeda members (mostly Sunnis) that it was permitted to cooperate with Shiites against the common enemy (JIR, June 1999, p. 36)
- Helped to negotiate a cooperative agreement among al Qaeda, Sudan's National Islamic Front, and Iran to work together against the USA (JIR, June 1999, p. 36)
- Helped arrange explosives training for al Qaeda members in Iran (JIR, June 1999, p. 36)
- In late 1993 he allegedly approved a scheme to obtain enriched uranium (JIR, June 1999, p. 36)

Ihab M. Ali

- A taxi driver from Orlando (WP, 8/1/99)
- He left the United States in 1989 and spent several years helping Afghan refugees on the Pakistan border before returning to central Florida (WP, 8/1/99)
- In February 1997, Wadih el Hage sent a coded fax from Kenya to an unnamed co-conspirator in Orlando, saying that he had just returned from a meeting with bin Laden's military commander, Muhammed Atef, in Pakistan (WP, 8/1/99)
- Five days later, the co-conspirator replied in code with an offer of support for bin Laden (WP, 8/1/99)
- Five months later, the co-conspirator in Orlando sent another coded message to el Hage warning to "be careful about possible apprehension by American authorities" (WP, 8/1/99)

[redacted]

[redacted]

Who's Who

Adel Mohammed Abdul Almagid Abdul Bary

Managed guesthouses and training camps for al Qaeda (WP, 8/1/99)

Arrested in London (WP, 8/1/99)

Ibrahim Hussein Abdelhadi Eidarous

Managed guesthouses and training camps for al Qaeda (WP, 8/1/99)

Arrested in London (WP, 8/1/99)

Ali Abul-Saud Mustafa

Was tasked by bin Laden in the mid 1990s with gathering information about U.S. embassies in Africa (JIR, June 1999, p. 3)

Visited Tanzania, Kenya, Uganda, Nigeria, and Somalia in 1995 and 1996 (JIR, June 1999, p. 3)

Had an important role in providing military training to members of Egypt's Islamic Jihad in their camps in Afghanistan (JIR, June 1999, p. 3)

Allegedly helped Ayman Al Zawahri enter the U.S. in 1995 to raise funds from mosques in North Carolina (JIR, June 1999, p. 3)

Was arrested by U.S. authorities in mid 1999 (JIR, June 1999, p. 3)

[redacted]

[redacted]

Events After The African Bombings

Aug 1998 Osama bin Laden was living in a hilltop complex near Kandahar, Afghanistan

Communications intercepts linked bin Laden to the African bombings

Communications intercepts also revealed his operatives discussing additional truck bombings

There was "a dispersement of people away from bin Laden's bases" in Afghanistan

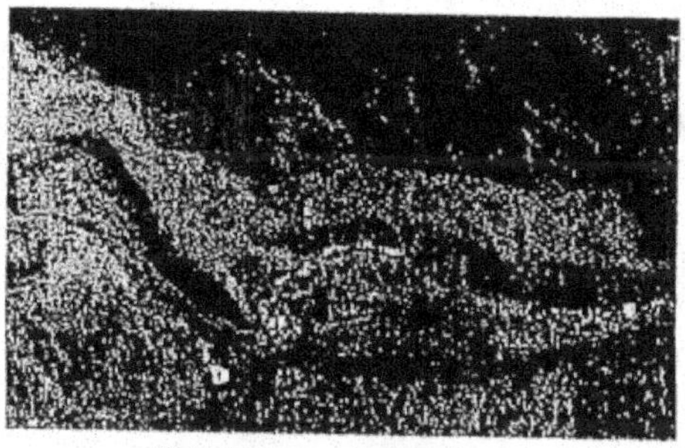

The bin Laden complex near Khost

[redacted]

[redacted]

Events After The African Bombings

Aug 1998 — Mohammed Saddiq Odeh took Pakistan Air flight 746 from Nairobi to Karachi, Pakistan

He had an onward ticket for a flight from Karachi to Kabul on 7 Aug (the day of the bombings)

Because the photograph in his Yemeni passport was a poor match for his face, Odeh was detained (Wash Post claims he was detained on his way to the Karachi to Kabul flight)

Odeh claimed that the embassy bombings were the work of Al Qaeda and bin Laden

Odeh was on his way to meet with bin Laden: He has reportedly stated that he expected to be greeted and thanked by bin Laden personally

He claimed he was on his way to Afghanistan with six other members of bin Laden's forces, who were able to evade security checks at Karachi airport

Pakistani officials claim that Odeh calming boasted of providing technical and logistical support for the Nairobi bombing

Aug 1998 — Fazul Abdullah Mohammed hired persons to clean the villa located at 43 Rundu Estates in Nairobi

[redacted]

[redacted]

Events After The African Bombings

Aug 1998	The World Islamic Front for Jihad Against Jews and Crusaders sent a message to the Arab world's leading newspaper, the Al-Hayt The statement said that: "Strikes will continue from everywhere, and Islamic groups will appear one after the other to fight American interests"
8 Aug 1998	President Clinton's advisors ordered the Pentagon Joint Staff and the CIA to draw up a list of sites connected to bin Laden and his organization that could be attacked (NYT, 10/27/99)
9 Aug 1998	Mohamed Rashed Daoud al-'Owhali was contacted by Kenyan officials and found to have numerous injuries and lacerations: He was subsequently taken into custody
11 Aug 1999	Iran expressed its deep sympathy for the victims of the embassy bombings (SGIU, "U.S. Faces Dilemma in Relations with Iran")
11 Aug 1998	Senior American intelligence officials met to discuss whether or not the Al Shifa factory in Sudan was an appropriate target for a retaliatory strike (NYT, 10/27/99)
12 Aug 1998	al-'Owhali claimed to have been standing in a bank near the embassy at the time of the bombing

[redacted]

Events After The African Bombings

12 Aug 1998 The Small Group of presidential advisors met with President Clinton with evidence that bin Laden was looking to obtain weapons of mass destruction and chemical weapons to use against US installations (NYT, 9/23/98; PBS Online)

President Clinton and key national security officials were briefed by General Shelton for the first time on possible targets for retaliation (NYT, 10/27/99)

12 Aug 1998 US intelligence reportedly intercepted a mobile phone conversation between two of bin Laden's lieutenants that implicated them in the African embassy bombings (Newsweek, 8/31/98; PBS Online)

13 Aug 1998 Intelligence showed that bin Laden and his key lieutenants would be meeting on 20 August at Khost and that he might be planning further attacks, possibly with chemical weapons (NYT, 10/27/99)

13 Aug 1998 Mohammad Sadiq Howaida was handed over to U.S. officials in Karachi and was then flown to Nairobi two days later (JIR, 10/98, p. 48)

14 Aug 1998 The U.S. Embassy in Accra, Ghana was closed for 3 days after a bomb threat, but later reopened on 17 August

14 Aug 1998 Odeh was flown back to Nairobi

With U.S. investigators, Odeh recanted his confession but did acknowledge that he is a member of al Qaida

Events After The African Bombings

14 Aug 1998	Abdallah Mohammed Fazul flew from Nairobi to the Comoros Islands on Air Madagascar
16 Aug 1998	Over 200 U.S. military personnel are sent to Albania to evacuate U.S. dependents and other nonessential personnel and to guard the American residential compound
17 Aug 1998	Sometime this week, a group founded by bin Laden issued a new threat to "continue shipping more American dead bodies to their unjust government"
18 Aug 1998	Investigators raided the Hill Top Hotel in Nairobi where the Nairobi bomb was believed to have been assembled
	Mohammed Saddiq Odeh was believed to have been the chief assembler of the bomb
	Sources indicated that the bomb consisted of 800 kilograms of TNT
18 Aug 1998	The U.S. evacuated over half of its diplomatic staff from Pakistan saying that there were "very serious indications of threat to US facilities and its citizens"
	The State Department evacuated more than 200 non-emergency personnel and family members from Islamabad

Events After The African Bombings

19 Aug 1998	In a White House meeting, officials chose to attack the Afghan camps and two sites in Sudan, the Al Shifa factory and a tannery in Khartoum that intelligence had linked to bin Laden (NYT, 10/27/99) However, General Shelton objected to attacking the tannery because of the potential that missiles might hit civilians and because it was not suspected of being involved in chemical weapons (NYT, 10/27/99)
20 Aug 1998	At about 2 a.m., President Clinton ordered that the tannery in Sudan be removed from the target list for the cruise missile strikes (NYT, 10/27/99)
20 Aug 1998	al-'Owhali stated that he had been trained in a number of camps in Afghanistan, including camps affiliated with al Qaeda; that he was trained in explosives, hijacking and kidnapping; and that he had attended meetings with Osama bin Laden
20 Aug 1998	The US added bin Laden's name to a list of terrorists whose funds are targeted for seizure by the US Treasury (WP, 8/28/98; PBS Online)

[redacted]

The Afghan Camps

The camps are hidden in the steep mountains and deep valleys of Paktia province, near the town of Khost

During the Soviet war in Afghanistan, all seven ranking Afghan resistance leaders maintained underground headquarters, mountain redoubts, and weapons stocks at these camps

The Soviets attacked with Scud missiles, aerial bombings, artillery, helicopter gunships, and special forces assaults, yet the Afghan resistance was able to maintain a decade-long siege on the Soviet-supported garrison town of Khost

Soviet accounts of the siege of Khost referred to the rebel camps as "the last word in NATO engineering techniques"

After the war with the Soviets, the Afghan resistance veterans hoarded the remaining weapons and set up military training centers at camps like those near Khost

Bin Laden built at least three training camps for veterans of the Afghan war

Bin Laden maintains well-defended camps in Loggar and Nangarhar, mountainous regions near the Pakistani border

Bin Laden keeps a safe house in Kandahar and two more in Jalalabad

One of these houses in Jalalabad is his favorite, which he has named "Star of the Jihad"

[redacted]

[redacted]

The Afghan Camps

Bin Laden helps run an Islamic training camp, Al-Badr, in the mountains near Khost

At this camp, Algerians, Egyptians, Sudanese, Pakistanis, and Kashmiris are trained in commando techniques

Thousands of Islamic radicals from around the world have come to these camps for training, many sponsored by bin Laden

The camps have trained fighters that went on to Turkey, Algeria, Egypt, Saudi Arabia, India, Bosnia, and Chechnya

During a 1994 interview, a commander named Noor Amin, who was loyal to the fundamentalist leader Gulbuddin Hekmatyar, stated that:

> "the whole country is a university for jihad"
>
> "There are many formal training centers. We have had Egyptians, Sudanese, Arabs, and other foreigners trained here as assassins."

Badr 1 and Badr 2 are two camps located near Khost: They house not only Arabs, but also many Kashmiri fighters who carry out attacks against the Indian army, Tajiks opposed to the government in Dushanbe, Turkomans, Filipinos, and Chinese

The main Arab Afghan camps are in the suburbs of Jalalabad and in the Khunar valley where bin Laden heads several hundred Saudi and Palestinian fighters

[redacted]

[redacted]

The Afghan Camps

Altogether, the camps house about 2,500 Arabs

Many other camps have been installed along the road that links Kandahar and Khost, inhabited mainly by Afghans, Pakistanis, and Kashmiris

The cruise missiles targeted the Zhawar Kili al-Badr training complex, 94 miles south of Kabul

This complex consists of a base camp, support camp, and four training camps

The training camps consist of numerous tents, obstacle courses, firing ranges, and explosive training areas

Egyptian Jihad and al-Gama'a al-Islamiya are among the groups that train there

A senior commander of the Hezbul Mujahedeen (Party of Holy Warriors), Bakht Zamin, has stated that over 20,000 men have trained at these camps in the six years prior to the attacks

Some reports claim that the camps targeted in Afghanistan were first established under the Reagan administration by the CIA (JIR, 10/98, p. 24)

Zamin described the training day as follows: Prayers, 1-2 hours of running in the mountains, breakfast military training (including the use of weapons such as rifles, mortars, RPGs, and explosives), lunch, more prayers, afternoon for study of the Koran and sports, dinner, and bed

Bin Laden's communications infrastructure in the camps is based on portable satellite telephones

[redacted]

[redacted]

The Afghan Camps

Bin Laden moved every 4 or 5 nights to avoid attack and always traveled with a group of his commandos

Bin Laden is reportedly accompanied everywhere by 12 to 100 masked or hooded bodyguards

His bodyguards carry Stinger missiles to protect against a surprise air attack

Four camps were hit in the cruise missile attack:

Two of the camps, in the Jarawah area near Khost, trained Pakistanis and Kashmiris for the war against India in Kashmir

These two camps have reportedly been supported by Pakistan

One of these two was run by a Pakistani fundamentalist Islamic organization called Harakat Mujahedeen, or Movement of Holy Warriors. (This group was formerly known as Harakat Ansar, but changed its name after the DoS put them on its list of terrorist organizations in 1997.)

The nearby camp of Al Farooq was used mainly by Arabs from several nations

The Al Badr camp, ten miles west, was also used mainly by Arabs and was run by Bin Laden

[redacted]

[redacted]

Attack on the Afghan Camps

20 Aug 1998 Approximately 70 BGM-109 Tomahawk cruise missiles were launched against bin Laden's Zhawar Kili terrorist training complex

Military officials later said that 66 missiles were fired into Afghanistan at the Shawar Kili base camp, support complex, and Al-Badr training facilities

Planners are believed to have timed the arrival of the Tomahawk missiles so that a few missiles with unitary warheads would strike first (to lure people outside to see what had happened), followed by D-model Tomahawks, each of which carries 166 CEM bomblets effective against personnel

The Zhawar Kili terrorist training complex was located 94 miles SE of Kabul, near Khost, in the southeastern province of Paktia, Afghanistan

The complex was used for training by the Egyptian Islamic Jihad, Algeria's Armed Islamic Group (GIA), and others presumed to be funded by bin Laden

The U.S. calls it the largest Sunni terrorist training facility in the world

It was the largest of at least 2 terrorist training camps established by bin Laden in Afghanistan

An estimated 24 people were killed (PBS Online, "The Controversial U.S. Retaliatory Missile Strikes")

Most of the dead were Pakistani recruits training to fight in Kashmir

[redacted]

Attack on the Afghan Camps

20 Aug 1998 A terrorist conference was expected at the time of the attack, but apparently did not take place as anticipated

Bin Laden survived "by the grace of God": He had dropped plans at the last minute to visit his Harkatul Jihad Al-Ismali military training camp in Khost for a visit and dinner

However, one communications intercept indicated that bin Laden was at an Al Qaeda camp in Afghanistan on the day it was struck

In fact, AW&ST reported that he was actually in mid-meeting with his terrorist command group at the time of the attack, but was in a hardened underground bunker immune to cruise missile attack

The Pentagon claims that 600 people were at the "Afghanistan terror complex" on the day of the attack

Military sources told The Washington Times on 24 August that one reason for the strict secrecy surrounding the strike was the Pentagon's desire to take advantage of the chaos of the raid to listen in on the communications of bin Laden and his associates. Thus, even though the raid did not kill large numbers of terrorists, it did provide priceless intelligence.

Bin Laden later admitted that 34 of his followers, including one top lieutenant, had been killed by the cruise missile attack (FYEO, 2/1/99, p. 466-3)

[redacted]

Attack on the Afghan Camps

20 Aug 1998 Missiles targeted the all-Arab Harkatul Jihad Al-Islami military training camp of bin Laden, and two camps run by Pakistani individuals (the Jamiatul Mujahideen and Harkatul Ansar camps) which are 21 kilometers away from bin Laden's camp

The Harkatul Ansar (HUA) camp was run by a Pakistani named Saiful Islam Akhter and produced hundreds of mujahideen fighters who fought against anti-Muslim forces from the Philippines to Kashmir and Bosnia

HUA trains guerrillas to fight in the Indian-held part of the disputed state of Jammu and Kashmir

Bin Laden provided financial support to HUA camps in Khost

The HUA were responsible for the December 1994 kidnappings (and presumed murders) of four western tourists in Kashmir

At least 7 HUA members were killed and 10 wounded in the attack

Other reports have said at least 7 HUA members were killed and two dozen were wounded (WP, 3/7/99)

Cruise missile damage at a camp in Afghanistan

[redacted]

[redacted]

Attack on the Afghan Camps

20 Aug 1998 A total of eight Pakistani militants belonging to the groups Lakshar-e-Taiba and Hizb-ul-Mujahideen were also killed in the attack (WP, 3/7/99)

The Jamiatul Mujahideen camp was commanded by a Pakistani named Mufti Bashir from Pakistan-controlled Kashmir

The Jamiatul Mujahideen camp was used almost exclusively to train people for the Kashmir struggle and was training at least 250 youth at the time

Bin Laden's Harkatul Jihad Al-Islami military training camp was extensively targeted and was "completely ruined" and "leveled to the ground" according to witnesses

Bin Laden is also tied to other Arab training facilities in the Khost area such as the Salman Farsi camp, and the Badar One and Badar Two camps

[redacted]

[redacted]

The Al Shifa Factory

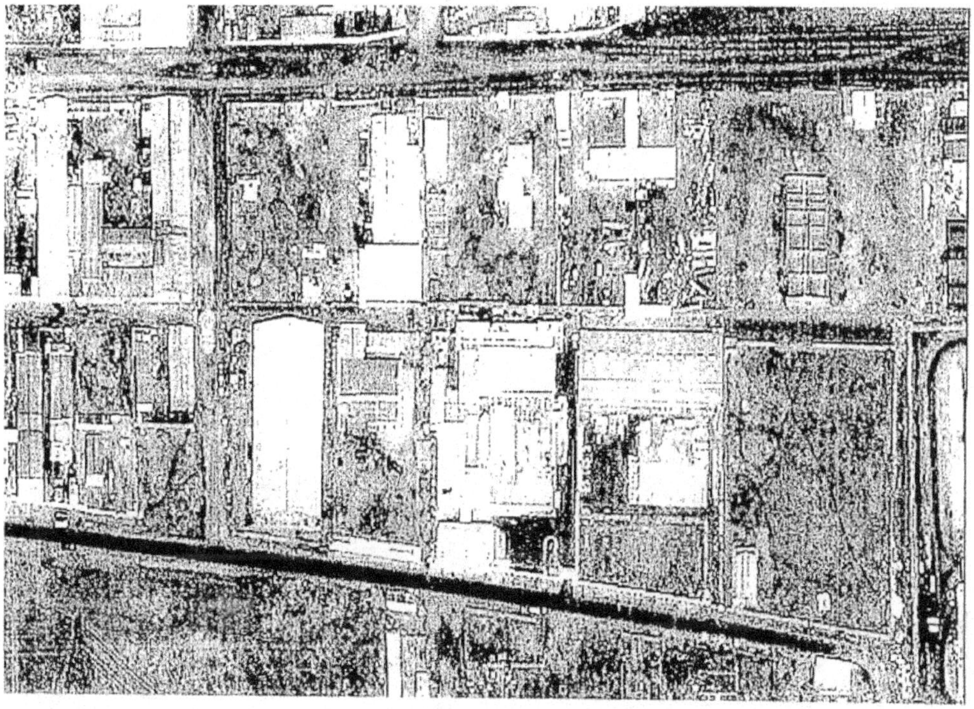

Satellite photograph of the Al Shifa plant

[redacted]

[redacted]

Attack on The Al Shifa Factory

20 Aug 1998 — 6 BGM-109 Tomahawk cruise missiles were launched against the Shifa Pharmaceuticals plant near Khartoum, Sudan

Military officials later said 13 missiles were fired into Sudan.

The attack caused a reported 10 injuries (JIR, Mar 1999, p. 49) and the night watchman was killed (PBS Online, "The Controversial U.S. Retaliatory Missile Strikes")

Just hours before the strike, President Clinton called off a planned attack on a second target in Sudan, a tannery, after senior military officials raised questions about the risk of civilian casualties and the evidence linking it to bin Laden (NYT, 10/27/99)

VX itself as not produced at the Shifa plant, but at another facility located a great distance from Khartoum

Scenes of the damage at the Shifa Pharmaceutical factory

[redacted]

[redacted]

Attack Analysis

Was the attack effective?

- Number dead: small and replaceable
- Facilities damage: minor and replaceable
- Degree of decapitation: Bin Laden emerged alive and unscathed
- Degree of deterrence: Bin Laden emerged undeterred (as evidenced by the 6+ post-attack bombing plots)
- Will it deter states that harbor terrorists (Sudan, Afghanistan) or those that seek to use terrorists to their advantage (Iraq, Iran)?

Scenes of the damage at the Shifa Pharmaceutical factory

[redacted]

Attack Analysis

Was the attack counter-productive?

- The attack succeeded in making bin Laden a hero in the Islamic world (NYT, 2/8/99)
- Two years after Reagan ordered the bombing of Libya, we experienced the Pan Am 103 bombing over Lockerbie, Scotland, which we are still grappling with: Will this attack similarly serve only to provoke rather than to deter?

Was the attack moral?

- Bin Laden delivered two truck bombs on foreign soil, killing many innocent people
- Our reply: We "air-delivered" 70 large bombs on foreign soil, killing many people not directly linked to the crimes
- Much of the world reacted to our attacks in outrage: Have we lost the moral high ground?
- Given the "wild west" nature of Afghanistan, is it fair to hold Afghanistan accountable for the actions of those located on its soil? (CRS Report 98-733F)

Scenes of the damage at the Shifa Pharmaceutical factory

[redacted]

[redacted]

Attack Analysis

Was the attack legal?

- To justify the missile attacks, the administration invoked Section 324(4) of the Antiterrorism and Effective Death Penalty Act of 1996 Pa. 1041321 (22 USC 22377) which states that: "The Congress finds that... The President should use all necessary means, including covert action and military force, to disrupt, dismantle, and destroy international infrastructure used by international terrorists, including overseas terrorist training facilities and safe havens" (CRS Report 98-733F)

Precedents for retaliation in response to terrorism

- The U.S. bombed Libya in 1986 following the Berlin Disco bombing (CRS Report 98-733F)
- The U.S. bombed Iraq in 1993 as a response to a plot to assassinate former President Bush (CRS Report 98-733F)

Some think that the attack was a sign of a new terrorism policy that is (CRS Report 98-733F):

- Based upon a new resolve
- More global
- More proactive
- More national-security oriented (as opposed to law enforcement oriented)
- More likely to use force
- Less likely to be constrained by national boundaries
- More unilateral

Miscellaneous

- The original list of possible targets for the cruise missile strikes contained one or more targets in a third country (other than Afghanistan or Sudan) which has not been named (NYT, 10/27/99)

[redacted]

[redacted]

Was the Attack Justified?

Initially, the U.S. justified the attack with several claims:

The plant produced a chemical unique to the manufacture of the nerve agent VX (JIR, Mar 1999, p. 49)

> This is a reference to the soil sample analysis which was not disclosed at first
>
> National Security Advisor Sandy Berger stated that "we know with great certainty" that the Al Shifa pharmaceutical plant produced "essentially the penultimate chemical to manufacture VX nerve gas" (PBS Online)

The plant was run by Sudan's Military Industrial Complex (JIR, Mar 1999, p. 49)

The plant had received financial support from bin Laden (JIR, Mar 1999, p. 49)

The plant did not produce any commercial pharmaceutical products (JIR, Mar 1999, p. 49)

> It has been asserted that this claim was made after conducting only an internet search on the plant (PBS Online, "The Controversial U.S. Retaliatory Missile Strikes")

The plant had an unusual level of security, including military guards and fences (JIR, Mar 1999, p. 49)

[redacted]

[redacted]

Was the Attack Justified?

Evidence of commercial activity contradicted the U.S. position

The plant had a contract to sell medicine to Iraq under the UN-sponsored "oil-for-food" deal (JIR, Mar 1999, p. 49; USNWR, 8/23/99, p. 28)

Foreign reporters were given free access to the site to see the medical supplies strewn throughout the rubble (JIR, Mar 1999, p. 49)

The US administration was forced to admit that the facility "may very well have been producing legitimate pharmaceuticals" (JIR, Mar 1999, p. 49)

Eventually the U.S. backtracked from some of the charges

The US government admitted that bin Laden only had an "indirect" investment in the plant, having provided funding to the Military Industrial Complex believed to be connected to it (JIR, Mar 1999, p. 49)

On 23 September 1998 senior US administration officials admitted that they had no evidence that directly linked bin Laden to the Al Shifa factory at the time of the missile strikes on 20 August, but that intelligence officials had found financial transactions between bin Laden and Sudan's Military Industrial Corporation (NYT, 9/23/98; PBS Online)

George J. Tenet, the Director of Central Intelligence at the time, reportedly warned that the link between bin Laden and the Al Shifa factory could be "drawn only indirectly and by inference" although the plant's involvement with chemical weapons was more certain (NYT, 10/27/99)

[redacted]

Was the Attack Justified?

Additional justifying statements and evidence

US officials revealed that a soil sample from the plant contained traces of a chemical known as EMPTA (O-ethylmethylphosphonothioic acid), a precursor said to be unique to the production of VX (JIR, Mar 1999, p. 50)

The soil sample had been collected in December 1997 by an agent working for the CIA (NYT, 10/27/99)

The soil sample was collected about 60 feet from the Al Shifa factory, directly across an access road from the main entrance (NYT, 10/27/99)

The soil was found to contain about 2.5 times the normal trace amounts of EMPTA, a chemical used in the production of VX nerve gas (NYT, 10/27/99)

The plant reportedly produced the chemical precursor QL and possibly others used in the production of VX

US officials told reporters that Iraq was the only country that "we are aware of that planned to use EMPTA" (JIR, Mar 1999, p. 50)

The media reported that one of the leaders of Iraq's CW program, Emad al-Ani, had close ties with senior Sudanese officials at the factory (JIR, Mar 1999, p. 50)

The media reported that Iraqi scientists working for al-Ani had attended the grand opening of the facility two years before it was destroyed (JIR, Mar 1999, p. 50)

Undersecretary of State Thomas Pickering stated that "El Shifa officials, early in the company's history, we believe, were in touch with Iraqi individuals associated with Iraq's VX program" (JIR, Mar 1999, p. 50)

[redacted]

Was the Attack Justified?

Additional justifying statements and evidence

Senior executives of the plant had ties to bin Laden

Bin Laden was an investor in the plant

Salih Idris, the owner of the plant, had financial dealings with members of the Egyptian Islamic Jihad according to reports in the New York Times

The general manager of the plant, Osman Sulayman, had been deported from Saudi Arabia in around 1995 for his suspected ties to bin Laden (JIR, Mar 1999, p. 50)

After the attack, the CIA conducted a study of Sudanese businessman Saleh Idris, saying it had found new evidence about his possible financial connections to the terrorist group Islamic Jihad, which has connection to bin Laden (NYT, 10/27/99)

Salih Idris, the owner of the Al Shifa plant, had had financial dealings with members of Islamic Jihad, the Egyptian group which receives money and sponsorship from bin Laden (JIR, Mar 1999, p. 50)

The CIA had received reports that Iraqi chemical weapons experts had visited Khartoum, prompting suspicions that Iraq was shifting some of its production of chemical weapons to Sudan, and bin Laden moved to Sudan at about this same time (NYT, 10/27/99)

The CIA had intelligence indicating that in 1995 bin Laden won tentative approval from Sudanese leaders to begin developing chemical weapons for use against American troops in Saudi Arabia (but he was later expelled from Sudan after pressure from the U.S. and Saudi Arabia) (NYT, 10/27/99)

In the summer of 1997 an informant reported that two sites in Khartoum might be involved in chemical weapons production and the informant also mentioned that Al Shifa, on which he had less information, was suspicious because it had high fences and stringent security (NYT, 10/27/99)

[redacted]

[redacted]

Was the Attack Justified?

Additional contradictory statements and evidence

U.S. and European engineers and consultants who helped to design, build, and supply the plant have claimed that it produced medicine and veterinary drugs

Earl Norbet Garrett, a former CIA station chief in the Middle East and Asia, and now head of inquiries at the London office of investigation company Kroll O'Gara, examined the evidence and concluded that there was no proof that chemical weapons were being made at the plant (IPIN, 2/25/99, p. 3)

Kroll Associates turned up no evidence of links between Idris and bin Laden except very tenuous connections through distant third parties (USNWR, 8/23/99, p. 28)

Saleh Idris hired a leading U.S. chemist who reported finding no nerve gas precursors in extensive samples from the site (WP, 5/4/99)

Officials have acknowledged that the soil sample from Al Shifa had been obtained about four months before Saleh Idris had purchased the plant in March 1998 (NYT, 10/27/99)

[redacted]

[redacted]

Retaliation: Pros & Cons

Possible benefits of military retaliation:

Shows strength and world leadership (CRS Report 98-733F)

Demonstrates resolve

Demonstrates capability (In fact, the Al Shifa attack was code-named "Infinite Reach" [NYT, 10/27/99])

Punishes the guilty

Appeases domestic calls for action

Provides disincentives for other terrorists (i.e., may deter future terrorism) (CRS Report 98-733F)

May deter the states that harbor terrorists from providing future support

May be a more cost-effective way to thwart enemy actions than to harden all possible targets (CRS Report 98-733F)

May be a more cost effective way to thwart enemy actions than other means (e.g., pursuit, arrest, and prosecution)

May be a more certain form of punishment than pursuit and prosecution (since we may loose in court)

May truly damage or disrupt the enemy (CRS Report 98-733F)

Provides governments unhappy with the response an incentive to pursue diplomatic and law enforcement remedies to international terrorism (CRS Report 98-733F)

[redacted]

[redacted]

Retaliation: Pros & Cons

Possible drawbacks of military retaliation:

- Undermines the rule of law (CRS Report 98-733F)
- Could increase incidents of terrorism by provoking and drawing retaliation (CRS Report 98-733F)
- Leaves allies and other nations feeling left out (CRS Report 98-733F)
- May be characterized as discriminatory (e.g., anti-Islamic) (CRS Report 98-733F)
- May radicalize some elements of populations and aid terrorist recruitment (CRS Report 98-733F)
- May result in the loss of innocent lives (CRS Report 98-733F)
- May result in embarrassment (e.g., missed targets, mistaken targeting, or other errors and blunders) (CRS Report 98-733F)
- May reveal shortcomings and vulnerabilities of our own forces and thus undermine deterrence (e.g., missiles fail, resulting damage is highly ineffective, or certain defensives prove impregnable)
- May cost more (in dollars, lives, ammunition expenditures, etc.) than other solutions

Other options besides military retaliation:

- More effective intelligence to provide indications and warning (e.g., better satellites, better coverage, etc.)
- New approaches to intelligence (e.g., more human sources) (CRS Report 98-733F)
- More intelligence sharing (e.g., other nations may be better able to penetrate an organization than is the U.S.)
- Minimize focusing on individuals like bin Laden because this glamorizes the individual and may draw support, funding, and recruits to their cause (CRS Report 98-733F)
- Enhanced use of covert operations (e.g., to have sabotaged the Al Shifa plant rather than to have openly attacked it) (CRS Report 98-733F)

[redacted]

[redacted]

The EMPTA Debate

The U.S. claims that soil samples from the site contained the chemical known as EMPTA (O-ethylmethylphosphonothioic acid), which is a precursor for the manufacture of the nerve agent VX

The presence of EMPTA could have been due to the use of the factory as a transshipment point (JIR, Mar 1999, p. 50): For example, the contract to supply medicine to Iraq under the UN-sanctioned "oil-for-food" program could have been used to mask the transfer of chemical precursors to Iraq (JIR, Mar 1999, p. 50)

One source has described the molecule discovered as "one half of a VX molecule, and the part which is most difficult to find or produce, containing not only a phosphorous-carbon bond, but sulphur as well" (JIRP, 10/98, p. 8)

Several non-governmental chemical weapons experts claimed that EMPTA is chemically similar to several commercial pesticides and herbicides (including the weed-killer known as Round-Up) and that the chemical tests of the soil sample could have misidentified the key ingredient if the sample had not been well preserved and tested quickly

Donato Kinigier-Passigli, a spokesman for the Organization for the Prohibition of Chemical Weapons, stated that EMPTA could be used "in limited quantities for legitimate commercial purposes", including the manufacture of fungicides and anti-microbial agents

Several American experts in chemical warfare stated that the chemical structure of EMPTA resembled that of an agricultural insecticide, known as FONOFOS, which is commercially available in Africa and that the two chemicals could be confused in lab tests performed under less-than-ideal conditions

An official with a chemical weapons organization in The Hague stated that EMPTA could be the byproduct of the breakdown of certain pesticides

[redacted]

[redacted]

Attack Analysis: Quotes

"US cruise missile strikes... failed to kill the Saudi but succeeded spectacularly in galvanizing Pakistan's Islamic hardliners while reinforcing bin Laden's image as an Islamic Che Guevara"

Jane's Intelligence Review, Jan 1999, p. 36

"If the U.S. is perceived by Arabs to be using a double standard and a heavy hand against Arab interests, then the terrorists will find more understanding among people who perceive the U.S. as an aggressor."

Khalid Abdalla, chief representative of the Washington office of the 22-nation Arab League

"We have to have a political and diplomatic strategy to attack him without aggrandizing him"

A US counter-terrorism official, (NYT, 2/8/99)

The missiles inflicted little lasting damage but helped to make Mr. Bin Laden a "revered figure" in the Islamic world

A US counter-terrorism official, (NYT, 2/8/99)

"What was served by the cruise missile attacks? You've inflated one individual to an enormous extent. Why would you want to create more like him? Such acts only help him proliferate."

Mohammad Saddique Kanju, Deputy Foreign Minister of Pakistan (NYT, 2/8/99)

"I know the guy.. and he's not that mighty... But the United States has created a hero out of him."

Ghazi Salah el-Din, Information Minister of Sudan (NYT, 2/8/99)

[redacted]

[redacted]

After the Cruise Missile Attacks

After the cruise missile attacks, bin Laden had been intercepted talking on satellite phones, trying desperately to get damage assessments and news of casualties (PBS Online, citing a report by ABC reporter John Miller)

After the cruise missile attacks, bin Laden ceased using his satellite telephones (which threatened to give away his whereabouts) and sought new hiding places (JIR, June, 1999, p. 6)

Bin Laden has said that just after the missile strikes, he survived an assassination plot ordered by a prince in Saudi Arabia (NYT, 12/25/98)

20 Aug 1998 The same day as the missile strikes, President Clinton signed executive order (E.O. 13099) which would freeze any assets owned by bin Laden, specific associates, their self-proclaimed Islamic Army Organization, and prohibiting U.S. individuals and firms from doing business with them (CRS Report 98-733F)

20 Aug 1998 In his televised address to the nation, President Clinton linked bin Laden to:

1. Ambushes of peacekeepers in Somalia in 1993
2. A plot to kill the pope (the Ramzi Yousef connection)
3. A plot to kill Egyptian President Mubarak
4. A scheme to blow up several U.S. airliners (the Ramzi Yousef connection)
5. A bus bombing in Egypt that killed 9 German tourists in 1997

After the attacks, bin Laden stayed in a remote mountain hide-out in the vicinity of Kandahar, in contrast to the lifestyle he led before the attacks

[redacted]

[redacted]

After the Cruise Missile Attacks

Aug or Sept 1998	Soon after the cruise missile attacks, Taliban leader Mullah Omar spoke with a Peshawar-based journalist, Rahimullah Yusufzai, and stated that "There cannot be two different and parallel emirates [governments] in Afghanistan. We have a central Taliban-led authority ruling the country and it ought to be obeyed."
22 Aug 1998	Abdallah Mohammed Fazul flew from the Comoros to Dubai
22 Aug 1998 led	Abdallah Mohammed Fazul (a.k.a. Haroun Fazil), a suspected explosives expert who the Kenyan cell of al-Qaida, boarded a flight from Moroni, Comoros to Dubai, United Arab Emirates and was never seen again
22 Aug 1998	The Egyptian group Jamma Islamiyya, one of the groups which was part of the umbrella group of Islamic militant organizations founded by bin Laden, called on Moslems around the world "to stand alongside the peoples of Sudan and Afghanistan, to besiege American embassies in Moslem countries and to force their leaders to close them and expel American diplomats who are spying on us"" (SGIU, 10/23/98)
24 Aug 1998	At a secret briefing at the UN Security Council, U.S. officials told western diplomats that bin Laden was linked to 18 separate attacks in recent years
24 Aug 1998	President Clinton stated that he stayed awake "up till 2:30 in the morning trying to make absolutely sure that at that chemical plant there was no night shift… I didn't want some person who was a nobody to me, but who may have a family to feed and a life to live, and probably had no earthly idea what else was going on there, to die needlessly"

[redacted]

After the Cruise Missile Attacks

26 Aug 1998 A Criminal Complaint was filed against Mohamed Rashed Daoud Al-'Owhali in the U.S. Federal Court, Southern District of New York for his involvement in the Nairobi embassy bombing (USIA)

Al-'Owhali was returned to the United States that night (USIA, "Text: Reno Statement on Transport to U.S. of Daoud Al-Owhali")

27 Aug 1998 The U.S. Embassy in South Korea received information that terrorist actions might be taken against U.S. installations or personnel in that country

31 Aug 1998 U.S. Embassies in Accra, Ghana and in Lome, Togo were closed because of security threats

31 Aug 1998 The Washington Times reported that the FBI had alerted U.S. companies and business people that bin Laden was offering bounties worth thousands of dollars to kill Americans

According to one source, bin Laden offered to pay more than $18,000 for every American killed

After the Cruise Missile Attacks

Sept 1998 — Charges were filed in Manhattan against a 46 year old former sergeant in the U.S. Special Forces, Ali Mohamed, who is suspected of aiding the terrorist campaign of bin Laden

Mohamed was a former Egyptian Army officer who acquired US citizenship in 1985 and enlisted in the US Army

Mohamed served in the special forces for 3 years and was honorably discharged in 1989

In 1989, while on active duty he had traveled to New York and provided military training to local Muslims preparing to fight the Soviets in Afghanistan. However, these visits were not part of his official duties.

Mohamed also began leaking classified documents

Sources claim that Mohamed has become a witness for the prosecution (PBS Online, "The Suspects & Charges")

Sept 1998 — The CIA broke up a bin Laden ring that had been planning an attack on the U.S. embassy in Baku, Azerbaijan

Egyptian terrorists identified in the plot were deported to Cairo

[redacted]

After the Cruise Missile Attacks

Sept 1998	The US embassy in Dushanbe, Tajikistan closed because of fear of terrorist attacks (JTWR, 1/19/99) Employees were relocated to neighboring Kazakstan and Uzbekistan during the closure, which lasted until January (JTWR, 1/19/99)
Sept 1998	The U.S. warned of a possible plot to blow up its embassy in Kuwait The embassy in Kuwait had been evacuated several times in 1998 in response to various threats
Sept 1998	Members of Abu Sayyaf, a Filipino Moslem terrorist organization sponsored by bin Laden, reportedly infiltrated Manila, where they may have been planning to attack the U.S. embassy (SGIU, 10/13/98)
1 Sept 1998	A handwritten note found in the toilet of a plane that arrived in Kuwait from Dubai claimed that the U.S. Embassy in Manila would be bombed on Sept 4
2 Sept 1998	The U.S. embassy in Kuwait issued a message stating that the U.S. had received information of a planned attack in Kuwait similar to the African embassy bombings
4 Sept 1998	The State Department issued a warning, distributed to embassies around the world, advising Americans to "maintain a high level of vigilance"
8 Sept 1998	Citing administration sources, the New York Times reported that terrorists associated with bin Laden were planning a new round of attacks

[redacted]

[redacted]

After the Cruise Missile Attacks

14 Sept 1998 Several Western embassies and agencies in Kampala, Uganda closed their offices for security reasons

Those shut down included the US Embassy, the UK High Commission, the Royal Danish Embassy, the World Bank Uganda office, the European Union Delegation of the European Commission and their agencies countrywide

There had been a wave of telephone callers allegedly warning of bomb attacks

Mid Sep 1998 Two men, believed to be associates of bin Laden, were arrested as they tried to enter Uganda from Kenya

They were allegedly leaders in a plot to bomb the U.S. Embassy in Kampala, Uganda

Law enforcement sources stated: "Bin Laden clearly wanted to demonstrate to the world that he was still in business. There was very credible information about this operation."

The Kampala embassy had been closed three times since august 7 because of concerns about a possible terrorist attack

The Tawheed Islamic Association in Kampala was described as a "holding pen" for would-be terrorists: "They don't conduct operations themselves, but they keep guys available for operations"

[redacted]

[redacted]

After the Cruise Missile Attacks

16 Sep 1998 Mahmduh Mahmud Salim, a 40 year old with a Sudanese passport, was arrested in Germany while visiting a friend near Freising (a town in Bavaria)

Another report says that he was arrested in Grueneck, Germany (SGIU, 12/1/98)

Salim is suspected of being a leading weapons procurer and financial accountant for bin Laden

One of the founders of al Qaida, Salim had managed terrorist training camps in Afghanistan, Pakistan, and Sudan; sought enriched uranium and nuclear weapons components for the development of nuclear weapons; and allegedly conspired to use weapons of mass destruction against U.S. nationals

Salim allegedly carried out financial and international business transactions for Al Qaeda, managed some of its accounts, and procured communications and electronic equipment for its use

He is believed to have run training camps and guest houses in Sudan and Afghanistan and ran a guest house in Pakistan

17-18 Sept '98 Eight Ugandans and ten Somalis were arrested in Uganda on suspicion of planning an attack on the U.S. Embassy in Kampala using a one-ton bomb in a dump truck

Police seized a large quantity of explosives and a dump truck

[redacted]

After the Cruise Missile Attacks

21 Sep 1998	The National Disaster Operation Center in Nairobi confirmed the death of another woman in the embassy bombing
	This brought to 254 the number of victims of the Nairobi embassy bombing
21 Sep 1998	Egyptian Mustafa Mahmoud Said Ahmed (a.k.a. Said Ahmed, a.k.a. Saleh Aben Alahales) and Tanzanian Rashid Saleh Hemed were charged with murder in connection with the Tanzanian embassy bombing
22 Sep 1998	Three suspects in the bombing of the U.S. embassy in Tanzania were released on bail in Tanzania
	One of them, Mustafa Mahmood Sayyed Ahmad, is an Egyptian citizen with links to a close associate of bin Laden
22 Sept 1998	Saudi Arabia announced that it was expelling the Afghan charge d'affaires in Riyadh and recalling its own representative from Kabul
	The decision was believed to have been taken because of the continued presence of bin Laden in Afghanistan

After the Cruise Missile Attacks

23 Sep 1998 Seven Middle Eastern men were arrested in London by Scotland Yard detectives on suspicion of having links with bin Laden

Egyptian police said that six of the seven men were Egyptian fundamentalists from the Egyptian Islamic Jihad group and that the seventh was a Saudi national and a key aide to bin Laden

The group included Adel Abdel Meguid Abdel Bari, an Egyptian who was sentenced to death in absentia in 1997 for conspiring to blow up the antique district of Cairo's Khan al-Khalili bazaar

The group also included Khaled al Fawaz, a Saudi dissident who has served as a London spokesman for bin Laden as head of bin Laden's London office

24 Sep 1998 German police deployed more than 100 officers to seal off the area around the U.S. consulate in Hamburg after receiving information that a terrorist attack was imminent

25 Sept 1998 U.S. authorities acknowledged that the FBI had won the secret cooperation of an admitted terrorist in al Qaeda as early as 1996 and had obtained extensive information about the group from the asset (NYT, 9/26/98)

The source was described in court papers as "a member of al Qaeda for a number of years" who was "personally familiar" with bin Laden (NYT, 9/26/98)

This source provided information to the FBI in the late summer and fall of 1996 (NYT, 9/26/98)

[redacted]

After the Cruise Missile Attacks

28 Sept 1998	Five militants from Egypt's Jihad movement (Hawi Sibai, Ibrahim Aidarus, Ussama Hassan, Sayyed Ahmed, and Sayyed Moawad) and the right-hand man of bin Laden (Khaled al Fawaz) were arrested in the U.K. (IPIN, 5/27/99, p. 6)
Late Sept 1998	Saudi Arabia's top intelligence official, Prince Turki bin Faisal, met privately with Mullah Mohammed Omar, leader of the Taliban's Supreme Council, to try to persuade Afghanistan to deport bin Laden (NYT, 10/18/98)
	Prince Turki reportedly presented evidence to the Taliban of bin Laden's involvement in terrorism, but it made no difference (NYT, 10/18/98)
Early Oct 1998	Federal prosecutors in New York released a 50-page indictment of four top aides to bin Laden
Oct 1998	All U.S. missions in Saudi Arabia closed for four days to review security after receiving information that the American Embassy in Riyadh was under threat of a terrorist attack
Oct 1998	It was reported that U.S. State Department officials had previously spoken to members of bin Laden's family in Saudi Arabia to gain their cooperation in bringing bin Laden to justice (NYT, 10/18/98)

After the Cruise Missile Attacks

7 Oct 1998 The London-based newspaper Al Hayat reported that the Taliban had communicated to Saudi Arabia that they might consider putting bin Laden on trial for the 1996 Khobar Towers bombing (NYT, 10/8/98)

7 Oct 1998 The U.S. embassy in Cairo was evacuated after a bomb hoax

10 Oct 1998 At a news conference in Delhi, Jayaram Jayalalitha, the leader of the regional All-India Anna Dravida Munnetra Khazagham, warned that some 200 Afghan-trained supporters of bin Laden were "roaming" in Tamil Nadu and other southern Indian states (SGIU, 10/13/98)

She claimed that bin Laden's agents might have been responsible for bombings in the city of Coimbatore earlier in the year (SGIU, 10/13/99)

She also said that suspicions that bin Laden may be active in India were reinforced following the recent arrest of a Moslem suspect in Hyderabad who reportedly confessed that he had received six months of training in Afghanistan (SGIU, 10/13/99)

12 Oct 1998 Reports of a truck bomb parked at the U.S. embassy in Thailand were found to be a hoax

After the Cruise Missile Attacks

19 Oct 1998 Mohamed Abed Abdel Aal, a leader of the Egyptian group Jamaa Islamiyya, which was a part of an umbrella group of Islamic militant organizations founded by bin Laden, was arrested at a hotel in Bogota, Columbia, two days after arriving in the city on a bus from Quito, Ecuador (SGIU, 10/23/98)

Abdel Aal was wanted by Egyptian authorities for his involvement in the terrorist attack in Luxor, Egypt in 1997 (SGIU, 10/23/98)

Abdel Aal had been in Italy under surveillance prior to his arrest in Columbia (SGIU, 10/23/98)

There was speculation that the most likely mission to take Aal to Columbia would be to conduct transactions with Columbia's rebels involving some mixture of arms, drugs, and cash (SGIU, 10/23/98)

20 Oct 1998 Abdelhakim Mujahid, the Taliban ambassador to Pakistan, stated that "Osama bin Laden has lived in Afghanistan for more the 15 years, where he is considered a hero for his fight against the Soviets. It would be very difficult for us to make a case to our people and our public opinion for pushing him outside now." (NYT, 10/22/98)

25 Oct 1998 The Taliban invited outsiders to provide evidence to the Taliban's supreme court on bin Laden's links to terrorism

[redacted]

After the Cruise Missile Attacks

Nov 1998 — The Pakistani militant group Lakshar-e-Taiba, some of whose members were killed in the August 1998 U.S. cruise missile attacks, organized a religious gathering of 50,000 youths near Lahore, Pakistan's second-largest city (WP, 3/7/99)

One large banner said "Soon the flames of holy war will engulf the United States of America" (WP, 3/7/99)

4 Nov 1998 — A federal jury in New York formally charged bin Laden with masterminding the 7 August bombings in a 238-count indictment that superseded the earlier October indictment and included bin Laden and his military commander Mohammed Atef, in addition to the four aides named in the earlier October indictment

US Attorney Mary Jo White charged that bin Laden engaged in business transactions on behalf of al Qaeda, including purchasing warehouses for the storage of explosives, transporting weapons, and establishing a series of companies in Sudan to provide income to al Qaeda and as a cover for the procurement of explosives, weapons, and chemicals, and for the travel of operatives (USIA, 11/4/98)

"In addition, al Qaeda reached an understanding with the Government of Iraq that al Qaeda would not work against that government and that on particular projects, specifically including weapons development, al Qaeda would work cooperatively with the Government of Iraq" according to the indictment (USIA, 11/4/98)

The State Department also announced a $5 million reward for information leading to their arrest and conviction

[redacted]

After the Cruise Missile Attacks

7 Nov 1998	US officials released a statement saying that the US embassy in Riyadh, Saudi Arabia, the US consulate in Jiddah, and the US consulate in Dhahran would be closed from 11 Nov until 14 Nov to review security
	The statement said that the US government had received information indicating that a terrorist attack may be planned on the US Embassy in Riyadh
20 Nov 1998	Taliban Chief Justice Noor Mohammed Saqib stated that he had closed a three-week inquiry into allegations that bin Laden is waging a war of terror against the US and pronounced bin Laden a "free man" because the US did not provide any evidence as requested
21 Nov 1998	Austrian Interior Minister Karl Schloegl stated that the Austrian government had tightened security at US missions in Vienna following indications that an attack on a US-linked organization in Vienna was being planned
Late Nov 1998	Four Afghan men hired to assassinate bin Laden were ambushed and killed about 2 kilometers from bin Laden's hideout in southern Afghanistan
	The Taliban was convinced that the assassination attempt was masterminded and financed by the US

[redacted]

After the Cruise Missile Attacks

27 Nov 1998 — The Pakistani newspaper "Ausaf" reported that the U.S. had attempted and failed to kill bin Laden in a plot involving Mola Humayun Taqi, a former commander of Hezb-e Eslami, who had recruited two friends and a relative to assist him (SGIU, 12/1/98)

The assassination was reported planned in a house belonging to an Afghan-Canadian national who was a representative of the UN Food Program in Kabul but Afghan intelligence learned of the plot and killed all four attackers in an ambush at bin Laden's residence (SGIU, 12/1/98)

30 Nov 1998 — A Munich court approved the extradition to the US of Mamdouh Mahmud Salim, who was allegedly bin Laden's finance chief

Early Dec 1998 — A Chechen Foreign Ministry official arrived in Kandahar to discuss opening diplomatic relations with the Taliban

The London-based Arabic-language Al-Hayat reported that bin Laden was ready to leave Afghanistan to seek asylum in Chechnya

Other media reports said that a delegation from Yemen was in Afghanistan for talks with bin Laden

Dec 1998 — The Pakistani newspaper Khabrain reported that "teams of American commandos" had recently spent two weeks in Afghanistan trying to track and capture bin Laden (FYEO, 1/4/99, p. 464-3)

[redacted]

[redacted]

After the Cruise Missile Attacks

Dec 1998 Bin Laden is reported to have met with the Iraqi ambassador to Turkey, who may be an agent of Iraqi intelligence (JIR, June 1999, p. 37)

3 Dec 1998 Pakistani Prime Minister Nawaz Sharif, while on an official visit to the US, admitted that discussions had taken place with US officials on the subject of Pakistan helping to seize bin Laden, who was hiding in neighboring Afghanistan

3 Dec 1998 Court documents first mentioned on this date by the New York Times, indicate that an aide to bin Laden, identified only as CS-1, had pleaded guilty to terrorism charges and had agreed to testify against bin Laden

6 Dec 1998 Police masquerading as a wedding procession raided a guest house in Islamabad, Pakistan acting on tips that bin Laden might be visiting there

7 Dec 1998 Police conducted two early morning raids in Lahore, Pakistan (on a guest house in the Defence Housing Society and on a downtown hotel) acting on tips that bin Laden might be visiting there

12 Dec 1998 The pro-Islamic Pakistani newspaper Khabrain reported that "teams of American commandos returned from Afghanistan to the U.S. after their futile two-week operation to arrest the mujahid of the Muslim nation, Osama bin Laden" (SGIU, 12/15/98)

However, the report also claimed that CIA agents had disguised themselves as Tablighi Jamat preachers, an ultra conservative type of Pakistani clergymen who would be very difficult to impersonate, thus casting doubt on the Pakistani news reports of assassination attempts (SGIU, 12/15/98)

[redacted]

[redacted]

After the Cruise Missile Attacks

14 Dec 1998 U.S. embassies in Bahrain, Kuwait, Saudi Arabia, and the United Arab Emirates were warned of a "strong possibility" that terrorists might attempt an attack over the next 30 days

The warning came after U.S. intelligence agents monitored conversations between bin Laden in Afghanistan in Afghanistan and some of his supporters during which a plot was discussed to attack one or more U.S. targets in the Gulf region

The warning was followed by a curfew on the 1,000 U.S. personnel at the U.S. Fifth Fleet headquarters in Bahrain (SGIU, 12/15/98)

15 Dec 1998 The DoD said that it was aware of intelligence reports that bin Laden was seriously ill

16 Dec 1998 Five men were indicted for bombing the U.S. Embassy in Dar es Salaam in August 1998: Mustafa Mohamed Fadhil, Khalfan Khamis Mohamed, Ahmed Khalfan Ghailani, Fahid Mohammed Ally Msalam, and Sheikh Ahmed Salim Swedan (NYT, 12/17/98)

All five men were at large at the time and rewards of up to $5 million each were offered for their arrest or capture (NYT, 12/17/98)

[redacted]

[redacted]

After the Cruise Missile Attacks

19 Dec 1998 The month of Ramadan began

There were fears that the month of Ramadan might be the starting point for new operations by bin Laden since Pakistani intelligence and diplomatic sources were saying that bin Laden's organization (al Qaeda) was preparing to send teams of militants on missions to bomb US targets in the Middle East

For six weeks leading up to Ramadan, Pakistani intelligence conducted secret raids in the border city of Peshawar in Pakistan and found safe houses used by Zainul Abideen, a 38-year-old Palestinian known as the "schoolteacher", who was the man responsible for moving men and money into new bin Laden facilities

The Pakistani agents also arrested men from Iraq, Saudi Arabia, and Bosnia who were carrying stolen and forged travel documents

Bin Laden had rebuilt the training camps destroyed by US missiles and was constructing a new bomb-proof headquarters in a cave in Kunduz Province in the Pamir mountains near the border with Tajikistan

Bin Laden's agents had stolen a "sizeable number" of passports and travel documents in London and other western European cities for use in future operations and hundreds of new recruits from North Africa, the Middle East and Bosnia had been smuggled into bin Laden's bases in Afghanistan

[redacted]

[redacted]

After the Cruise Missile Attacks

16 Dec 1998	Administration officials said that bin Laden had ordered a terrorist attack on American targets in the Persian Gulf within the next few days or weeks (NYT, 12/16/98)
	American intelligence learned of the preparations for a strike by eavesdropping on conversations between bin Laden and members of his terrorist organization (NYT, 12/16/99)
20 Dec 1998	Germany extradited Mamduh Mahmud Salim to the US (FYEO, 1/4/99, p. 464-3)
21 Dec 1998	TIME Magazine reported that intelligence officials have evidence that bin Laden may be planning a strike on Washington or New York City
22 Dec 1998	Bin Laden summoned reporters for Pakistan's The News, Time Magazine, and ABC News to his tented encampment in Afghanistan's Helmand province for interviews (PBS Online)

[redacted]

[redacted]

After the Cruise Missile Attacks

23 Dec 1998 — A correspondent for Time Magazine conducted an interview with bin Laden (PBS Online)

The interview with Time Magazine included the following question-answers excerpts (PBS Online, Osama bin Laden v. the U.S.: Edicts and Statements):

TIME: "Are you responsible for the bomb attacks on the two American embassies in Africa?"

Bin Laden: "Our job is to instigate and, by the grace of God, we did that, and certain people responded to this instigation"

TIME: "The U.S. says you are trying to acquire chemical and nuclear weapons."

Bin Laden: "It would be a sin for Muslims not to try to possess the weapons that would prevent the infidels from inflicting harm on Muslims."

24 Dec 1998 — In a second interview with ABC reporter John Miller, bin Laden denied that he was behind the bombings of the U.S. embassies in East Africa but described two of the suspects, whom he said he knew, as "two men whom we respect and hold in the highest esteem" (PBS Online, Osama bin Laden v. the U.S.: Edicts and Statements)

Bin Laden also did not deny charges that he tried to develop chemical and nuclear weapons, saying "If I seek to acquire such weapons, this is a religious duty. How we use them is up to us." (PBS Online, Osama bin Laden v. the U.S.: Edicts and Statements)

[redacted]

After the Cruise Missile Attacks

24 Dec 1998 In comments to a reporter from the Afghan news agency Bakhtar and a Pakistani journalist, bin Laden said that he is "innocent" but "not sorry" for the August 1998 East African embassy bombings

"I was not involved in the bomb blasts... but I don't regret what happened there."

Dec 1998 Bin Laden granted interviews with Pakistani reporters, including stringers for Time and Newsweek magazines, over the course of several successive days

For Newsweek, he repeated his earlier denial of any involvement in the 7 Aug 1998 bombings in East Africa, but then he told Time that "if the instigation for jihad against the Jews and the Americans is considered a crime, then let history be a witness that I am a criminal"

Bin Laden said that he "instigated" the bombings but did not directly order them

He also defended the acquisition of weapons of mass destruction for the "defense of Muslims"

He denied that he was ill, as some reports had earlier indicated

His aides said that bin Laden relied solely on radio and newspapers for outside contact and avoided using his portable satellite phone for fear that the US might use the signal to target his location

[redacted]

After the Cruise Missile Attacks

Dec 1998 — Bin Laden's agents stole a sizeable number of passports and travel documents in London and other Western European cities and hundreds of new recruits from North Africa, the Middle East, and Bosnia had been smuggled into his bases in Afghanistan (JIR, Feb 1999, p. 56)

Pakistan's Inter-Services Intelligence conducted raids in Peshawar and found safe houses used by bin Laden followers and arrested men from Iraq, Saudi Arabia, and Bosnia who were carrying stolen and forged travel documents (JIR, Feb 1999, p. 56)

Dec 1998 — US diplomatic facilities on every continent were targeted by the bin Laden network (CNN, 6/17/99)

17 Dec 1998 — In an FBI release, the US offered a $5 million reward for the arrest of five more suspects in the embassy bombings: Tanzanians Khalfan Khamis Mohamed and Ahmed Khalfan Ghailani; Kenyans of Yemeni descent Sheikh Ahmed Salim Swedan and Fahad Mohamed Ally Msalam; and Kenyan Mustafa Fadhil (a.k.a. Hussein) (FYEO, 1/4/99, p. 464-3)

20 Dec 1998 — The Sunday Times reported that bin Laden had rebuilt the training camps destroyed by a cruise missile attack on 20 Aug 1998 and was building a new bomb-proof headquarters in a natural cave system in Kunduz Province in the Pamir Mountains, near the border with Tajikistan (JIR, Feb 1999, p. 56)

Pakistani intelligence confirmed that al Qaeda was opening a new camp in Kunduz Province (FYEO, 1/4/99, p. 464-3)

[redacted]

After the Cruise Missile Attacks

24 Dec 1998 Bin Laden denied in an interview that he had been behind the US embassy bombings (FYEO, 1/4/99, p. 464-3)

25 Dec 1999 Bin Laden called on Muslims to avenge the US and British air strikes on Iraq, stating that "it is the duty of Muslims to kill American and British nationals in retaliation for the air strikes against Iraq" (SGIU, 1/13/99)

26 Dec 1998 A Pakistani newspaper, The News, reported that the governor of Riyadh, Saudi Arabia, Prince Salman bin Abdul Aziz, offered about $267,000 to Siddiq Ahmad and two accomplices to kill bin Laden

The paper quoted bin Laden as saying that the assassination attempt failed

The next day (27 Dec), Saudi Arabia denied that a senior government official had plotted to assassinate bin Laden

28 Dec 1998 The Taliban newspaper Hawad reported that the commander of the Northern Alliance (which was fighting the Taliban for control of Afghanistan), Ahmad Shah Masood, had recently met US officials in Tajikistan who gave him $5 million in return for the arrest of bin Laden

Masood denied that he had struck a deal with the US to capture bin Laden and claimed that the Taliban was receiving aid from the US

[redacted]

After the Cruise Missile Attacks

Aug 98 – Jan 99 During this six month period, US outposts overseas received more than 650 threats from the bin Laden network (CNN, 6/17/99)

Jan 1999 A US Navy P-3C Orion patrol plane was operating over Pakistan in an attempt to eavesdrop on communications from bin Laden's bases (FYEO, 2/1/99, p. 466-3)

Jan 1999 Indian police arrested Sayed Abu Nasir on suspicion of involvement in a plan to bomb the US Embassy in New Delhi and the consulates in Madras and Calcutta (FYEO, 2/1/99, p. 466-3)

Nasir was arrested with two kilograms of the explosive RDX and was allegedly plotting to blow up the U.S. Embassy in New Delhi and two American consulates elsewhere in India (WP, 2/17/99)

Indian police said he was part of a nine-member team backed by bin Laden (FYEO, 2/1/99, p. 466-3)

Other reports said that Indian authorities believed that Nasir was part of a seven-member cell funded by bin Laden (WP, 2/17/99)

Jan 1999 Bin Laden was interviewed by journalists working for Time and Newsweek magazines (JIR, June 1999, p. 37; DOE TSD, Feb 1999, p.2)

[redacted]

After the Cruise Missile Attacks

Jan 1999 Secret arrests and unpublicized detentions of several suspects linked to bin Laden took place, according to US officials (NYT, 2/8/99)

However, arrests do not always stick: Seven people detained in England and Albania at the behest of the United States were quietly released for lack of evidence (NYT, 2/8/99)

Jan 1999 Al-Babour Habib, a Tunisian national suspected of having links to bin Laden was arrested at Karachi's international airport upon his arrival from London via Kuwait, traveling on a forged French passport (JTWR, 2/4/99)

Habib was deported from Pakistan in 1993 after returning from Afghanistan (JTWR, 2/4/99)

French authorities said that Habib is wanted in connection with at least one killing in France (JTWR, 2/4/99)

Habib has been linked to bin Laden (FYEO, 2/15/99)

5 Jan 1999 The London-based Asharq al-Awsat reported that in an interview in Afghanistan, Mohammad Atef, the military commander of al Qaeda, had denied US charges that he was involved in the August 1998 East African embassy bombings (JTWR, 1/7/99)

[redacted]

After the Cruise Missile Attacks

7 Jan 1999 Malaysia arrested seven Afghan nationals travelling on forged Italian passports who were apparently en route to London to conduct a terrorist attack after the end of Ramadan (FYEO, 2/1/99, p. 466-3; SGIU, 1/13/99)

The individuals were arrested at the Bayan Lepas International Airport when they tried to board a Singapore Airlines flight for London (SGIU, 1/13/99)

An Italian national, who most likely supplied the forged passports, was also arrested (SGIU, 1/13/99)

They are believed to have acquired the forged Italian passports from the Italian national after they entered Malaysia and to have tested them by entering Singapore on 8 December 1998 and returning to Malaysia on 15 December (SGIU, 1/13/99)

The seven Afghani individuals, who had been under investigation since they entered Malaysia on 7 December 1998, may have been connected with bin Laden (SGIU, 1/13/99)

[redacted]

After the Cruise Missile Attacks

11 Jan 1999 In separate interviews with journalists working for Time and Newsweek that were published on this date, bin Laden made the following statements (DOE TSD, Feb 1999, p.2):

"Our job is to instigate [acts of terrorism] and by the grace of God, we did that, and certain people responded to this instigation" [referring to the August 1998 East African embassy bombings]

"Acquiring [nuclear and chemical] weapons for the defense of Muslims is a religious duty... and if I seek to acquire these weapons, I am carrying out a duty"

"... any American who pays taxes to his government... is our target"

12 Jan 1999 Bin Laden renewed his call for attacks on Americans, Jews, and Christians during an interview broadcast this day (FYEO, 2/1/99, p. 466-3)

16 Jan 1999 The US Attorney's office filed its most complete indictment to date of bin Laden and 11 other members of his organization (PBS Online)

17 Jan 1999 Police in India arrested four people suspected of plotting to bomb the US Embassy in New Delhi and the US consulates in Madras and Calcutta (JTWR, 1/20/99)

Police said that the attacks were to have taken place before 26 January (JTWR, 1/20/99)

After the Cruise Missile Attacks

18 Jan 1999	French internal security agents arrested Said Laidouni, a French citizen of Algerian descent (WP, 2/17/99)
	Press reports described Laidouni as a close associate of bin Laden (WP, 2/17/99)
19 Jan 1999	The London Evening Standard reported that bin Laden was planning to kidnap a high-profile US national through his London connections (JTWR, 1/19/99)
	US intelligence sources said that the US was on high alert the week before, expecting bin Laden to attempt a kidnapping or assassination in the UK (JTWR, 1/19/99)
	Documents seized at the home of Khalid Al-Fawaz, bin Laden's alleged connection in London, showed fax numbers in ten US cities, where orders were allegedly sent to murder US citizens (JTWR, 1/19/99)
	Also, two US post office box numbers were rented by bin Laden operatives in Denver and Kansas City (JTWR, 1/19/99)
20 Jan 1999	The UN Security Council demanded that Afghanistan's ruling Taliban militia stop providing sanctuary to international terrorists (JIR, Feb 1999, p. 3)
20 Jan 1999	Bin Laden made a rare public appearance when he joined Taliban leaders in prayer (FYEO, 2/1/99, p. 466-3)

[redacted]

After the Cruise Missile Attacks

22 Jan 1999 — Richard Clarke said that US intelligence and law enforcement agencies had foiled bin Laden's network from carrying out truck-bomb attacks against at least two US embassies since August of 1998 (JTWR, 2/5/99)

23 Jan 1999 — US officials said that the US had blocked two attacks on embassies by bin Laden's group (FYEO, 2/1/99, p. 466-3)

Late Jan* 1999 — The Taliban announced that bin Laden had "disappeared" (JIR, June, 1999, p. 6)

This was followed by reports of a rift between bin Laden and Taliban leader Mullah Omar and that Omar had taken away bin Laden's satellite telephones (JIR, June, 1999, p. 6)

These developments raised hopes that the Taliban was bowing to international pressure and would restrain bin Laden's terrorist activities (JIR, June, 1999, p. 6)

*This should probably be early Feb (see below)

29 Jan 1999 — Uruguayan police arrested three members of the Egyptian-based Islamic Group in the small border town of Chuy (FYEO, 2/15/99)

A fourth member was arrested on 3 February (FYEO, 2/15/99)

All four had been involved in two attacks in Egypt that killed 80 people and were arrested after the CIA had told Uruguayan police where they would be (FYEO, 2/15/99)

[redacted]

[redacted]

After the Cruise Missile Attacks

30 Jan 1999	Said Mohkles, an Egyptian suspected of having close links with bin Laden, was arrested in South America (TST, 2/8/99)
	The CIA said that he was about to fly to London to assemble a terrorist cell (TST, 2/8/99)
	Western security sources reportedly believed that bin Laden had put "high profile" British targets on a hit list, including embassies in Brussels and Paris (TST, 2/8/99)
	Evidence of these plans is believed to have been collected by British security services from intercepts of coded telephone calls made to Britain by Said Mohkles (TST, 2/8/99)
Feb 1999	A trial of 107 Islamic fundamentalists began in Egypt (IPIN, 4/22/99, p. 8), 63 in absentia (JDW, 2/24/99, p. 22)
	The defendants were allegedly members of Egypt's Al Jihad group (JDW, 2/24/99, p. 22)
Feb 1999	Bin Laden again issued a fatwa declaring jihad against the USA (JIR, June 1999, p. 34)

[redacted]

After the Cruise Missile Attacks

Feb 1999 — In an interview, bin Laden said of his possible acquisition of WMD: "If I seek to acquire these weapons I am carrying out a duty" (JIR, June 1999, p. 34)

2 Feb 1999 — George J. Tenet, Director of Central Intelligence delivered a statement to the Senate Armed Services Committee in which he stated that the U.S. had recently noted activity similar to what occurred prior to the African embassy bombings (Statement as prepared for delivery to the Senate Armed Services Committee)

3 Feb 1999 — US Assistant Secretary of State for South Asian Affairs, Karl Inderfurth, met Pakistani Foreign Minister Sartaj Azaz in Islamabad to express concern over bin Laden's latest threats and to seek Pakistani support for his extradition from Afghanistan (JTWR, 2/4/99)

Inderfurth also met with the Taliban's Deputy Foreign Minister, Jalil Akhund, who had arrived from Afghanistan on 3 February (JTWR, 2/4/9; NYT, 3/4/99))

It was later reported that Inderfurth had handed to a Taliban Deputy Foreign Minister a sealed letter from the US government (JTWR, 2/10/99) and repeated American demands that Afghanistan turn over bin Laden (NYT, 3/4/99; WP, 2/17/99)

It has also been reported that in meetings with the Taliban, the U.S. reserved the right to take any necessary military action against bin Laden or countries that support him (SGIU 2/18/99)

After the Cruise Missile Attacks

4 Feb 1999 FBI agents arrested Ali Mohfoudh Salim, a Kenyan mechanic whose garage might have been used to build the vehicle that transported the bomb to the Nairobi embassy in August 1998 (JTWR, 2/8/99)

5 Feb 1999 A Kenyan high court in Mombasa stopped the FBI from extraditing Ali Mohfoudh Salim, who had been arrested the day before, to the US (JTWR, 2/8/99)

8 Feb 1999 The minister of state in the UK Foreign Office, Derek Fatchett, met with Taliban Deputy Foreign Minister Abdul Rahman Zahid in Islamabad, Pakistan to talk about bin Laden and other issues (JTWR, 2/9/99)

Taliban officials later said that they considered the demands of the UK government to control bin Laden as "more reasonable" than the earlier demand by the US to have him extradited or forced out of Afghanistan (JTWR, 2/11/99)

9 Feb 1999 The Taliban government said that it would try bin Laden if specific evidence of his direct involvement in terrorism were produced, but it would not expel him from the country (JTWR, 2/10/99)

The statement was made by telephone with the Pakistan-based Afghan Islamic Press after the Taliban leadership considered the letter from the US government which had been delivered to them on 3 February (JTWR 2/10/99)

10 Feb 1999 A source claimed to have met bin Laden in Jalalabad, at which time bin Laden was complaining of kidney pain (SGIU, 2/18/99)

[redacted]

After the Cruise Missile Attacks

10 Feb 1999 A Taliban spokesman said that the Taliban took bin Laden's satellite telephone and banned him from meeting anyone (NYT, 3/2/99)

Bin Laden was also expelled from Kandahar and isolated in the countryside where he and his Taliban guards moved from place to place (NYT, 3/4/99)

Abdul Hakeem Mujahid, a senior Taliban official, said that "our leadership decided to cut all communications from him, and even his telephone set has been taken from him", that "he has been told no foreigner can talk to him", and that "ten bodyguards were provided for him" (NYT, 3/4/99)

A Taliban representative also said that the Afghans had sent an emissary to the United States asking how to deal with bin Laden without seeming to double-cross him and had asked Saudi Arabia if it would take care of his wives and children (NYT, 3/4/99)

The Taliban also assigned Afghan agents to escort bin Laden, who job was to protect him and "to spy on him" (NYT, 3/2/99)

A senior Taliban official, Moulvi Wakil Ahmad Muttawakil, told the BBC that Taliban authorities had imposed restrictions on bin Laden, had withdrawn his telephone and radio facilities, and had appointed a special commission to keep an eye on him (JTWR, 2/11/99)

[redacted]

After the Cruise Missile Attacks

10 Feb 1999 (contd)

The London-based Arabic newspaper Al-Quds al Arabi told CNN on 15 February that bin Laden's "disappearance" came after he was snubbed by Taliban leader Mullah Mohammad Omar in January during the three-day Eid ul-Fitr holiday that follows the holy fasting month of Ramadan: Bin Laden had been left to wait for two hours when he went to greet Omar, who had been unhappy over bin Laden's statements calling for the deaths of all Americans (and who had also been under intense pressure from the US to extradite bin Laden) (JTWR, 2/16/99)

The New York Times reported on 4 March that the Taliban leadership and bin Laden had had "a violent falling-out" (JTWR, 3/4/99)

Three US officials and two Taliban representatives confirmed that a fight broke out on 10 February in Kandahar between bin Laden's bodyguards and a group of Taliban officers sent to replace the bodyguards (JTWR, 3/4/99; NYT, 3/4/99)

The fight broke out on 10 Feb when bin Laden's bodyguards became furious that a group of ten or more Taliban officers tried to replace them (NYT, 3/4/99)

The Taliban later officially denied that bin Laden had been thrown out of his stronghold or that members of the militia were involved in a gunfight with his guards (SGIU, 3/1/699)

Despite speculation that bin Laden may have fled from Afghanistan, he was widely believed to be still hiding in that country (JTWR, 2/16/99; NYT, 3/4/99)

[redacted]

After the Cruise Missile Attacks

11 Feb 1999 Taliban spokesman Wakil Ahmad Muttawakil told Reuters that reports of bin Laden planning attacks on Western targets were "hollow rumors" which the US was fabricating in order to justify a strike against Afghanistan and that any new US strike against bin Laden in Afghanistan would demonstrate "US dictatorship" and be an "unforgettable mistake" (JTWR 2/12/99)

12 Feb 1999 Afghanistan's ruling Taliban said that it had placed new restrictions on bin Laden (that his satellite telephone had been shut off and that he was barred from talking to the news media) (WP, 2/12/99)

12 Feb 1999 Agence France Presse, citing a "high-placed Pakistani intelligence source" in a report on 13 February, claimed that bin Laden had been seen on this date on Afghan territory along the Iranian border (SGIU, 2/17/99; SGIU 2/18/99)

Some reports claimed that bin Laden had crossed into Iran this morning at Torghundi in Herat Province although the Iranian Foreign Ministry has categorically rejected the claim (SGIU, 2/17/99; SGIU 2/18/99)

13 Feb 1999 The Taliban leadership formally replaced bin Laden's bodyguards with members of its intelligence service and the foreign ministry, instructing them to keep bin Laden from public view (JTWR, 3/4/99; NYT, 3/4/99)

Ten bodyguards were provided to "supervise him and observe that he will not contact any foreigner or use any communication system in Afghanistan" (NYT, 3/4/99)

Bin Laden was then expelled from Kandahar, leaving him isolated in the countryside without his satellite phones (JTWR, 3/4/99)

[redacted]

[redacted]

After the Cruise Missile Attacks

13 Feb 1999 Taliban leader Mullah Omar announced that bin Laden had disappeared (NYT, 3/2/99; SGIU 2/18/99)

Taliban spokesman Mohammed Tayyab told journalists: "He has disappeared. We didn't ask him to leave. We don't know where he is." (SGIU 2/18/99)

Taliban rulers said they had no idea where he was, even though, according to a top Taliban official, he was accompanied by ten Afghan agents sent both to protect him and to spy on him (NYT, 3/2/99)

Prior to his "disappearance", bin Laden had lived in Kandahar, only six miles away from Taliban leader Mullah Omar (NYT, 3/2/99)

Because scores of Arabs began arriving there two weeks before his "disappearance", some believe that bin Laden had moved to Islam Dara, about 50 miles away, where there exists a warren of caves and stone barracks that had been used by Afghans during the war against the Soviets: These facilities are said to be concealed in the crevices of Sheikh Hazrat Mountain, protected by land mines, and reachable only by a maze of foot paths (NYT, 3/2/99)

A Taliban spokesman said that bin Laden's four wives and an unknown number of children had remained at Kandahar, where they lived near the airport in a compound of 300 homes built by bin Laden to house his Arab followers (NYT, 3/2/99)

[redacted]

[redacted]

After the Cruise Missile Attacks

15 Feb 1999 The London-based newspaper Al-Hayat reported that informed Afghan sources were "unanimous" that bin Laden was still in Afghanistan (SGIU, 2/17/99)

Various sources claimed that bin Laden had moved into territory in northern Afghanistan controlled by Golboddin Hekmatyar'sHezb-e-Islami (SGIU, 2/17/99)

Other sources claimed that bin Laden had sent a reconnaissance mission to the Kiyan Valley in Baghlan Province prior to his departure from Kandahar, and might be relocating to that valley, or might be relocating to Kunduz Province (both of which are controlled by Hezb-e-Islami) (SGIU, 2/17/99)

However, on 16 Feb, Hezb-e-Islami denied that bin Laden had arrived in an area controlled by the group (SGIU, 2/17/99)

Al-Hayat also reported that eyewitnesses to bin Laden's departure from Kandahar claimed that he was with ten companions, including the leader of Egypt's Jihad group, and that they were escorted from town by ten Taliban guards (SGIU, 2/17/99)

15 Feb 1999 AP reported that police in France had arrested Said Laidoni, an Islamic militant believed to have links with bin Laden (JTWR, 2/16/99)

Laidoni, a 31-year-old Frenchman of Algerian origin, was a petty criminal in Paris before becoming a mercenary for Bosnian Muslims (JTWR, 2/16/99)

Laidoni is believed to have been trained in weapons and explosives in Pakistan and Afghanistan (JTWR, 2/16/99)

[redacted]

[redacted]

After the Cruise Missile Attacks

16 Feb 1999 An anti-Taliban alliance spokesman said that troops opposed to the Taliban regime had spotted bin Laden inside of Afghanistan (SGIU, 2/17/99)

16 Feb 1999 The Voice of the Islamic Republic of Iran cited Pakistani news sources as having claimed that bin Laden was killed by factions within the Taliban (SGIU, 2/17/99)

16 Feb 1999 Car bombings in Tashkent, Uzbekistan killed 15 people and injured more than 100 (JTWR, 2/25/99)

Uzbek authorities have linked the bombings to Islamic extremists who are suspected of getting help from abroad (JTWR, 2/25/99)

17 Feb 1999 US Assistant Secretary of State Karl Inderfurth met with the Taliban's New York representative, Abdul Mujahid, in Washington to press again for action regarding bin Laden (JTWR, 2/17/99)

17 Feb 1999 An anonymous Taliban spokesman told the Pakistan-based Afghan Islamic Press that "we have no specific information about Osama bin Laden but we strongly suspect now that he has left Afghanistan" (SGIU, 2/17/99)

[redacted]

[redacted]

After the Cruise Missile Attacks

17 Feb 1999 — An aide to Northern Alliance commander Ahmed Shah Masood said that bin Laden was still in Afghanistan (JTWR, 2/19/99)

He said that the Taliban contention that he had "disappeared" was a ploy to ease US pressure (JTWR, 2/19/99)

Dr. Abdullah, aide to anti-Taliban leader Ahmed Shah Massoud, said that allegations of bin Laden's departure from Afghanistan were a ploy to ease US pressure on Afghanistan (SGIU, 2/17/99)

He also said that bin Laden had a big network with two bases in Kandahar, one in Oruzgan Province and another in Farah Province (SGIU, 2/17/99)

17 Feb 1999 — The London-based newspaper Al Hayat cited a source close to bin Laden as saying that bin Laden was at the Tora Bora base in the mountains near Jalalabad in Nangarhar Province in eastern Afghanistan (SGIU, 2/17/99)

"Bin Laden chose this base because he has known it ever since 1989, when he fought alongside the Afghan mujahedeen in repelling an offensive by troops of the former Soviet Union on the town of Jalalabad" (SGIU, 2/17/99)

Al-Hayat claimed that bin Laden also chose Tora Bora over northern Afghanistan, where he allegedly had planned to go, because he has kidney troubles that require treatment (SGIU, 2/17/99)

[redacted]

[redacted]

After the Cruise Missile Attacks

17 Feb 1999 Bayan Jaber of the Iraqi opposition group the Supreme Council for Islamic Revolution in Iraq (SCIRI), told the Kuwaiti newspaper Al-Rai Al-Aam that Saddam Hussein had "offered to shelter bin Laden under the precondition that he carry out strikes on targets in neighboring countries" (SGIU, 2/17/99)

Jaber said that bin Laden had recently settled in Iraq and that groups of Arab Afghans in Iraq could be used to carry out Saddam's threats against his neighbors in the form of bomb attacks (SGIU, 2/17/99)

24 Feb 1999 Citing intelligence officials, USA Today reported that U.S. intelligence agencies had prevented bin Laden from carrying out at least 7 vehicle bomb attacks on U.S. facilities overseas since the August 1998 East African embassy bombings (USAT, 2/24/99)

The targets were Prince Sultan Air Base in Saudi Arabia (a base for U.S. aircraft) and embassies in Tirana, Albania; Baku, Azerbaijan; Abidjan, Ivory Cast; Dushanbe, Tajikistan; Kampala, Uganda; and Montevideo, Uruguay (USAT, 2/24/99)

Officials said that these embassies were chosen because they were housed in older buildings lacking modern security (USAT, 2/24/99)

Prior warning of the embassy attacks came from reconnaissance satellite intercepts of bin Laden telephone calls, after which local officials were tipped off, who then arrested the suspects (USAT, 2/24/99)

Dozens of arrests had been made: In Uganda police arrested 20 suspects in September (USAT, 2/24/99)

[redacted]

[redacted]

After the Cruise Missile Attacks

24 Feb 1999 — The London-based Arabic newspaper Al Hayat reported that a Taliban delegation, including Deputy Foreign Minister Mullah Abdul Jalil, had visited bin Laden in Jalalabad in an effort to mend relations (JTWR, 2/26/99)

25 Feb 1999 — The chairman of the Joints Chiefs of Staff, General Henry Shelton, when asked at a news conference in Bangkok, refused to rule out new bombing raids against bin Laden in Afghanistan (NYT, 2/25/99)

25 Feb 1999 — The Taliban refuted a newspaper report that Taliban officials had met with the "missing" bin Laden a few days ago (JTWR, 2/26/99)

25 Feb 1999 — The London-based Arabic newspaper Al Hayat reported that UK Islamic militant Abu Hamza Al Masri had threatened to blow up Western military and civilian aircraft in mid-air in an attempt to end the West's monopoly on global aviation (JTWR, 2/26/99)

Abu Hamza told the newspaper that the full extent of his plot would be revealed on 26 February at a conference in London sponsored by his group, the Supporters of Shari (JTWR, 2/26/99)

The plot reportedly involved attaching "flying mines" to balloons that would be released into the air to disrupt aircraft flights (JTWR, 2/26/99)

[redacted]

After the Cruise Missile Attacks

Mar 1999 Three militant Muslim groups based in Pakistan, angered because some of their comrades were killed in the August 1998 U.S. missile attacks on terrorist training camps in Afghanistan, were threatening to carry out revenge killings against Americans
(WP, 3/7/99)

The threats came mainly from the group Harkat Ansar and from Lakshar-e-Taiba and Hizb-ul-Mujahideen (WP, 3/7/99)

A senior Harkat member said that "The veterans of the Khost bombing form the nucleus of Osama bin Laden loyalists whose sole mission in life is to settle the score with the United States. For each of us killed or wounded in the cowardly U.S. attack, at least 100 Americans will be killed..." (WP, 3/7/99)

Mar 1999 It was reported that in recent meetings with the Taliban, the U.S. reserved the right to take any necessary military action against bin Laden or countries that support him (SGIU, 3/16/99)

5 Mar 1999 The London newspaper Al Hayat reported that some members of the Taliban militia had exchanged gunfire with bin Laden's Arab and Afghan guards during the February falling out between bin Laden and the Taliban (SGIU, 3/16/99)

The Taliban had officially denied that bin Laden was thrown out of his stronghold or that members of the militia were involved in a gunfight with his guards (SGIU, 3/16/99)

[redacted]

After the Cruise Missile Attacks

12 Mar 1999 — Agence France Presse reported that Saudi Arabia and Afghanistan's Taliban authorities had signed a protocol allowing only Afghans who have been certified by Taliban officials to enter Saudi Arabia during the annual Moslem pilgrimage to Mecca (SGIU, 3/16/99)

21 Mar 1999 — The Sunday Telegraph reported that bin Laden was living in eastern Afghanistan near Jalalabad and was moving between three camps in Taliban territory near the border with Pakistan (JIR, May 1999, p. 56)

Agents who located bin Laden said that he is concerned for his safety, has abandoned his distinctive convoy of 20 land cruisers for an inconspicuous white family car, and has cut his bodyguard to only two trusted lieutenants (JIR, May 1999, p. 56)

26 Mar 1999 — Rifai Ahmed Taha and Mostafa Hamza, leaders of Egypt's Jamaa Islamiya who are living in exile, agreed to halt bloodshed after seeking assurances concerning the release of sympathizers from jail and the movement's future in Egypt (IPIN, 6/10/99, p. 7)

This came at a time when many members of Egypt's fundamentalist movement were renouncing violence and debating the pros and cons of becoming a legal political party under the name Islamic Social Party or Reform Party (IPIN, 6/10/99, p. 7)

Ayman al Zawahiri, mastermind of Egypt's Al Jihad, denounced the Gamaat's cease-fire and vowed to fight on against the "new crusade" of Israel and America (ECON, 5/1/99, p. 44)

[redacted]

After the Cruise Missile Attacks

March 1999 — Published reports suggest that US intelligence agencies have disrupted at least seven planned bin Laden attacks between August 1998 and March 1999 (JIR, June 1999, p. 34)

April 1999 — Senior American officials stated that American commandos were poised near the Afghan border, hoping to capture bin Laden (NYT, 4/13/99)

14 Apr 1999 — Assistant Secretary of State for South Asia Karl Inderfurth told a Senate panel that the U.S. is convinced that bin Laden was planning further attacks and that Afghanistan's ruling Taliban appeared to be divided over whether or not to hand bin Laden over to the U.S. (SGIU, 4/20/99)

15 Apr 1999 — The Afghan newspaper Wahdat reported that the U.S. was setting up secret bases on the Afghan border to launch an operation against bin Laden (SGIU, 4/20/99)

18 Apr 1999 — At a trial in Cairo, nine leaders of the Egyptian Jihad, including Ayman al Zawahiri, were sentenced to death in absentia (IPIN, 4/22/99, p.6)

Following the trial, the Egyptian Jihad organization moved and altered some of its branches, particularly those in Albania where their members were infiltrated into humanitarian organizations in Tirana, Shkoder, Mitrovica, Oblic, and Glogavac (IPIN, 4/22/99, p. 6)

[redacted]

After the Cruise Missile Attacks

19 Apr 1999 The London-based newspaper Al-Hayat quoted Ahmad Salama Mabrouk, a jailed member of the Egyptian militant group Al-Jihad, as saying that bin Laden's umbrella group (the International Islamic Front for Fighting Jews and Crusaders) not only possessed biological and chemical weapons, but was planning about 100 operations against U.S. and Israeli interests around the world (SGIU, 4/20/99)

The report said that details of these planned attacks were found on a computer program, which was confiscated by the CIA in September 1998 at the time Mabrouk was taken into custody in Azerbaijan (SGIU, 4/20/99)

Apr 1999 Ayman al Zawahiri, leader of Egypt's Jihad, held a series of meetings with his closest associates in the Jalalabad region of Afghanistan to reorganize the movement which had been rocked over the previous six months by the arrest of many of its members in several countries and their extradition to Egypt (IPIN, 4/22/99, p.6)

His brother, Mohammed al Zawahiri, head of the organization's military wing, reportedly ordered units stationed in Africa and Southeast Asia to prepare for assaults against Egyptian and American diplomatic posts (IPIN, 4/22/99, p.6)

Late Apr 1999 The Egyptian government released some 1,200 jailed members of Gamaat Islamiya (ECON, 5/1/99, p. 42)

One month earlier, the group had declared a unilateral cease-fire (ECON, 5/1/99, p. 42)

[redacted]

[redacted]

After the Cruise Missile Attacks

30 April 1999 The Independent, a London-based newspaper, reported that bin Laden may be looking at Somalia as a safe haven for the future (SGIU, 5/5/99)

The newspaper quoted U.S. States Department sources as saying that bin Laden had visited Somalia and that his men were setting up a secure communication system in southern Somalia, possibly in Ras Kamboni, a coastal town near the Kenyan border (SGIU, 5/5/99)

These sources said that this information emerged while U.S. security officers were in Ras Kamboni investigating the March 20 murder of a U.S. aid worker by Islamic extremists (SGIU, 5/5/99)

Ras Kamboni is known for its fundamentalist activity, particularly for the Islamic movement Al Ittihad, which reportedly has links to bin Laden (SGIU, 5/5/99)

According to unconfirmed reports, bin Laden was running military training camps on islands off the Somali coast and was believed to be funding Islamic militias in the Gedo region of Somalia (SGIU, 5/5/99)

May 1999 There was a report that the US military, CIA, and FBI had launched several missions into Afghanistan to track bin Laden and that three Americans were missing from one such operation (FYEO, 5/24/99, p. 474-3)

[redacted]

[redacted]

After the Cruise Missile Attacks

1 May 1999 — The Arab daily Al-Sharq Al-Awsat cited Islamic sources in London as claiming that bin Laden was attempting to establish a base in Somalia (SGIU, 5/5/99)

The paper claimed that the U.S. State Department threatened to withdraw the U.S. passports of Somali warlord Hussein Mohammad Aideed and his family if he offered help to bin Laden (SGIU, 5/5/99)

3 May 1999 — Somali warlord Hussein Mohammad Aideed issued a statement refuting claims that bin Laden was setting up operations in his area of Somalia although he did not rule out that some of bin Laden's operatives may have been in the Gedo region of southern Somalia which borders Ethiopia and Kenya (SGIU, 5/5/99)

3 May 1999 — The U.S. Treasury Department ended its freeze on the $24 million held by Saleh Idris in American banks (ECON, 5/8/99, p. 48)

A senior White House official said that the U.S. was not prepared to expose sensitive intelligence sources and methods to block Idris's money (WP, 5/4/99)

Idris had filed a civil suit on 26 February to recover $24 million deposited in the Bank of America (JTWR, 5/5/99)

On 4 May Sudan asked the US to compensate everyone affected by the missile strike on 20 August 1998 (JTWR, 5/5/99)

[redacted]

After the Cruise Missile Attacks

5 May 1999	BBC reported that police in Kyrgystan had arrested 12 people suspected of planning bomb attacks in crowded public places in the capital of Bishkek and seized firearms, ammunition, and explosives from the suspects (JTWR, 5/6/99)
13 May 1999	Pakistani senator Syed Muhammad Jawad Hadi told the Pakistani Senate that "US commandos" were present in the tribal agency of Waziristan and in the town of Chaman in the province of Baluchistan bordering Afghanistan combing the area in an effort to apprehend bin Laden (JTWR, 5/14/99)
24 May 1999	It was reported that Pakistani authorities had asked a Somali national to leave Pakistan on the suspicion that he was a close aide of bin Laden (JTWR, 5/24/99)
Mid 1999	After lying low for a while, bin Laden began to receive a "considerable" number of visitors in Afghanistan (JIR, June, 1999, p. 6)
	He was apparently enjoying as much freedom of movement as ever and met with invited guests mainly in the Jalalabad region at settlements owned by contacts and sympathizers whom he knew from the days of the jihad against the Soviet Union (JIR, June, 1999, p. 6)
	This activity dashed hopes that bin Laden's disappearance, announced by the Taliban in January, was a sign that his hosts were bowing to international pressure and would restrain bin Laden's involvement in terrorist activities (JIR, June, 1999, p. 6)

[redacted]

[redacted]

After the Cruise Missile Attacks

Mid 1999 — US authorities arrested Ali Abul-Saud Mustafa, an Egyptian Islamist who had been tasked by bin Laden in the mid-1990s to gather information about US embassies in Africa, had traveled extensively in Africa in 1995 and 1996, and had been responsible for providing training for members of Egypt's Islamic Jihad in Afghanistan and for helping Jihad to raise money in the US in 1995 (JIR, June 1999, p. 3)

4 Jun 1999 — It was reported that, Mahmoud Azam, a follower of bin Laden who was awaiting deportation from Israel was looking for a country to grant him asylum (JTWR, 6/4/99)

Azam, whose uncle is a business partner of bin Laden, reportedly confessed that he was a member of bin Laden's group (JTWR, 6/4/99)

8 Jun 1999 — Qatar's satellite TV station Al-Jazira announced that bin Laden would be telling his side of the story in a television program on 10 June titled "A Man Against a State, a State Against a Man" and based upon an interview with bin Laden that was previously recorded in Afghanistan (JTWR, 6/9/99)

10 Jun 1999 — Bin Laden told a Qatar television station that his mission was to incite Muslims to rebel against the American "occupation" of Saudi Arabia (ABCN, 6/25/99)

He told the al-Jazeera satellite television station that "We are demanding the liberation of our land from the enemy, that our land be liberated from the Americans" and that "Every American man is an enemy to us" (Reuters, 6/17/99)

Following this, the State Department issued a reminder to American citizens worldwide to stay vigilant about their security (ABCN, 6/25/99)

[redacted]

[redacted]

After the Cruise Missile Attacks

7 June 1999	The FBI added bin Laden to its "Ten Most Wanted" list (ABCN, 6/25/99; USIA, 6/7/99)
June 1999	A week after the FBI put bin Laden on its Ten Most Wanted list, U.S. intelligence said that bin Laden was in the advanced stages of planning another attack (WP, 6/17/99)
	A U.S. official said that there had been indications in recent weeks that bin Laden had been moving unspecified materials that could be used in a terrorist operation
	They also indicated that U.S. facilities in African nations such as Ghana or Mozambique could be targets (WP, 6/17/99)
16 June 1999	U.S. intelligence officials were quoted by ABC-TV as saying that they believe bin Laden is suffering from Marfan's syndrome
	Marfan's syndrome is an illness that would put him at risk of having a stroke (WP, 6/17/99)

[redacted]

[redacted]

After the Cruise Missile Attacks

16 Jun 1999 A federal grand jury in New York indicted Ayman al-Zawahiri and Khalid al-Fawwaz on charges of involvement in the East Africa embassy bombings (JTWR, 6/17/99; NYT, 6/17/99)

Mr. Fawwaz allegedly ran media operations for al Qaeda: His duties included publicizing statements made by bin Laden, recruiting military trainees, transmitting confidential messages to members of the group, and purchasing communications equipment, including a satellite telephone (NYT, 6/17/99)

Before setting up the media office in London in 1994, Mr. Fawwaz briefly lived in Nairobi where he established businesses with Abu Ubaidah al-Banshiri, the al Qaeda military commander who died in 1996 (NYT, 6/17/99)

Mr. Fawwaz was being held by British authorities and al-Zawahiri was thought to be in Afghanistan with bin Laden (NYT, 6/17/99)

On 8 Sept 1999 a UK magistrate ordered the extradition of Khalid al-Fawwaz to the U.S. on suspicion of conspiring with bin Laden's al Qaeda group to bomb the US embassies in Nairobi and Dar es Salaam (JTWR, 9/8/99)

An informer identified Khalid al-Fawwaz as the UK head of al Qaeda (JTWR, 9/8/99)

[redacted]

After the Cruise Missile Attacks

16 Jun 1999 — A US official stated that there were indications that bin Laden had recently been moving unspecified materials that could be used in a terrorist attack on US facilities in African countries with poor security (such as Ghana or Mozambique) (JTWR, 6/18/99)

17 Jun 1999 — A counterterrorism official told CNN that the terrorist network headed by bin Laden had targeted American diplomatic facilities on every continent (CNN, 6/17/99)

Intelligence officials stated that they had been receiving about six credible threats a day from people believed to be affiliated with bin Laden (CNN, 6/17/99)

Based on, US officials believed that bin Laden "may be in the final stages" of planning an attack against the US (CNN, 6/17/99)

This was based upon intercepted conversations and other information (CNN, 6/17/99)

The most specific concerns were about embassies in Mozambique, Senegal, and Ghana (CNN, 6/17/99)

These were believed to have been under surveillance by possible terrorists (CNN, 6/17/99)

[redacted]

After the Cruise Missile Attacks

24 Jun 1999	The US announced that it was temporarily closing six of its embassies in Africa because they are believed to have been under surveillance by "suspicious individuals" (BBCN, 6/25/99; ABCN, 6/25/99; JTWR, 6/25/99; and JIR 8/99)
	The embassies to be closed were located in Gambia, Togo, Madagascar, Liberia, Namibia, and Senegal
	Another report says that there were indications that they were under surveillance by "members of bin Laden's network" (WP, 7/29/99)
	Earlier, ABC News had quoted intelligence sources as saying that attempts had been made to penetrate security systems at the embassies in Accra and Dakar (BBCN, 6/25/99)
	The embassies were closed for three days (JIR, 8/99, p. 5)
	The U.S. announced on July 12 that it was reopening the embassy in Madagascar, the last of the closed embassies to be re-opened (STRATFOR Country Profile, Madagascar, 0005 GMT 990713)
25 Jun 1999	The UK announced the temporary closure, starting 26 June, of its embassies in Gambia, Madagascar, Namibia, and Senegal (JTWR, 6/25/99; JIR 8/99)

[redacted]

After the Cruise Missile Attacks

28 Jun 1999 The London-based Al Hayat reported that Yasser Tawfiq el-Siri, head of the Islamic Observation Center (and wanted in Egypt for an attempted assassination of a former prime minister in 1993), warned that Islamic fundamentalists would launch attacks on US facilities (JTWR, 6/28/99)

He advised the UK to distance itself from the US (JTWR, 6/28/99)

"the continuation of the subordination policy to the US will only bring trouble for the British people" (JTWR, 6/28/99):

28 June 1999 The U.S. reopened its embassies in Gambia, Togo, Liberia, Namibia, and Senegal (which had closed on 24 June)

However, they left closed the embassy in Madagascar (JTWR, 6/28/99)

29 June 1999 Bin Laden was reportedly seen in a convoy of trucks on the road to the village of Farmihadda, a few miles south of Jalalabad (JTWR, 7/6/99; STRATFOR, Countries, Afghanistan, 0100 GMT 990705)

Bin Laden had reportedly moved into an old collective farm in Farmihadda (JTWR, 7/6/99)

He was reportedly moving part of his operation from its previous base near Kandahar into a former military base near Farmihadda known as Tora Bora (JTWR, 7/6/99)

[redacted]

After the Cruise Missile Attacks

Late June or Early July, 1999

U.S. officials, including Treasury Department and National Security Council officials, traveled to the United Arab Emirates to discuss U.S. concerns that bin Laden had a financial relationship with a bank controlled by the UAE government, the Dubai Islamic Bank in Dubai (NYT, 7/8/99)

They were also concerned that Qatari officials may have warned a wanted fugitive (Khaled Shaikh Mohammad) that an FBI counterterrorism team was on its way to Qatar to arrest him on charges in connection with a plot to blow up 12 American airliners over the Pacific (NYT, 7/8/99)

The CIA allegedly had evidence that bin Laden had been allowed to funnel money through the bank, and that bin Laden's relationship with the bank had been arranged with the approval of officials who control the bank (NYT, 7/8/99)

The attempt to arrest Khaled Shaikh Mohammad, a suspected lieutenant of Ramzi Yousef, took place in 1996: He had been secretly indicted in January 1996 as an accomplice in the airliner plot after which American authorities learned that he was living in Doha, the capital of Qatar (and working at the Public Works Ministry) and sent agents to arrest him, only to find that he had disappeared (NYT, 7/8/99)

American officials say that Mohammad was warned by someone in the Qatar government and that he had been staying at the estate of Abdallah bin Khalid, a fundamentalist who has provided support for other Islamic radicals (NYT, 7/8/99)

[redacted]

[redacted]

After the Cruise Missile Attacks

July 1999 The State Department, having received reports of terrorist plots against Americans in Pakistan, issued a ban on travel there (NYT Op-Ed, 8/13/99)

July 1999 Mustafa Elnore, a small businessman from Jersey City, NJ, was arrested and charged with lying about his relationships to a number of alleged and convicted terrorists (WP, 8/1/99)

July 1999 The FBI halted public tours of its headquarters in Washington after receiving what it considered credible information about a potential attack by bin Laden operatives (WP, 7/29/99)

Potential attackers had reportedly scouted the building by slipping in on the tour (USN&WR, 8/30/99, p. 8)

U.S. intelligence later overheard the perpetrators bragging about the penetration and about their plans to return (USN&WR, 8/30/99, p. 8)

[redacted]

[redacted]

After the Cruise Missile Attacks

July 1999

The Taliban launched a massive offensive north of Kabul against the Northern Alliance: Western intelligence sources estimated that a force of 8,000 Pakistani volunteers were serving at that time among the Taliban's country-wide total of 50,000 troops (JIR, 10/99, p. 32)

Sources claim that the Taliban's offensive involved an estimated 3,000-4,000 Pakistani citizens backed by Arabs loyal to bin Laden (JIR, 10/99, p. 32)

Other sources have given different numbers:
London's Daily Telegraph reported that 400 bin Laden-backed Arabs had joined masses of Taliban fighters preparing for an all-out offensive against the Northern Alliance (which still held parts of northern Afghanistan) (STRATFOR Commentary, "Noose Closing on Bin Laden")
Russian Foreign Ministry spokesman Vladimir Rakhmanin said on 3 August that over 400 Arab gunmen who were followers of bin Laden had joined the Afghan fighting on the side of the Taliban (JTWR, 8/5/99)

Whatever the numbers, it is known that training for foreign volunteers was centralized since late 1998 at the former 7th Division base at Rishkhor (JIR, 10/99, p. 33)

This base, located to the south of the city, ringed by mountains, and accessible from the city by only a single road guarded by the Taliban, was run by the HUA/HUM and Arabs loyal to bin Laden (JIR, 10/99, p. 33)

[redacted]

[redacted]

After the Cruise Missile Attacks

July 1999 (contd)

This base had been set up following the August 1998 cruise missile strikes against several training camps for foreigners in the Khost area on the Pakistan border (JIR, 10/99, p. 33)

This base at Rishkhor was bigger and better organized than the Khost camps (JIR, 10/99, p. 33)

One individual who trained there was subsequently captured by the Northern Alliance

This individual has said that the Rishkhor camp can accommodate 1,000-1,500 trainees, divided into 8 or 9 classes (JIR, 10/99, p. 33)

He also said that most trainees were put through an intensive 40-day course by Pakistani or Arab trainers, 20-30 of whom were in the camp (JIR, 10/99, p. 33)

Weapon training, theoretical and practical, covered small arms (the SKS carbine, AK/AKM-type assault rifles, and light machine guns) and infantry support weapons (12.7mm and 14.5mm heavy machine guns, recoilless rifles, and mortars) (JIR, 10/99, p. 33)

Advanced courses were also taught in specific weapons, demolitions, and escape-and-evasion techniques (JIR, 10/99, p. 33)

[redacted]

[redacted]

After the Cruise Missile Attacks

3 July 1999 According to a report in a Kuwaiti newspaper on 8 July, Kuwaiti police arrested an unidentified Arab man who was trying to exit Kuwait illegally at the southwestern border crossing point of Al-Salmi carrying a forged Kuwaiti citizenship certificate bearing the photograph of bin Laden (JTWR, 7/9/99)

The man told police that he was commissioned to deliver the false citizenship paper to bin Laden and that bin Laden had visited Kuwait in disguise in 1996, at which time he was hosted by a big Kuwaiti family (JTWR, 7/9/99)

4 July 1999 The UK newspaper Observer reported that bin Laden had been seen in the Hadda agricultural farm area near Jalalabad (JTWR, 7/21/99)

Another source quotes the Observer report as saying that bin Laden moved to the village of Farmihadda, a few miles south of Jalalabad, two months previously (see 29 June) and had established a new operational base near Jalalabad (STRATFOR, Countries, Afghanistan, 0100 GMT 990705 and 0040 GMT 990704)

Following this report, families in the area left their homes, fearing that the site could be the target of another US missile strike (JTWR, 7/21/99)

4 July 1999 President Clinton met in Washington with Pakistani Prime Minister Nawaz Sharif (STRATFOR Special Report, "Was There More to the Clinton-Sharif Talks?")

[redacted]

[redacted]

After the Cruise Missile Attacks

5 July 1999 — President Clinton signed an executive order imposing financial and commercial sanctions against the Taliban regime for harboring bin Laden (JTWR, 7/7/99)

An administration official said that bin Laden provided fighters and finances to the Taliban in exchange for sanctuary (JIR, 8/99, p. 56)

7 July 1999 — Taliban leader Mullah Mohammad Omar told the Pakistan-based Afghan Islamic Press that "I don't know where he [bin Laden] is. We have neither asked him to leave Afghanistan nor asked him to live in Afghanistan" (JTWR, 7/8/99)

According to another report, two days after the sanctions went into effect (see 5 July), the Taliban admitted that bin Laden was living in the portion of Afghanistan that was under their control (WP, 7/29/99)

8 July 1999 — Taliban spokesman Wakil Ahmad Mutawakil insisted that the Taliban would survive the recently-imposed U.S. sanctions (see 5 July) (STRATFOR Special Report, "Was There More to the Clinton-Sharif Talks?")

He also acknowledged that bin Laden was in Afghanistan, under the protection and supervision of a special Taliban security detail (STRATFOR Special Report, "Was There More to the Clinton-Sharif Talks?")

[redacted]

After the Cruise Missile Attacks

9 July 1999 Taliban spokesman Wakil Mutawakil told the Afghan Islamic Press that "We are ready to hold talks with the United States on Osama" (STRATFOR, Countries, Afghanistan, 1700 GMT 990709)

Taliban spokesman Wakil Ahmad Mutawakil also stated that a Taliban intelligence unit was overseeing bin Laden's movements and activities in Afghanistan and that his whereabouts were being kept secret to ensure the safety of ordinary Afghans (JTWR, 7/9/99)

9 July 1999 State Department spokesman James Foley said that the U.S. was willing to negotiate with the Taliban for the purpose of bringing bin Laden to justice (STRATFOR, Countries, Afghanistan, 2150 GMT 990709)

11 July 1999 Two Egyptian men were arrested in London after being linked by fingerprint evidence to a conspiracy with bin Laden in the 7 August 1998 embassy bombings (JTWR, 7/12/99)

Another sources claims the date of these arrests was 10 July (CS, 8/13/99, p. 5)

The fingerprints of both men were found on statements claiming responsibility for the bombings at the London offices of The Advice and Reform Council (JTWR, 7/12/99)

[redacted]

After the Cruise Missile Attacks

15 July 1999 — The London-based Asharq Al-Awsat newspaper published an interview with Taliban spokesman Wakil Ahmad Mutawakel during his visit to the UAE in which Mutawakel said that "we have no objections if bin Laden accepts [the idea of leaving Afghanistan], but we will not take the initiative to hand him over to another party and we will not force him to leave Afghanistan" (STRATFOR Commentary, "Proposal To Extradite Bin Laden To A Neutral Third Country Emerges")

The newspaper said that Mutawakel was in the UAE to examine the possibility of having bin Laden tried for his alleged role in the East African embassy bombings in a neutral third country where he has not been indicted (STRATFOR Commentary, "Proposal To Extradite Bin Laden To A Neutral Third Country Emerges")

16 July 1999 — The US State Department issued a travel advisory warning that supporters of bin Laden were preparing to attack US interests in Pakistan (JTWR, 7/19/99)

18 July 1999 — The UK's Sunday Times reported that a fanatical Islamic group, known as Takfiris or "judge of the infidels" (a breakaway faction of the Islamic Jihad movement that was formed in the 1970s in the prison cells of Cairo), was seeking to kill bin Laden for betraying its cause (JTWR, 7/20/99; JIR, 9/99, p. 56)

A handwritten fatwa in Arabic issued by the group, and first seen by Arab relief workers outside the city of Peshawar, accused bin Laden of diverting resources away from other jihad groups and of refusing to listen to allied organizations and called for the "death of the infidel" (JTWR, 7/20/99)

[redacted]

[redacted]

After the Cruise Missile Attacks

18 July 1999	Taliban leader Mulla Mohammad told the Shariat weekly that the U.S. had "no right" to demand the expulsion of bin Laden from Afghanistan (STRATFOR, Countries, Afghanistan, 2152 GMT 990719)
19 July 1999	The U.S. Embassy in Maputo, Mozambique closed because of security concerns after receiving a threat (NYT, 7/23/99; JTWR, 7/30/99)
	Agence France Presse reported that the closure was in response to the presence in Maputo of elements belonging to bin Laden's terrorist group (STRATFOR, Country Profile, Mozambique, 1815 GMT 990722)
	The embassy reopened on 30 July (JTWR, 7/30/99)
20 July 1999	There were reports that bin Laden was returning to Jalalabad, his previous home (STRATFOR, Countries, Afghanistan, 2103 GMT 990720)
20 July 1999	The Pakistani government refuted claims by opposition leader (and former intelligence chief) General Ghul that Pakistani Prime Minister Nawaz Sharif had promised the U.S. that he would attempt to arrest and extradite bin Laden (STRATFOR Commentary, "Noose Closing on Bin Laden")
	Ghul also stated that Sharif's visit to the U.S. to meet with President Clinton (see 4 July) was to negotiate a deal to arrest bin Laden in exchange for a U.S. promise not to criticize Pakistan over Kashmir (STRATFOR Commentary, "Noose Closing on Bin Laden")

[redacted]

[redacted]

After the Cruise Missile Attacks

21 July 1999 — Pakistan's ruling Moslem League disputed claims from the opposition that Prime Minister Sharif had promised to arrest and extradite bin Laden (STRATFOR, Countries, Afghanistan, 1235 GMT 990721)

20 July 1999 — Taliban leader Mullah Mohammed Omar said that he would not extradite bin Laden to any country, even another Islamic one (STRATFOR Commentary, "Noose Closing on Bin Laden")

Omar made these comments after U.S. Assistant Secretary of State Karl Inderfurth, head of the U.S. delegation to the Afghanistan Six-Plus-Two Contact Group, met with Taliban representatives to renew a request that the Taliban hand over bin Laden to the U.S. government (STRATFOR Commentary, "Noose Closing on Bin Laden")

21 July 1999 — According to a report by the Voice of the Islamic Republic of Iran on 22 July, a U.S. commander and elite troops landed inside Pakistan at Peshawar airport with the intent of capturing bin Laden (STRATFOR, Countries, Afghanistan, 2006 GMT 990722)

These troops reportedly traveled to Dera Ismail Khan in western Pakistan and then on to the southern Waziristan area which borders Afghanistan (STRATFOR, Countries, Afghanistan, 2006 GMT 990722)

Residents of the area began leaving the area days before in fear of a potential attack (STRATFOR, Countries, Afghanistan, 2006 GMT 990722)

[redacted]

[redacted]

After the Cruise Missile Attacks

22 July 1999 — A Taliban official claimed that three U.S. military ships had anchored near Pakistani waters in order to prepare for a possible attack on Afghanistan (STRATFOR, Countries, Afghanistan, 1357 GMT 990722)

22 July 1999 — Thousands of demonstrators from the Jamiat i-Ulema i-Islam demonstrated in Pakistan against any attack on bin Laden or the Taliban (STRATFOR Commentary, "Noose Closing on Bin Laden")

22 July 1999 — The U.S. Embassy in Chad was closed because of a telephoned bomb threat, but reopened the next day (NYT, 7/23/99)

26 July 1999 — The Taliban reportedly detained a group of four men who were hunting for Osama bin Laden (STRATFOR Country Profile, Afghanistan, 2120 GMT 990726)

The men, who were equipped with a car and modern weapons, reportedly had contact with U.S. troops in Peshawar, Pakistan (STRATFOR Country Profile, Afghanistan, 2120 GMT 990726)

26 July 1999 — The Taliban's minister of culture and information said that the issue of bin Laden could not be resolved through force, that bin Laden is not a threat to society, and that the U.S. should start negotiations faithfully and without any preconditions (STRATFOR Country Profile, Afghanistan, 0004 GMT 990726)

[redacted]

[redacted]

After the Cruise Missile Attacks

27 July 1999 The London-based Al Hayat newspaper reported that bin Laden had abandoned his hideout near Jalalabad in eastern Afghanistan for fear of an "imminent" US attack (JTWR, 7/30/99; STRATFOR Country Profile, Afghanistan, 1410 GMT 990727)

They claimed that he had moved, under Taliban supervision, to a secret location elsewhere in Afghanistan accompanied by family members and supporters, including his military chief Mohammad Atef and Egyptian Jihad leader Ayman Zawahiri (JTWR, 7/30/99; STRATFOR Country Profile, Afghanistan, 1410 GMT 990727)

The Pakistani newspaper Jang reported that bin Laden had moved to a secret hideout made up of fortified bunkers guarded by some 450 Arab guerillas along with hundreds of local Afghan fighters (JTWR, 7/30/99)

27 July 1999 Pakistani Minister of State for Foreign Affairs, Mohammad Siddiq Kanju, said that there was a danger of a US missile strike against Afghanistan (STRATFOR Country Profile, Afghanistan, 1520 GMT 990727)

29 July 1999 US security officials, using new "highly sensitive" detection equipment at a roadblock installed to screen cars, found traces of plastic explosives in a US jeep-type vehicle outside the US embassy in Antananarivo, the capital city of Madagascar (JTWR, 7/29/99)

However, the acting ambassador said that it remained to be seen whether or not this was a false reading (JTWR, 7/29/99)

[redacted]

[redacted]

After the Cruise Missile Attacks

30 July 1999 — Bin Laden announced that he will leave Afghanistan and take refuge in an unnamed Islamic country (FYEOX, 8/1/99)

Later that day, a Taliban spokesman said that bin Laden was still in Afghanistan under tight security and that a report about his leaving was baseless (JTWR, 7/30/99)

August 1999 — Since the East African bombings a year previous, an estimated 2,400 threats or incidents had been aimed at U.S. interest overseas, more than double the number from the same period one year previously (CS, 8/13/99, p. 5)

Nearly 70 embassies or consulates had been closed at some point for 24 hours or more in response to these threats (CS, 8/13/99, p. 5)

August 1999 — Khalid Sharaf-al-Din reported in the Arabic-language Al-Sharq-al-Awsat in Cairo that members of the Islamic Jihad group had managed to buy anthrax from a source in an East Asian country for the equivalent of $3,695 plus freight (JIR, 8/99, p.5)

Ahmad Ibrahim al-Najar, a defendant in the recent Egyptian court proceedings against Islamic militants, had confessed details of the transactions (JIR, 8/99, p. 5)

Factories in former Warsaw Pact countries and some Eastern states supply deadly diseases such as Ebola, anthrax, and Salmonella to whoever wants to buy them without verifying the identity of the importer (JIR, 8/99, p. 5)

For example, a Czech laboratory apparently agreed to supply what appeared to be botulinum toxin for $7,500 per sample (JIR, 8/99, p. 5)

[redacted]

[redacted]

After the Cruise Missile Attacks

6 Aug 1999 Citing Russian and Saudi intelligence sources, Yosef Bodansky, a researcher attached to the House counter-terrorism task force, said that bin Laden had as many as 20 suitcase nuclear bombs that had been smuggled out of Russia by Chechen rebels who had managed to steal them from the Russian military and then sold them to bin Laden (WND, 8/12/99)

According to Bodansky, "The Russians believe that he has a handful [of nuclear weapons], the Saudi intelligence services are very conservative... [and] believe that he has in the neighborhood of 20." and "Most of them have been transferred through Pakistan" (WTC, 8/9/99)

He also said that bin Laden was attempting to recruit former Russian special forces to operate the bombs (WND, 8/12/99)

Bodansky also claims that bin Laden has biological and chemical weapons and has received technical help from Iraq (WTC, 8/9/99)

Bodansky has also said that bin Laden was located in Islam Darva, about 80 kilometers northwest of Kandahar and that he travels to Jalalabad when he wants to communicate with the outside world (WTC, 8/9/99)

7 Aug 1999 After rising unrest in the region, a Muslim rebel offensive was unleashed in Dagestan by Chechen leader Shamil Basayev on the first anniversary of the bomb attacks against American embassies in East Africa (IPIN, 8/26/99, p. 1)

[redacted]

[redacted]

After the Cruise Missile Attacks

10 Aug 1999 A report on this date claimed that a satellite television station in Qatar had said that two US military planes carrying "commandos" had landed in Pakistan, presumably to carry out an operation against bin Laden (JTWR, 8/10/99)

The Qatari station quoted "informed Pakistani sources" (JTWR, 8/10/99)

These sources said that the planes had landed in Islamabad and Quetta and that Pakistani personnel at the two airports had been prevented from approaching the two aircraft (JTWR, 8/10/99)

The report also said that the US embassy in Islamabad had been secretly evacuating the dependants of diplomatic personnel and that more than 75 US citizens had been evacuated in recent days (JTWR, 8/10/99)

10 Aug 1999 The US State Department issued a travel warning advising US citizens not to travel to Pakistan (JTWR, 8/10/99)

12 Aug 1999 In a statement, the Taliban government in Afghanistan rejected claims that bin Laden maintained training camps in Afghanistan (JTWR, 8/12/99)

15 Aug 1999 Taliban and U.S. diplomats had been holding regular meetings to negotiate a surrender of bin Laden (FYEOX, 8/16/99)

The most likely solution at the time was for bin Laden to be sent to a third world country (like Saudi Arabia) for trial (FYEOX, 8/16/99)

[redacted]

[redacted]

After the Cruise Missile Attacks

18 Aug 1999 A report said that at a public meeting in the Pakistani border town of Chaman in western Baluchistan province, Maulana Fazlur Rehman, the leader of the Islamic political party Jamiat-ul Islami, said that "US terrorism" would not be tolerated (JTWR, 8/18/99)

He reportedly warned the Pakistani government against allowing US forces to use Pakistani soil to launch an attack against the Taliban or bin Laden (JTWR, 8/18/99)

He also said that his followers would fight alongside the Taliban against any US attack to apprehend bin Laden (JTWR, 8/18/99)

19 Aug 1999 On this date the AP reported that the Taliban's deputy leader, Mullah Mohammed Rabbani, warned the U.S. not to use force to capture bin Laden (JTWR, 8/19/99)

23 Aug 1999 Over 4,000 Islamic activists marched in Lahore, Pakistan to protest U.S. actions against bin Laden (JIR, 10/99, p. 5)

Members of the group Jamiat-Ulema-Islami shouted anti-U.S. slogans and waved posters that read (JIR, 10/99, p. 5):

"Down with America"

"Osama is a Muslim World Hero"

"We Will Protect Osama with Our Blood"

[redacted]

After the Cruise Missile Attacks

24 Aug 1999 A truck bomb exploded near the home of Taliban leader Mullah Mohammed Omar in southern Kandahar (JIR, 10/99, p. 5; JTWR 8/26/99)

It was later announced that some 40 people were killed, including two brothers and a brother-in-law of Taliban leader Mullah Mohammed Omar (FYEOX, 9/12/99)

The Taliban later declared this bombing an act of terrorism and said that "the material in this explosion was very advanced material and of the very best quality" (JTWR, 8/27/99)

The Sunni Taliban later detained a number of Shia Afghans in connection with the truck bombing, which fueled speculation that the Taliban may suspect Iran of being behind the attack (JTWR, 9/8/99)

Early Sept 1999 One of bin Laden's right-hand men, a Libyan named el Mouaz Hallali, arrived in Yemen to try to protect and to reorganize two fundamentalist networks in the country (IPIN, 9/23/99, p. 7)

The two groups were Tarek el Fodhil's Jihad and the Aden Islamic Army (IPIN, 9/23/99, p. 7)

Earlier assaults by Yemeni authorities had either destroyed or seriously mauled a number of secret units (IPIN, 9/23/99, p. 7)

After the Cruise Missile Attacks

Sept 1999 — President Clinton wrote to Iranian President Mohammed Khatami to ask for his support in fighting terrorism (SGIU, 10/12/99)

This is not as outlandish as it may seem, for two reasons:

Ramzi Yousef, who was convicted in the bombing of the World Trade Center, has been linked to a June 1994 bombing of a Shia holy place in Iran (ECON, 10/9/99, p. 26)

President Khatami had worked hard to try to moderate the fiery anti-Western rhetoric of Iran and to open a dialog with the West

Washington had also dangled the prospect of official diplomatic recognition in front of the Taliban in exchange for certain concessions, which included the extradition of bin Laden (SGIU, 10/12/99)

Sept 1999 — It was reported that U.S. efforts to nab bin Laden were being restricted to political pressure on the Taliban (offering inducements to hand him over or to arrange for him to be expelled to a country that would do so) rather than more drastic measures (FYEOX, 9/7/99)

The concern was that more drastic measures would risk raising Islamic anger against the U.S. in the aftermath of the goodwill that was generated in Arab and other Islamic states after U.S. backing for the Muslim rebels in Kosovo) (FYEOX, 9/7/99)

After the Cruise Missile Attacks

Sept 1999 There was a series of bomb attacks in Russian cities which Russia blamed on Islamic militants associated with fighting in Dagestan and Chechnya: (JIR, 10/99, p. 2):

1. 31 August 1999: A bomb in a shopping mall near the Kremlin killed 1 and injured over 40
2. 4 September 1999: A bomb in a building housing Russian servicemen and their families in Buinaksk, Dagestan killed 64
3. 9 September 1999: A bomb in an apartment block of the Pechatniki suburb of Moscow killed 94
4. 13 September 1999: A bomb attack at Block 3, Number 6 Kashirskoyoe Highway in southern Moscow killed 118
5. 16 September 1999: A truck bomb outside a nine-block apartment building in Volgodonsk in southern Russian killed 18

There was evidence that bin Laden, while not the instigator of the urban bombing campaign, had offered financial support to its perpetrators (ECON, 10/9/99, p. 25)

Furthermore, fighters under the influence of bin Laden were active in Chechnya and Dagestan, although their presence was probably not the main reason why the war was raging there (ECON, 10/9/99, p. 25)

8 Sept 1999 A UK magistrate ordered the extradition of Khalid al-Fawwaz, a Saudi Arabian, to the U.S. on suspicion of conspiring with bin Laden's al Qaeda group to bomb the US embassies in Nairobi and Dar es Salaam (JTWR, 9/8/99)

An informer identified Khalid al-Fawwaz as the UK head of al Qaeda (JTWR, 9/8/99)

After the Cruise Missile Attacks

12 Sept 1999 Mahrez Amduni, a terrorist on Interpol's list of most wanted criminals and a leading associate of bin Laden, was captured in Turkey carrying a Bosnian passport (FYEOX, 9/24/99; IPIN, 9/23/99, p. 7)

He was captured after a tip-off from the CIA and an investigation that shed light on a widespread drive to recruit Arab fundamentalists for service in the Caucasus (IPIN, 9/23/99, p. 7)

Authorities believe that Amduni may also have intended to assassinate either Italian foreign minister Lamberto Dini or US Under Secretary of State Marc Grosman when they visited Istanbul (FYEOX, 9/24/99)

Amduni went to Bosnia in 1993, fought with the Islamic "freedom fighter" el-Mujaheed unit during the Bosnian war, lived in Bosnia from 1 May 1993 to 5 May 1995, and applied for Bosnian citizenship in December 1997 (FYEOX, 9/24/99)

Bosnian police believe that he may have been involved in the attempted assassination of Pope John Paul II in 1997 (FYEOX, 9/24/99)

12 Sept 1999 Russian Prime Minister Vladimir Putin said that Russia had information that bin Laden's followers were involved in the fighting in Dagestan and Chechnya (JIR, 10/99, p. 56; JTWR, 9/13/99) [See item above regarding Mahrez Amduni]

After the Cruise Missile Attacks

17 Sept 1999 — Michael Sheehan, US Coordinator of Terrorism, and senior Indian government officials met (JTWR, 9/21/99)

Following this meeting, the U.S. formally asked Pakistan to "distance itself" from the activities of bin Laden and Harkat-ul Ansar, which was involved in the separatist insurgency in the Indian state of Jammu and Kashmir (JTWR, 9/21/99)

18 Sept 1999 — Afghan scholar Abdul Rahim Muslim Dost, noting that the U.S. has offered $5 million for Osama bin Laden, offered a reward of 5 million Afghanis ($113) for the assassination of President Clinton (FYEOX, 9/19/99)

19 Sept 1999 — The Turkish newspaper Milliyet reported that six followers of bin Laden were in Turkey, presumably planning bomb attacks on US and UK diplomatic missions (JTWR, 9/20/99)

Turkish police went on alert after intelligence reports that the six-man team loyal to bin Laden had arrived to launch bomb attacks on US and British diplomatic facilities (FYEOX, 9/23/99)

The six men, four Kurds and two Algerians, entered Turkey from Iran to plan the attacks (JTWR, 9/20/99)

Two Iranians were reported to be "on standby" in Iran (JTWR, 9/20/99)

After the Cruise Missile Attacks

22 Sept 1999	Rockets, apparently launched by the Afghan Taliban, struck a village in Pakistan which was close to bin Laden's suspected hideout in Afghanistan (SGIU, 10/12/99)
	It is possible that the Northern Alliance, which was fighting the Taliban for control of Afghanistan, may have set up in Pakistan, close to bin Laden's bases, and might therefore pose a threat to bin Laden (SGIU, 10/12/99)
Oct 1999	Senior administration officials said that they believe that bin Laden was trying to develop chemical weapons in Afghanistan and may have obtained them (NYT, 10/27/99)
5 Oct 1999	U.S. State Department spokesman James Rubin hinted that cooperation against terrorists could lead to an easing of U.S. sanctions against Iran (SGIU, 10/12/99)
6 Oct 1999	The US, backed by Russia, introduced a draft resolution in the UN Security Council calling for the imposition of an air embargo and financial sanctions on the Taliban regime (JTWR, 10/7/99)
7 Oct 1999	Khalfan Khamis Mohamed, the man who allegedly rented a house in Tanzania to manufacture bombs for the August 1998 US embassy bombings in East Africa, was arrested in Cape Town's airport as he was about to be deported for illegally entering South Africa (JTWR, 10/8/99)
	He was then flown into New York by FBI agents (JTWR, 10/8/99)

After the Cruise Missile Attacks

7 Oct 1999	Radio Pakistan announced that Pakistani Prime Minister Nawaz Sharif sent the director-general of the Inter-Services Intelligence Service, General Khawaja Ziauddin, to Kandahar, Afghanistan to demand the closure of terrorist training camps (SGIU, 10/12/99; also see IPIN, 10/21/99, p. 7) Sharif had been blaming terrorists trained in Afghanistan for a wave of sectarian violence in Pakistan and had begun a high-profile campaign abroad to pressure the Taliban to close down the camps (SGIU, 10/12/99)
9 Oct 1999	The London-based Daily Telegraph reported that Taliban leader Mullah Omar had said that the Taliban was "ready to cooperate fully with the international community to combat terrorism by vested interests in the name if Islam" (SGIU, 10/12/99)
11 Oct 1999	Pakistani Prime Minister Nawaz Sharif and the director-general of the Inter-Services Intelligence Service, General Khawaja Ziauddin, traveled to Dubai for talks with UAE leaders (because the UAE is one of only three nations to recognize the Taliban) on violence in Pakistan and its relationship to terrorist training camps in Afghanistan (SGIU, 10/12/99; IPIN, 10/21/99)
11 Oct 1999	Taliban leader Mullah Mohammad Omar said that he was ready for talks with anyone on the fight against terrorism, but he demanded that a clear distinction be made between "terrorists and freedom fighters" (JTWR, 10/12/99)

After the Cruise Missile Attacks

15 Oct 1999	The UN Security Council gave unexpectedly strong backing to a resolution to impose sanctions in 30 days that will freeze the Taliban's economic assets abroad and curtail international flights by the Afghan national airline if bin Laden and one of his aides are not turned over (NYT, 10/19/99)
	Two Islamic nations, Bahrain and Malaysia, joined in the unanimous 15-0 vote for sanctions (NYT, 10/19/99)
16 Oct 1999	The Taliban rejected a UN demand to hand over bin Laden and instead proposed that a group of Islamic scholars be convened to advise them on a proper solution (JTWR, 10/18/99)
16 Oct 1999	Pakistani Islamic militants vowed that they would prevent any attempt to arrest bin Laden if he chose to move to Pakistan (FYEOX, 10/18/99)
18 Oct 1999	Michael A. Sheehan, the State Department's coordinator for terrorism, met with Abdul Hakeem Mujahid, the Taliban representative in New York, to press for action on bin Laden (NYT, 10/19/99; JTWR, 10/20/99)
19 Oct 1999	The State Department warned that American citizens and facilities in the Balkans were being targeted by Islamic extremists (FYEOX, 10/19/99)
19 Oct 1999	The UN Security Council, in a unanimous resolution, condemned all forms of terrorism (JTWR, 10/20/99)

After the Cruise Missile Attacks

20 Oct 1999	Reuters reported that U.S. Secretary of Defense William Cohen said that UAE President Sheikh Zaid bin Sultan al-Nahayan had assured him that the UAE (one of only three nations that had recognized the Taliban regime) would meet all of its obligations under the recent UN Security Council resolution that imposed sanctions on the Afghan Taliban regime (JTWR, 10/21/99)
23 Oct 1999	The Taliban announced that they would be willing to discuss the fate of bin Laden (FYEOX, 11/1/99; JTWR, 10/25/99)
24 Oct 1999	Saudi Interior Minister Prince Nayef told reporters that his government was not interested in extraditing bin Laden because he was no longer a Saudi citizen (JTWR, 10/25/99)
25 Oct 1999	Abdul Hakeem Mujahid, the Taliban's representative at the UN, visited Washington to meet with Karl Inderfurth to discuss pending UN sanctions against Afghanistan and the fate of bin Laden (BBCN, 10/26/99)
	The UN sanctions were due to take effect on 14 November unless bin Laden was handed over to face trial for his role in the August 1998 African embassy bombings (BBCN, 10/26/99)
25 Oct 1999	U.S. State Department spokesman James Rubin said that the Taliban regime was responding to U.S. demands for the expulsion of bin Laden from Afghanistan with "some ideas" (JTWR, 10/26/99)

After the Cruise Missile Attacks

26 Oct 1999 Abdul Hakeem Mujahid, the Taliban's representative at the UN, and Karl Inderfurth, the Assistant Secretary of State for South Asia, discussed pending UN sanctions against Afghanistan and the fate of bin Laden (BBCN, 10/28/99)

27 Oct 1999 Mr. Wakil Ahmad Muttawakil was appointed as Afghan Foreign Minister and said that he would make special efforts to improve ties with the U.S. (BBCN, 10/28/99)

28 Oct 1999 Tayeb Agha, a Taliban spokesman, said that "the reports which say that Taliban are about to hand over Osama or extradite him are totally baseless" (BBCN, 10/28/99; JTWR, 10/29/99)

The Taliban's newly appointed Foreign Minister Abdul Wakil Muttawakil also told the Pakistan-based Afghan Islamic Press that no agreement had been reached with the U.S. to hand over bin Laden (JTWR, 10/29/99)

Speculation about a possible handover had increased after recent U.S. talks with the Taliban and after Pakistan's new military ruler, General Perez Musharraf, had visited Saudi Arabia and the United Arab Emirates (the only two nations other than Pakistan to have recognized the Taliban government) (BBCN, 10/28/99)

There were reports hat General Musharraf had pledged to secure the extradition of bin Laden in return for U.S. support for his new government (BBCN, 10/28/99)

However, General Musharraf has been careful not to appear being too conciliatory towards the U.S. for fear of stirring up Pakistan's fundamentalists (IPIN, 11/4/99, p.6)

After the Cruise Missile Attacks

29 Oct 1999 A Pakistan-based Afghan news service reported that, in a letter to Taliban leader Mullah Omar, bin Laden had offered to leave Afghanistan under two conditions: that the Afghan government help him reach his destination and that only Omar and one other person in his Islamic movement should know his destination (Reuters, 10/29/99; JTWR, 11/1/99)

30 Oct 1999 There were reports that terrorists linked to bin Laden intend to strike at British, Russian, and American embassies and diplomatic consulates in Turkey (FYEOX, 11/2/99)

30 Oct 1999 Bin Laden offered to leave Afghanistan (FYEOX, 11/1/99)

30 Oct 1999 In an interview published on this date, Saudi Interior Minister Prince Nayef bin Abdul Aziz said that "the case of Osama bin Laden" had been "grossly inflated" and that it was not worthy of being taken up by the UN Security Council (JTWR, 11/1/99)

He also said that bin Laden was not a security concern for Saudi Arabia (JTWR, 11/1/99)

31 Oct 1999 Taliban Foreign Minister Wakil Ahmed Muttawakil told AP that Taliban leader Mullah Mohammad Omar had assured bin Laden that he would not be handed over to the U.S., but that if he wanted to leave Afghanistan, he was free to go (JTWR, 11/1/99)

After the Cruise Missile Attacks

Nov 1999	There were reports that the Taliban had begun disarming "Arab Afghan" units and moving their camps in eastern Afghanistan to the Kabul area (IPIN, 11/4/99, p. 6)
	Elements base at the Dronthe camp near Jalalabad who belong to the Egyptian Jihad movement led by Ayman al Zawahiri were among those moved (IPIN, 11/4/99, p. 6)
	The real motive for the moves may have been to preclude a strike by U.S. special forces (IPIN, 11/4/99, p. 6)
2 Nov 1999	Michael Sheehan, the U.S. State Department's Coordinator for Counterterrorism, told a Senate Foreign Relations subcommittee that Pakistan was supporting the training of militant groups in Afghanistan as well as providing "material support" to Kashmiri militants (JTWR, 11/5/99)
3 Nov 1999	The Taliban regime accused the U.S. of "bad faith" in talks conducted to get bin Laden out of Afghanistan (JTWR, 11/3/99)
	Taliban Foreign Minister Wakil Ahmad Muttawakil was speaking after the U.S. had dismissed an offer by bin Laden to leave Afghanistan for another Islamic country provided that Afghanistan help him relocate and that only Taliban leader Omar and one other person would know his destination (JTWR, 11/3/99)

After the Cruise Missile Attacks

3 Nov 1999 A three-day conference began in Muridke, Pakistan of the Lashkar-e-Tayyaba militant Islamic group at which militants praised holy wars and condemned India and the United States (NYT, 11/4/99)

The meeting was attended by 300,000 followers from Sudan, Afghanistan, Egypt, and Saudi Arabia (NYT, 11/4/99)

Hafiz Saeed, chief of Dawaad-al Arshad, the umbrella organization that includes Lakshar-i-Tayyaba, blamed the U.S. for the worsening plight of Muslims around the world (JTWR, 11/5/99)

At least 50,000 young men reportedly signed up to fight in jihads anywhere in the world (JTWR, 11/5/99)

9 Nov 1999 In a letter, Taliban leader Mullah Mohammed Omar warned the American people that thee would be "surprises" if a UN resolution calling for sanctions against Afghanistan was carried out (NYT, 11/9/99)

Where To Next?

If bin Laden were to leave Afghanistan, where might he go:

Iran
- Unlikely because bin Laden is a Wahhabi Sunni Muslim and Iran is Shiite (SGIU, 2/17/99)

Yemen
- Yemeni factions have offered bin Laden sanctuary in the past (SGIU, 2/17/99)
- Bin Laden has said that he would like to relocate to Yemen (SGIU, 2/17/99)
- But Yemen is under careful watch (SGIU, 2/17/99)

Iraq
- Iraqi President Saddam Hussein has offered asylum to bin Laden (WP, 2/14/99)
- Unlikely because even bin Laden would not trust Saddam Hussein (SGIU, 2/17/99)

Libya

Sudan
- Khartoum is not eager to find itself in the Taliban's dilemma (SGIU, 2/18/99) after themselves having been subject to U.S. pressure to expel bin Laden in the early 1990s and after having targeted in the U.S. cruise missile strikes of 20 August 1998

Chechnya
- Has offered bin Laden sanctuary (SGIU, 2/17/99)
- But hard to reach and under constant threat from Russia (SGIU, 2/17/99)

Where To Next?

The Philippines

The military is doing well enough against bin Laden's Muslim separatists allies that this is an unlikely destination (SGIU, 2/17/99)

Also unlikely because of the high probability that the US could snatch bin Laden from the Philippines (SGIU, 2/17/99)

Pakistan

Bin Laden enjoys hero status there among a large and growing fundamentalist movement (SGIU, 2/17/99)

But he would be vulnerable there to US commando operations against him (SGIU, 2/17/99)

Somalia

Bin Laden has always maintained strong ties with friends in Somalia (JIR, 7/99)

Aideed and bin Laden share a passionate hatred of the West in general and of the US in particular (JIR 7/99)

Somalia's anarchy could be used defensively, especially by bin Laden who has made a career out of structuring an ad hoc organization from many disparate extremist groups (SGIU, 5/5/99)

But Somalia, in a constant state of anarchy, cannot guarantee security (SGIU, 2/17/99)

Summary: Al Qaeda (The Base)

Origins

- Grew out of the "mekhtab al khidemat" ("Services Office") which had maintained offices in various parts of the world, including Afghanistan, Pakistan, and the U.S. (particularly at the Alkifah Refugee Center in New York)
- Called itself Al Qaeda from on or about 1989
- PBS Online, citing a document provided by a source close to bin Laden, reports that in 1988 Bin Laden realized that his system of documentation was backward and that he was unable to answer the questions of some families whose loved ones were missing in Afghanistan, so he decided to organize better and arranged for better documentation and tracking of all visitors and mujahedeen: It was at this time that the whole bin Laden complex was named Al-Qa'edah, which means "The Base"
- Was originally a way station in Peshawar where Egyptian and Saudi volunteers rested before setting off for battle in Afghanistan (NYT, 4/13/99)

History

- Headquartered in Afghanistan and Peshawar, Pakistan from 1989 until in or about 1991
- Leadership relocated to Sudan in or about 1991
- Leadership relocated to Afghanistan in or about 1996

Leadership

- At all relevant times, Al Qaeda was led by its "emir", Osama bin Laden
- Members pledged an oath of allegiance (called a "bayat") to bin Laden and Al Qaeda (Other reports say that some members swear allegiance to bin Laden, but not all)
- A consultation council ("majlis al shura") which discussed and approved major undertakings
- A military committee which considered and approved military matters

Summary: Al Qaeda (The Base)

Composition

- Training camps and guest houses in Afghanistan, Pakistan, Sudan, Somalia, and Kenya
- At least six front companies in Sudan
- 2,000 to 3,000 operatives around the world in Africa, the Mideast, Afghanistan, Pakistan, Bosnia, Chechnya, Tajikistan, and Kosovo
- Other reports claim that bin Laden enjoys the active support of only a small number of individuals whose allegiance both to him and to each other is highly informal (JIR, June, 1999, p. 6)
- The loose-knit nature of the alliance among al Qaeda members, based on an oath of allegiance and a common militant interpretation of Islam, makes the organization rather more like a mafia than a tightly controlled paramilitary force
- "Bin Laden's organization has contacts virtually worldwide, including in the United States" according to George J. Tenet, Director of Central Intelligence, 2/2/99 (Statement as prepared for delivery to the Senate Armed Services Committee)
- "...in truth this network is more often inspired by him [bin Laden] than controlled by him" - Milt Bearden, former CIA chief in Pakistan (NYT Op-Ed, 8/13/99)

Mamdouh Mahmud Salim, an associate of bin Laden who was arrested in Germany in September 1998, has said that there were three kinds of men in Al Qaeda: "people who had no success in life, had nothing in their heads and wanted to join just to keep from falling on their noses", "people who loved their religion but had no idea what their religion really meant", and "people who have nothing in their heads but to fight and solve all the problems in the world with battles" (NYT, 4/13/99)

Summary: Al Qaeda (The Base)

Affiliates

Egyptian Islamic Jihad, led by Ayman al Zawahiri

The Islamic Group (Gamaa Islamiya), led by Sheik Omar Abdel Rahman and later by Ahmed Refai Taha (a.k.a. Abu Yasser al Masri)

Jihad groups in Sudan, Egypt, Saudi Arabia, Yemen, Somalia, Eritrea, Djibouti, Afghanistan, Pakistan, Bosnia, Croatia, Albania, Algeria, Tunisia, Lebanon, the Philippines, Tajikistan, Azerbaijan, the Kashmiri region of India, and Chechnya

Cells in Kenya, Tanzania, the United Kingdom, and the United States

The Egyptian affiliates consider Sheik Omar Abdel Rahman as their spiritual leader

"Bin Laden has taken over the sheik's old network" (Kenneth Katzman)

Key players

Ahmed Refai Taha serves as military commander

Mohammad Jamal Khalifa, bin Laden's brother-in-law, serves as chief fund-raiser and operates mainly from the Philippines

The Majlis al Shura (consultative council) decides on terrorist operations

The fatwa committee issues religious rulings

Summary: Al Qaeda (The Base)

Strengths

"Enormous replicating ability" (Bruce Hoffman)

May be heavily compartmentalized, with as many as six layers of intermediaries between bin Laden and any terrorist activity

Bin Laden's skillful oratory and use of the media stir the passions of militant Muslims around the world: There is widespread support among ordinary people in the Muslim world for his central political argument that American troops should get out of Saudi Arabia (NYT, 4/13/99)

He has been successful in forging links based on Islam that bring together such ethnically, socially, and politically diverse groups as Sudanese, Bangladeshis, and Filipinos (SGIU, 1/27/99)

He has forged a new militant, fundamentalist, Islamic identity that is divorced from Arabic or Persian identity (SGIU, 1/27/99)

It has been difficult to find direct evidence linking bin Laden to the East African bombings of August 1998 because he is more of an inspiration for terrorism than a commander who orders and directs his troops (NYT, 4/13/99)

Links to states

Allied with the National Islamic Front in Sudan

Allied with representatives of the government of Iran

Close ties to the Taliban in Afghanistan

Summary: Al Qaeda (The Base)

Weaknesses

Not as disciplined as past state-sponsored terrorists

Not as sophisticated as past state-sponsored terrorists

Bin Laden may already have exhausted his inheritance

The organization is penetrated by spies: For example, two key defectors from the group (who may have been agents of Saudi intelligence) have provided information to the United States and the U.S. has had a spy inside bin Laden's organization since 1996 who has provided key information on the team that attacked the embassy in Kenya

Its foot soldiers are often amateurs

Bin Laden is not as globally powerful as some people have asserted

Security

Bin Laden is known to be extremely cautious about his own security, employing various bodyguards (who have reportedly wielded surface-to-air missiles in order to guard against air attack)

He is known to take pains to conceal himself during transport, either traveling in large convoys with darkened windows or, later, attempting to travel inconspicuously in a family car (JIR, May 1999, p. 56)

He reportedly dislikes relocating because he suffers from chronic back pain (JIR, June 1999, p. 6)

He imposes elaborate checks even on many of his hand-picked guests (JIR, June 1999, p. 6)

Summary: Al Qaeda (The Base)

Supporters & Financing

Revenues from businesses

Donations (including donations from members of the Saudi royal family and gulf state merchants)
Money donated to charities*

Protection money (including money from wealthy Saudis who have paid him not to conduct operations in Saudi Arabia)

Bin Laden receives money and political support from princes of the Saudi royal family and from powerful people and financial institutions in Kuwait and Qatar (NYT, 2/8/99)

Among the legitimate fronts used by anti-American groups which bin Laden has financed are schools and mosques (NYT, 8/14/96)

Bin Laden solicits contributions from religious businessmen and Islamic leaders (NYT, 8/14/96)

Bin Laden communicates with his adherents through audiotapes (just like Abdel-Rahman) and also spreads his beliefs through Web sites on the internet

Vince Cannistraro, former director of the CIA's counterterrorism department, has said that: "People don't send a check into bin Laden directly. They provide money to so-called charities for Islamic causes."

*As a result of this, the FBI has dramatically expanded investigations of Muslim Americans suspected of aiding overseas organizations that mix charity with terrorism (WP, 10/31/98)

Summary: Al Qaeda (The Base)

The good financial news

Several sources have been quoted as saying that he appears to control only a fraction of the $250 million fortune that he is said to possess (this number is arrived at by dividing the estimated $5 billion family fortune by 20, the number of male heirs) (NYT, 4/13/99)

Business associates have said that his family cut him off years ago and are managing his share of the inheritance for him (NYT, 4/13/99)

His Saudi assets have been frozen (NYT, 4/13/99)

The bad financial news

He receives a generous allowance from his eldest brother (NYT, 4/13/99)

Because he can still probably tap into a limitless supply of funds from supporters (who make willing donations through secret channels) and from ordinary Muslims worldwide (who make unwitting donations via charities and other Muslim causes which they believe to be legitimate), he is unlikely ever to be seriously constrained in the long run by serious financial difficulties

After decades of focusing on state sponsors of terrorism, the emergence of sophisticated privately-financed networks of terrorists poses new diplomatic and legal challenges (NYT, 8/14/96)

Tracing the financial trail of privately-funded terrorists is complicated by the use of untraceable telephone numbers, cash-carrying couriers, and layers of business and religious organizations (NYT, 8/14/96)

Identifying and taking action against individuals who support terrorism can be more complicated than moving against rogue states (NYT, 8/14/96)

Summary: Economic Holdings

Kenya
- Trading companies
- A construction firm he controls maintains an office in Nairobi

Yemen
- Ceramic manufacturing company

Sudan
- Bank
- Construction company
- Investment firms
- Near monopoly on gum arabic, the country's leading export
- One of the largest privately-owned farms in Sudan, located south of Khartoum (JIRP, 10/98, p. 8)

Kenya
- Yemeni sources say that bin Laden owns commercial firms in Kenya that deal in electrical appliances and make a great deal of profit that is transferred to his financial department and is spread in several European capitals, including Rome
- Saudi officials estimated in 1998 that bin Laden owned at least 70 to 80 companies
- Other reports have said that he had a financial empire of more than 60 companies, some in the West (NYT, 8/14/96)
- Bin Laden's companies provide cover for his activities, playing the same role as the diplomatic immunity provided by state sponsors of terrorism

Summary: Egypt's Islamic Jihad

(From IPIN, 2/25/99, p. 7)

Headed by

- A nine-member consultative council (Majlis Shura) made up mainly of imams established in Afghanistan
- A constitutional council (Majlis Taassisi) composed of operational leaders in several countries, including Albania, Kenya, Tanzania, the United States, Britain, and Pakistan

The Majlis Shura, chaired by Ayman al Zawahiri, also includes:

- Mohamad al Zawahiri (a.k.a. "the engineer" or Samir), Ayman's brother, who was based in Jalalabad in Afghanistan
- Sarwat Salah Shehata (a.k.a. Mohamad Ali, Abu Samah, and Abu Mohamad), a lawyer who was residing in Kandahar in southern Afghanistan
- Abdullah Mohamed Rajab Abdul Rahman (a.k.a. Ahmed Hassan Abu Kheir), who was based in Peshawar, Pakistan
- Abel Abdul Kudus (a.k.a. Hazem, Alaa, or Osman) who was living in the suburbs of Vienna
- Ahmed Salame Mabruk (a.k.a. Abu Faraj al Masri), who was living in the Badr-1 camp at Khost in the Jalalabad region
- Nasr Fahmi Nasr (a.k.a. Mohamad Salah or Abu Ibrahim), who was living in the Badr-2 camp at Khost
- Murjan Mustapha Salem al Jawhjari, who was living in the Konar valley in eastern Afghanistan
- Hani Mohamed al Sayed Sibai (a.k.a. Abu Karim), who was arrested by Scotland Yard in December 1998

Summary: Egypt's Islamic Jihad

(From IPIN, 2/25/99, p. 7)

The Majlis Taassisi is organized into several committees:

- The Internal Civil Organization Committee was being led by Mabruk and ensured contact with imams and preachers in Egypt
- The Security Committee, headed by Shehata, was in charge of collecting intelligence on the Egyptian regime's leading civilian and military figures and on Egyptian interests abroad; oversaw counter-espionage; and organized logistic support for Jihad's militants and sympathizers in Egypt
- The Documents Committee, which was headed by Salameh until he was extradited from Tirana in July of 1998, was in charge of furnishing travel tickets and visas
- The Financial Committee, was headed by Nasr (who is very close to bin Laden) and saw to the collection of money from mosques and welfare associations in the United States and in the Gulf nations
- The Sharia Committee, under Salem, issued fatwas and published edicts on the Sharia
- The Media Committee was headed by Hani al Sibai until his arrest in London

Jihad has roots in the U.S. (Chicago and San Francisco), Pakistan (Peshawar), Sudan, Albania, Azerbaijan, the United Kingdom, Austria, and Saudi Arabia (Riyadh)

Al Zawahiri communicates with his operational chiefs through an American activist of Egyptian origin named Ali Abu Seoud

Jihads main military camp, Al Khilafa, was located in the Konar valley in Afghanistan near Jamaa Islamiya's camp at Al Mourabitoun

Summary: Incidents Linked to bin Laden

Assassination of Sadat

Plot to assassinate Mubarak

Aden bombings

Attempted assassination of Jordan's Crown Prince Abdullah

World Trade Center bombing

Plot to kill the pope

Plot to bomb airlines

Ambush in Somalia

Operation of terrorist camps

Attempt to assassinate Clinton

Riyadh bombing

Seven bombings in France

Khobar Towers bombing

Bus bombing in Cairo

Kidnappings in Kashmir

Kenya and Tanzania bombings

Numerous foiled bombing plots

Summary: The Reach of bin Laden and the "Arab Afghans"

- Afghanistan
- Algeria
- Azerbaijan
- Bangladesh
- Bosnia
- Chechnya
- China
- Croatia
- Egypt
- Eritrea
- France
- India
- Indonesia
- Kenya
- Kashmir
- Kosovo
- Lebanon
- Libya
- Malaysia
- Pakistan
- The Philippines
- Saudi Arabia
- Somalia
- Sudan
- Tajikistan
- Tanzania
- Turkey
- Tunisia
- Uganda
- United States
- Yemen

The federal indictment of bin Laden and his accomplices names 20 countries where al Qaidia is allegedly operating, including the United States

What's the Beef?

A Summary of the bin Laden Philosophy

Righteous Indignation

- The U.S. is regarded as an infidel because it is not governed in a manner consistent with the extremists interpretation of Islam
- The U.S. supports other infidels, such as Israel
- A general sense that the Islamic world is trod upon by the west and fails to realize its full potential because it is fractured
- A specific hatred of the U.S. and of the Saudi royal family for defiling Islam with the stationing of U.S. troops in Saudi Arabia
- A specific hatred of the U.S. because of the arrest and imprisonment of persons belonging to al Qaeda or its affiliated terrorist groups (such as Sheik Omar Abdel Rahman)
- A conviction that the Gulf War in 1991 and Operation Restore Hope in Somalia in 1992 and 1993 were preparations for an American occupation of Islamic countries

Sudanese protestors after the Al Shifa attack

Historical Lessons

- The U.S. is weak and has no stomach for body counts (e.g., the U.S. in Somalia)
- A superpower can be defeated by persistent opposition from determined forces (e.g., the USSR in Afghanistan)

What's the Beef?

A Summary of the bin Laden Philosophy

Al Qaeda seeks to:

Overthrow nearly all Muslim governments, which bin Laden views as corrupt

Drive Western influence from Muslim countries

Eventually abolish state boundaries

Al Qaeda advocates:

Destruction of the United States, which it sees as the main obstacle to reform in Muslim societies

Support for Muslim fighters in places such as Afghanistan, Algeria, Bosnia, Chechnya, Eritrea, Kosovo, Pakistan, Somalia, Tajikistan, and Yemen

Bin Laden spends hundreds of thousands of dollars for satellite time to broadcast his anti-U.S. message to sites in the Middle East

What's the Beef?
A Summary of the bin Laden Philosophy

Goals

In general, to unite the Islamic world and place it in a position of strength in the world

Specifically, to unite, train, and coordinate fundamentalist Islamic fighters worldwide

Specifically, to force the U.S. out of Saudi Arabia

Means

Attacks against U.S. interests worldwide

Manipulation of the media

The Muslim militant's view of President Clinton

"You will leave [Saudi Arabia] when the bodies of American soldiers and civilians are sent [home] in the wooden boxes and coffins... That is when you will leave."

Osama bin Laden, in an interview with ABC's Nightline, 1998

[redacted]

Quotes

"It will further motivate people. They consider it a matter of pride and a blessing of God to become a martyr."

Bakht Zamin, commander of a Kashmir unit trained in Afghanistan, on the cruise missile attacks against the training camps near Khost

"If, with the blessing of God, I become a martyr, please show extreme patience, because life is the trust of God and if He gets his trust back, there is no reason to cry."

A letter found on the body of Hafiz Shabir Ahmad after being killed in Kashmir in June of 1998. (Before being sent into battle, each fighter must write such a letter for his family.)

"Being killed for Allah's cause is a great honor achieved by only those who are the elite of the nation. "We love this kind of death... It is something we wish for."

Osama bin Laden, March 1997

"Al that has been proved is our joy at the killing of the American soldiers in Riyadh and Khobar..."

Osama bin Laden, 1996

"We deal with the Islamic world as a single state"

Osama bin Laden, 1996

[redacted]

[redacted]

Quotes

"Having borne arms against the Russians for ten years, we think our battle with the Americans will be easy by comparison"

Osama bin Laden, interview with Al Quds Al Arabi in a cave near Kandahar, Afghanistan, Nov 1996

"They could get rid of bin Laden tomorrow and plenty of new bin Ladens would step up to take his place"

Harvey Kushner, a Long Island University professor who studies terrorism

"We are openly against this organization. They are looking for people who are not well in the mind, who are poor, who need new visions."

Said Toihir Ben Said Maoulana, the grand mufti (top religious leader) of the Comoros Islands, referring to the Islamic organization based in Nairobi which offered a scholarship to study Islam in Sudan to Abdallah Mohammed Fazul, who became leader of the Kenyan cell of al-Qaida

"Are we ready for that big clandestine battle? Did we take the necessary measures to avoid having one of us fall in the trap, knowing we were counting on God's blessing with our limited resources?"

Haroun Fazul, in a letter before the East African bombings, warning about security compromises that could threaten the bin Laden cell that later carried out the bombings

[redacted]

[redacted]

Quotes

"We want [war] clean and they want it dirty. Right now we're in the feel-good stage because we struck back. But I guarantee you it's not over."

An aerospace industry official after the Aug 20 cruise missile attacks

"We deal with the Islamic world as a single state... We are a single nation with one religion."

Osama bin Laden, shortly after his return to Afghanistan in 1996

"Despite the great devastation inflicted on the Iraqi people by the crusader-Zionist alliance, and despite the huge number of those killed, in excess of one million... despite all this, the Americans are once again trying to repeat horrific massacres... the aim is also to serve the Jews' petty state and divert attention from its occupation of Jerusalem and murder of Muslims there."

From the Fatwa issued in February 1998 calling on Muslims to kill US military personnel and civilians

"The US is the enemy of Islam and we must fight it. Our order throughout the world is to kill any member of its army and its leaders, and this is a religious duty"

From a fatwa issued by bin Laden in retaliation for the US government's detention of Shaykh Omar Abdur Rahman

[redacted]

[redacted]

Quotes

"The Americans should learn a lesson from the Muslims of Afghanistan who, armed only with sticks, started their jihad against the Russian aggressors. Even so, they brought about the destruction of the superpower of their time... Let it be known that we, under any circumstances, cannot accept and tolerate the presence of the American military force in Saudi Arabia."

> From a 29-page fatwa issued by one of the highest religious officials of Saudi Arabia, Imam Abdur Rahman al-Hudhayfi, grand imam of Masjid an-Nabawi of Madina al-Munawwara of Saudi Arabia, during Jumah prayer 13 March 1998

"Somebody approached me at the mosque and asked me, 'if I see a Jew in the street should I kill him?' Don't ask me. After you kill him come and tell me. What do you want from me, a fatwa? Really, a good deed does not require one."

> Bassam Alamoush, a Jordanian Islamic militant, at an Arab conference in Chicago, Dec 1994 (JCSI, Spring 1998, p. 25)

""You have been supporting Israel throughout all the years in killing and torturing peoples, innocent peoples... You enjoy seeing people have war together. You enjoy sucking blood and shedding blood... you are the first one who introduced this type of terrorism to the history of mankind when you dropped an atomic bomb... it was necessary to use the same means against you because this is the only language you understand."

> Ramzi Yousef after being sentenced to life in prison (JCSI, Spring 1998, p. 32)

[redacted]

[redacted]

Quotes

"Jihad means do jihad with the sword, with the cannon, with the grenades, and with the missile. This is Jihad. Jihad against God's enemies for God's cause and His word."

Sheik Omar Abdul Rahman (JCSI, Spring 1998, p. 56)

"We can now state that the security position of the cell is at 100 percent danger. ...there is American-Kenyan-Egyptian intelligence activity in Nairobi aiming to identify the names and residences of the cell members. We are really in danger. We are 100 percent convinced that Kenyan intelligence is aware of us. Our security situation is extremely bad."

Haroun Fazil, in a letter written in Aug 1997 (one year before the embassy bombings) and later discovered among the computer files of Wadih el Hage (CTSR, vol. 8, no. 1, p. 11)

"We read in the British Daily Telegraph that there is an individual from the bin Laden finance department currently in the hands of the American Central Intelligence Agency in Saudi Arabia. The newspapers also mentioned that a man called Sidi Tayib had advised the Americans about the scope of distribution of money to various Arab communities who cooperate with the sheik in the United States, especially in Brooklyn and Jersey City."

Haroun Fazil, in a letter written in Aug 1997 (one year before the embassy bombings) and later discovered among the computer files of Wadih el Hage (CTSR, vol. 8, no. 1, p. 11)

[redacted]

[redacted]

Quotes

"We ask you to keep in touch with us through the internet from Pakistan, as we get a lot of information now about the Shaykh [bin Laden] from that network"

Haroun Fazil, in a letter written in Aug 1997 (one year before the embassy bombings) and later discovered among the computer files of Wadih el Hage (PBS Online, "The Letter from El Hage's Computer))

"Our job is to instigate [acts of terrorism] and by the grace of God, we did that, and certain people responded to this instigation"

Bin Laden in an interview, while speaking about the August 1998 embassy bombings (JIR, June 1999, p. 34)

"If the majority of the American people support their dissolute president, this means the American people are fighting us and we have a right to target them. Any American who pays taxes to his government is our target because he is helping the American war machine against the Muslim nation."

Bin Laden, in a January 1999 interview with Time magazine (JIR, June 1999, p. 37)

"Osama is a hero. Every young man here wants to be like him."

Sami ul-Haq, a leading Islamic politician in Pakistan (NYT, 2/8/99)

[redacted]

[redacted]

Quotes

"When bin Laden speaks, he is reflecting the aspirations of the people."

Naseerullah Babar, a retired Pakistani general who has served as Pakistan's Interior Minster (NYT, 2/8/99)

"People [in Pakistan] feel they have no voice... They resent the personal corruption of the Saudis" and the power of the United States

Robert B. Oakley, a former American ambassador in Pakistan (NYT, 2/8/99)

"I swear to Allah, I wish to fight for Allah's cause and be killed, I'll do it again and be killed, and I'll do it again and be killed"

Muslim prophet quoted by bin Laden

While Americans may see aid for anti-Communist Afghan Muslims or Bosnian government soldiers as moral, as opposed to support for Islamic Holy War and Hamas, "in Islamic terms, it's all defensive and hence moral"

A Saudi businessman (NYT, 8/14/96)

"For each of the 5,000 Pakistani and Afghan [students] in my two universities, Osama bin Laden is an ultimate hero... Our youth are getting desperate to pay back the Americans in their own coin."

Sami ul-Haq, the cleric who directs the largest Sunni seminary in Pakistan (WP, 3/7/99)

[redacted]

[redacted]

Quotes

"When my son was born on September 1 last year [1998], our family unanimously decided to name him Osama. We thought it was the most respectful name a Muslim can give to his newborn."

Abdul Aziz, a 43 year old carpenter in Pakistan (WP, 3/7/99)

"One should go to the refugee camps throughout Pakistan and find out how many boy children have been named Osama since last August. That's scary."

Former CIA official Milt Beardon (WP, 7/29/99)

"For all of us, he was almost an unseen god"

Jalil Chisti, a 19 year old Pakistani youth who was injured in the U.S. cruise missile attack on the Salman Farsi camp near Khost (WP, 3/7/99)

"Every state and every civilization and culture has to resort to terrorism under certain circumstances for the purpose of abolishing tyranny and corruption"

Osama bin Laden in a May 1998 interview with ABC (PBS Online)

"In today's wars, there are no morals"

Osama bin Laden in a May 1998 interview with ABC (PBS Online)

[redacted]

[redacted]

Quotes

"The two explosions that took place in Riyadh and in Khobar recently were but a clear and powerful signal to the governments of the countries which willingly participated in the aggression against our countries and our lives and our sacrosanct symbols"

Osama bin Laden in a May 1998 interview with ABC (PBS Online)

"The truth is that the whole Muslim world is the victim of international terrorism, engineered by America at the United Nations"

Osama bin Laden in a May 1998 interview with ABC (PBS Online)

"It is far better for anyone to kill a single American soldier than to squander his efforts on other activities"

Osama bin Laden in a May 1998 interview with ABC (PBS Online)

"We believe that the worst thieves in the world today and the worst terrorists are the Americans. Nothing could stop you except perhaps retaliation in kind. We do not have to differentiate between military or civilian. As far as we are concerned, they are all targets..."

Osama bin Laden in a May 1998 interview with ABC (PBS Online)

"We hope Allah receives them as holy martyrs"

Osama bin Laden in a May 1998 interview with ABC, referring to the Riyadh bombers (PBS Online)

[redacted]

[redacted]

Quotes

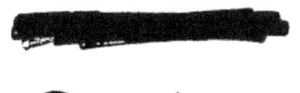

"We have instigated and they have responded"

Osama bin Laden in a May 1998 interview with ABC, referring to the Riyadh and Khobar bombers (PBS Online)

"Our battle against the Americans is far greater than our battle was against the Russians. Americans have committed unprecedented stupidity. They have attacked Islam and its most significant sacrosanct symbols."

Osama bin Laden in a May 1998 interview with ABC (PBS Online)

"After our victory in Afghanistan... the legend about the invincibility of the superpowers vanished"

Osama bin Laden in a May 1998 interview with ABC (PBS Online)

"Our boys were shocked by the low morale of the American soldier and they realized that the American soldier was just a paper tiger. He was unable to endure the strikes that were dealt to his army, so he fled..."

Osama bin Laden in a May 1998 interview with ABC, referring to events in Somalia (PBS Online)

"After a few blows, [America] forgot all about those titles [world leader] and rushed out of Somalia in shame and disgrace..."

Osama bin Laden in a May 1998 interview with ABC (PBS Online)

[redacted]

[redacted]

Quotes

"Our mothers and daughters and sons are slaughtered every day with the approval of America"

Osama bin Laden in a May 1998 interview with ABC (PBS Online)

"We say to the Americans as people and to American mothers... they must elect an American patriotic government that caters to their interests not the interests of the Jews."

Osama bin Laden in a May 1998 interview with ABC (PBS Online)

"If the present injustice continues... it will inevitably move the battle to American soil, just as Ramzi Yousef and others have done. This is my message to the American people."

Osama bin Laden in a May 1998 interview with ABC (PBS Online)

"We do not differentiate between those dressed in military uniforms and civilians; they are all targets in this fatwa"

Osama bin Laden (PBS Online, citing a report by ABC reporter John Miller)

"We are involved in a long-term struggle... This is unfortunately the war of the future..."

Secretary of State Albright in TV interviews after the 20 August 1998 cruise missile strikes (CRS Report 98-733F)

[redacted]

[redacted]

Quotes

"We don't recognize frontiers... I am not afraid of America and shall continue my work... nobody can stop me"

> Osama bin Laden, quoted in posters placed in northern Pakistan near the border with Afghanistan urging Muslim youth to contact him to wage jihad against Americans (AP, "Pakistani group claims its chief met bin Laden")

"If someone can kill an American soldier, it is better than wasting time on other matters"

> Osama bin Laden (U.S. Dept of State, "1997 Global Terrorism: Overview of State-Sponsored Terrorism")

[redacted]

[redacted]

Interest in Chem/Bio Agents

State Ties

- A "sensitive source" has said that bin Laden asked Sudanese officials to help him obtain chemical weapons that could be used against U.S. installations (NYT, 9/21/98)
- According to a U.S. intelligence official, "Bin Laden directly involved himself with the Sudanese government, trying to get it to test poisonous gases in case they could be tried against U.S. troops in Saudi Arabia" (NYT, 9/21/98)
- In February 1999 US National Security Advisor Sandy Berger told a press conference that prior to the attack on Al Shifa, "we knew bin Laden was seeking chemical weapons" and "we knew that he had worked with the Sudanese government to acquire chemical weapons" (JIR, June 1999, p. 37)
- CIA Director George Tenet is said to have told a small group of Presidential advisors that about three years before the cruise missile attack on the Al Shifa plant, bin Laden had asked Sudanese officials to help him make poison gas with which to attack U.S. troops in Saudi Arabia (NYT, 9/21/98)
- Bin Laden worked with the Sudanese to develop low-cost ways to store and dispense chemical weapons (USAT, 8/24/98)
- It is suspected that bin Laden tested, with the help of Sudanese officials, nerve agents that would be dispersed from bombs or artillery shells (TIME, 12/21/98, p. 34)
- Mamdouh Mahmud Salim (a.k.a. Abu Hajer al Iraqi or Abu Hajer), a close associate of bin Laden, conspired to use weapons of mass destruction against U.S. nationals and sought to develop chemical weapons while in Sudan (AWST, 10/12/98, p. 58)
- Mamdouh Mahmud Salim was involved in the procurement of the ingredients necessary for chemical weapons and involved in negotiating a joint weapons production agreement among al Qaeda and the Sudanese and Iranian governments (JIR, June 1999, p. 37)
- Financial transactions had been found between bin Laden and Sudan's government-run Military Industrial Corporation, which oversaw chemical weapons development (NYT, 9/21/98)

[redacted]

[redacted]

Interest in Chem/Bio Agents

State Ties

- Al Qaeda allegedly worked closely with Sudan's National Islamic Front to develop chemical weapons (AWST, 10/12/98, p. 58; USNWR, 10/5/98, p. 12)
- The CIA received reports indicating that in 1995 bin Laden won tentative approval from Sudanese leaders to begin developing chemical weapons for use against American troops in Saudi Arabia (but he was later expelled from Sudan after pressure from the U.S. and Saudi Arabia) (NYT, 10/27/99)
- Available evidence suggests than Sudan had acquired and used chemical weapons as early as 1992 (JIR, June 1999, p. 37)
- There is also evidence of Sudanese-Iraqi CW cooperation and bin Laden-Iraqi connections (JIR, June 1999, p. 37; USAT, 8/24/98)
- In December 1998 bin Laden is reported to have met with the Iraqi ambassador to Turkey, who may be an agent of Iraqi intelligence (JIR, June 1999, p. 37)
- There are reports of possible contacts between bin Laden's operatives and Iraq's special security organization, which is responsible for protecting Iraq's chem/bio programs (JIR, June 1999, p. 37)
- According to the 4 November 1998 indictment against bin Laden, "al Qaeda reached an understanding with the Government of Iraq that al Qaeda would not work against that government and that on particular projects, specifically including weapons development, al Qaeda would work cooperatively with the Government of Iraq" (USIA, 11/4/98)
- The CIA had received reports that Iraqi chemical weapons experts had visited Khartoum, prompting suspicions that Iraq was shifting some of its production of chemical weapons to Sudan, and bin Laden moved to Sudan at about this same time (NYT, 10/27/99)
- After Operation Desert Storm, Saddam Hussein managed to shift some of his biochemical agents to Sudan by moving them overland through Libya (JIRP, 10/98, p.8)
- The Clinton administration began to claim that Iraqis had been helping the NIF to develop chemical weapons (JIR, 10/98, p. 22)

[redacted]

[redacted]

Interest in Chem/Bio Agents

Al Shifa

- The Al Shifa plant had been built by bin Laden and originally belonged to him (JIRP, 10/98, p.8)
- In the summer of 1997 an informant reported that two sites in Khartoum might be involved in chemical weapons production and the informant also mentioned that Al Shifa, on which he had less information, was suspicious because it had high fences and stringent security (NYT, 10/27/99)
- In December of 1997 an agent working for the CIA collected a soil sample about 60 feet from the Al Shifa factory, directly across an access road from the main entrance: The soil was found to contain about 2.5 times the normal trace amounts of EMPTA, a chemical used in the production of VX nerve gas (NYT, 10/27/99)
- On 24 July 1998 the CIA issued its first intelligence report on the Al Shifa factory in Sudan based on the soil sample, satellite imagery, and other intelligence: The report highlighted apparent links between Al Shifa and bin Laden but one key paragraph, titled "Next Steps", called for more soil samples and additional satellite imagery and the report also raised questions by noting that there were no longer signs of heavy security around Al Shifa (NYT, 10/27/99)
- On 4 August 1998 a new CIA report assessed the possible connection between Sudan and bin Laden regarding bin Laden's efforts to acquire chemical weapons: New intelligence indicated that bin Laden had acquired chemical or nuclear materials and "might be ready" to conduct a chemical attack (NYT, 10/27/99)
- On 6 August 1998, State Department intelligence analysts responded to the 4 August CIA report with skepticism, arguing that even with the new intelligence, the evidence linking Al Shifa to bin Laden and chemical weapons was weak (NYT, 10/27/99)
- Shortly after the cruise missile attack, Secretary of Defense William Cohen stated that bin Laden had helped finance the plant: "We do know that he had contributed to this particular facility" (NYT, 8/29/98)

[redacted]

[redacted]

Interest in Chem/Bio Agents

Al Shifa

- Bin Laden was an investor in the plant (MSNBC, 8/17/98)
- The owner of the Al Shifa plant at the time of the attack, Salih Idris, was purportedly a front-man for bin Laden (NYT, 9/21/98)
- The owner of the Al Shifa plant at the time of the attack, Salih Idris, had financial links to the Islamic Jihad group in Egypt (JTWR, 10/5/98), and through it to bin Laden (source?)
- The general manager of the Al Shifa plant at the time of the attack, Osman Sulayman, was deported from Saudi Arabia around 1995 for his suspected ties to bin Laden (NYT, 9/21/98)
- John Gannon, chairman of the CIA's National Intelligence Council, stated on 16 Nov 1998 that bin Laden had known ties to the al Shifa plant in Sudan (CNN, 11/19/98)
- Bin Laden had made significant financial contributions to the plant (MDNC, "Afghanistan")

Miscellaneous

- A U.S. citizen, Wadih el Hage, who was arrested in Texas, allegedly tried to help bin Laden procure chemical weapons (WP, 9/21/98; WP, 9/26/98, p. A19)
- Hage is under investigation for "the extent to which [his] international travels concerned efforts to procure chemical weapons and their components on behalf of Osama bin Laden" (WP, 9/21/98)
- John Gannon, chairman of the CIA's National Intelligence Council, stated on 16 Nov 1998: "We know that bin Laden's organization has attempted to develop poisonous gases that could be fired at U.S. troops in the Gulf States" (CNN, 11/19/98)
- Court documents unsealed in Nov 1998 charge that bin Laden had made attempts to obtain the components of chemical weapons as early as 1993 (USDCNY indictment)
- In November 1998, CIA officials confirmed that bin Laden has attempted to develop or buy chemical weapons for use against US troops in the Persian Gulf area (JIR, June 1999, p. 37)

[redacted]

[redacted]

Interest in Chem/Bio Agents

Miscellaneous

In January 1999, Richard Clarke, a senior counterterrorism official, said that there was no evidence that bin Laden had yet acquired chemical or biological weapons (IHT, 2/3/99)

US officials have said that bin Laden was trying to obtain chemical and biological weapons from a number of sources – including former Soviet-bloc nations – for possible use in terrorist attacks (CNN, 6/17/99)

On 12 Aug 1998 the Small Group of presidential advisors met with President Clinton with evidence that bin Laden was looking to obtain weapons of mass destruction and chemical weapons to use against US installations (NYT, 9/23/98; PBS Online)

One U.S. official has said that bin Laden has "actively sought to acquire chemical weapons, and it is possible that he could conduct some type of [small-scale] chemical attack" (WP, 7/29/99)

On 19 April 1999 the London-based newspaper Al-Hayat quoted Ahmad Salama Mabrouk, a jailed member of the Egyptian militant group Al-Jihad, as saying that bin Laden's umbrella group (the International Islamic Front for Fighting Jews and Crusaders) not only possessed biological and chemical weapons, but was planning about 100 operations against U.S. and Israeli interests around the world (SGIU, 4/20/99)

In October 1999, senior administration officials said that they believe that bin Laden was trying to develop chemical weapons in Afghanistan and may have obtained them (NYT, 10/27/99)

[redacted]

[redacted]

Interest in Chem/Bio Agents

The Islamic Jihad mail-order revelations

In the summer of 1999 it was reported by Khalid Sharaf-al-Din in the Arabic-language Al-Sharq-al-Awsat in Cairo that members of the Islamic Jihad group had managed to buy anthrax from a source in an East Asian country (JIR, 8/99, p.5)

The cost was the equivalent of $3,695 plus freight (JIR, 8/99, p.5)

Ahmad Ibrahim al-Najar, a defendant in the recent Egyptian court proceedings against Islamic militants, confessed details of the transactions (JIR, 8/99, p. 5)

Factories in former Warsaw Pact countries and some Eastern states supply deadly diseases such as Ebola, anthrax, and Salmonella to whoever wants to buy them without verifying the identity of the importer (JIR, 8/99, p. 5)

For example, a Czech laboratory apparently agreed to supply what appeared to be botulinum toxin for $7,500 per sample (JIR, 8/99, p. 5)

Important questions

- How much was acquired?
- Was it a vaccine strain or a deadly strain?
- Could Islamic Jihad culture and weaponize it?

[redacted]

[redacted]

Interest in Nuclear Weapons

U.S. court documents allege that bin Laden's organization sent emissaries around the world in an effort to procure nuclear weapons (WP,9/26/98, p. A19)

In late 1993, Mamdouh Mahmud Salim, a top bin Laden aide who was arrested in Bavaria on 16 Sep 1998, had signed off on a scheme by al Qaida to obtain enriched uranium for the purpose of developing nuclear weapons (JTWR, 9/28/98; WP, 9/26/98, p. A19)

In late 1993 , following a bin Laden appeal to Al Qaeda members to attack "the U.S. enemy", his lieutenants launched an effort to obtain uranium (AWST, 10/12/98, p. 58)

Al Qaeda made an attempt to acquire weapons-grade uranium (USNWR, 10/19/98, p. 37)

A document relating to a proposed purchase of purported uranium was routed to Mamdouh Mahmud Salim for his review; after which he indicated that the project to make the purchase should go forward (AWST, 10/12/98, p. 58)

Authorities reportedly have copies of a document relating to a proposed purchase of enriched uranium (NYT, 9/26/98)

Other reports state that Salim tried to obtain components for nuclear weapons (AWST, 10/12/98, p. 58; ICT, 9/28/98)

The indictment states that at various times from at least 1993, bin Laden and others made efforts to obtain the components of nuclear weapons (USDCNY indictment)

[redacted]

[redacted]

Interest in Nuclear Weapons

Bin Laden first wanted to buy a Russian nuclear warhead on the black market, but abandoned that effort when no warhead could be found (TIME, 12/21/98, p.34)

Instead, his agents began to scour former Soviet Republics for enriched uranium and weapons components (TIME, 12/21/98, p. 34)

By late 1993 Mamdouh Mahmud Salim was enlisted in efforts in the Sudan and elsewhere to obtain the components of nuclear weapons (AWST, 10/12/98, p. 58)

Fortunately, they encountered scam artists who tried to rip them off: they were offered low grade reactor fuel and radioactive waste (TIME, 12/21/98, p. 34)

Bin Laden reportedly got frustrated by these efforts and decided to pursue chemical weapons instead (TIME, 12/21/98, p. 34)

On 7 Oct 1998 the London-based Arabic language newspaper al-Hayat claimed that bin Laden had acquired two or more nuclear weapons from former-Soviet Central Asian countries using a network of "influential friends" (UPI, 10/7/98; PBS Online; FYEO, 10/26/98; also see JIR, June 1998, p. 35)

Another more likely report suggests that he tried and failed to buy Russian nuclear warheads on the black market (JIR, June 1999, p. 35)

"Despite... several years of effort and a lot of money at their disposal, there is no evidence that bin Laden's agents have succeeded in buying a [nuclear] warhead. However, there is also no reason to believe that they have given up their search." (JIR, June 1999, p. 36)

[redacted]

[redacted]

Interest in Nuclear Weapons: Lack of Technical Know-How

The publicly available evidence suggests that bin Laden's agents have been nuclear novices, who apparently have lacked the most fundamental expertise and had quickly become targets of nuclear scams of the sort that have victimized others (JIR, June 1999 p. 36)

According to one government official: "Osama's buyers weren't physicists, and the people selling to him were trying to rip him off" (JIR, June 1999 p. 36)

In late 1993 Mamdouh Mahmud Salim (a.k.a. Abu Hajer al Iraqi) allegedly approved a scheme to obtain enriched uranium, but he and his associates were reportedly offered low-grade reactor fuel (enriched to less than 20% U235) by people who claimed that it was weapons-useable material (JIR, June 1999, p. 36)

Reports also indicate that Mamdouh Mahmud Salim and his associates were also offered "nuclear garbage", claimed by sellers to be Red Mercury (JIR, June 1999, p. 36)

[redacted]

[redacted]

Interest in Nuclear Weapons: The Bodansky Claims

On 6 Aug 1999 Yosef Bodansky said that bin Laden had as many as 20 suitcase nuclear bombs that had been smuggled out of Russia by Chechen rebels who had managed to steal them from the Russian military and then sold them to bin Laden (WND, 8/12/99)

Yosef Bodansky was a researcher attached to the House counter-terrorism task force (WND, 8/12/99)

He claimed that his sources of information were Russian and Saudi intelligence sources (WND, 8/12/99)

He also said that:

> Bin Laden was attempting to recruit former Russian special forces to operate the bombs (WND, 8/12/99).
>
> "The Russians believe that he has a handful [of nuclear weapons], the Saudi intelligence services are very conservative... [and] believe that he has in the neighborhood of 20." (WTC, 8/9/99)
>
> "Most of them have been transferred through Pakistan" (WTC, 8/9/99)
>
> Bin Laden has biological and chemical weapons and had received technical help from Iraq (WTC, 8/9/99)

[redacted]

[redacted]

Interest in Nuclear Weapons
The Bodansky Claims

There are many compelling questions raised by Bodansky's claims:

Would the anti-Soviet bin Laden really work with Soviet commandos who were his deadly enemies in the past? He apparently did work with a former U.S. Army employee of the Special Forces base at Fort Bragg, as well as with other Islamic Americans. Therefore, there seems to be no reason to believe that he would not employ renegade former Russian spetsnaz.

How could bin Laden buy what countries like Iran, Iraq, and Libya, with billions at their disposal, have sought for so many years? He has apparently had contacts with Chechen rebels in the past, in the form of Arab Afghans who went to fight for Chechnya. Perhaps it is possible that such ties would serve him where Islamic nations have had lesser influence or support.

Why would Chechen rebels sell what would be so valuable to them? Can we really believe that they could have obtained so many of these devices that they should be willing to sell 20? If this is true, then surely they must have kept some for themselves, and there would also be a high probability that they could have sold some to other buyers as well, all of which would mean that this problem, if true, is likely to be much greater than bin Laden alone.

Are Bodansky's sources credible? WND states that "one must always treat the claims of Russian officials with near-total skepticism" (WND, 8/12/99). Although such blanket put-downs border on racism, it is true that Bodansky's sources should be treated with a great deal of skepticism.

[redacted]

[redacted]

Quotes Regarding WMD

"If I seek to acquire these weapons I am carrying out a duty"

Osama bin Laden, in an interview in February 1999, while discussing his possible acquisition of WMD (JIR, June 1999, p. 34)

"How we use them is up to us"

Osama bin Laden, referring to chemical, biological, and nuclear weapons (George J. Tenet, Director of Central Intelligence, 2/2/99, statement as prepared for delivery to the Senate Armed Services Committee)

"We can't tell you for certain that they have acquired it, but they certainly have demonstrated an interest in it in the past"

U.S. intelligence official, speaking about the interest by bin Laden's group in obtaining chemical and biological warfare material (Reuters, 6/17/99)

"Acquiring [nuclear and chemical] weapons for the defense of Muslims is a religious duty... and if I seek to acquire these weapons, I am carrying out a duty"

Osama bin Laden, in interviews with journalists working for Time and Newsweek, Jan 1999 (DOE TSD, Feb 1999, p.2):

[redacted]

[redacted]

Quotes Regarding WMD

"It would be a sin for Muslims not to try to possess the weapons that would prevent the infidels from inflicting harm on Muslims."

> Osama bin Laden, 23 Dec 1998, in an interview with a correspondent for Time Magazine, when asked whether he was trying to acquire chemical and nuclear weapons (PBS Online, Osama bin Laden v. the U.S.: Edicts and Statements)

"If I seek to acquire such weapons, this is a religious duty. How we use them is up to us."

> Osama bin Laden, 24 Dec 1998, in an interview with ABC reporter John Miller, when discussing charges that he tried to develop chemical and nuclear weapons (PBS Online, Osama bin Laden v. the U.S.: Edicts and Statements)
> [Other reports say that the interview was conducted by Ramiullah Yusufzi, the ABC news producer in Pakistan at the time (NYT, 12/25/98)]

[redacted]

[redacted]

Nuclear Weapons Issues

Even if bin Laden were able to purchase a nuclear warhead, he would have to figure out how to bypass its arming, fail-safe, or use control systems

Could he build a gun-assembled HEU-based nuclear explosive?

He could build an RDD using materials such as Cesium 137 or Cobalt 60, which are widely used for medical and industrial purposes and, therefore, readily available (JIR, June 1999, p. 36)

If he were to try to manufacture a nuclear explosive device, he would need technical expertise in many areas in addition to a source of fissile material:

- Electronics
- Conventional explosives
- Physics
- Materials science
- Engineering

At the present time, it seems that attacks with conventional explosives are still more likely than any chem/bio or nuclear attacks

[redacted]

[redacted]

Al Qaeda Shows Little Evidence of Technical Sophistication

Bin Laden

- Some reports claim that bin Laden obtained an engineering degree in the U.S. (JIRP, 10/98, p. 8)
- However, his background is in civil engineering projects, such as construction, (as opposed to more scientific engineering disciplines such as electrical or mechanical engineering)

Documents

- Al Qaeda provide operatives with false identification
- However, this is sometimes very crude (as in the case of Odeh)

Communications

- Al Qaeda operatives engage in coded communications
- However, their effectiveness is this regard is unknown (from open sources)
- Bin Laden also spreads his beliefs through Web sites on the internet
- El Sayyid Nosair, a volunteer in the anti-Soviet jihad network in the US who conspired to kill Rabbi Meir Kahane, was very adept at communicating with fellow radicals even while serving a prison term at Attica (JCSI, Fall 1998, p. 25):
  Knowing he was under surveillance, he used other inmates' telephone PIN numbers to call terrorist contacts as far away as Iran (JCSI, Fall 1998, p. 25)
  He also wrote secretly coded letters to top clerics in Iran and elsewhere using codes inscribed on the backs of stamps and in elaborate Arab calligraphy that prison officials mistook for simple embroidery of his writings (JCSI, Fall 1998, p. 25)

Use of satellite telephones

- Provides a cheap, portable, and effective communications tool for bin Laden
- Easy to intercept, although this can be offset by the use of a one-time code book to conduct cryptic conversations
- Easy to locate, although this is easy to offset by frequent moves

[redacted]

[redacted]

Bombing Analysis
Lessons Learned

The Bad News

Even with <u>many</u> warning signs, the African bombings were not prevented

Al Qaeda cells and operatives were either very numerous or very crafty (or both) in order to evade an extensive dragnet by the world's most sophisticated intelligence agencies

"Contrary to popular myth, terrorist attacks are not easy to carry out. The mere act of acquiring or moving weapons and explosives, identifying and monitoring targets, acquiring and using bases of operations and transportation, involves both trusting increasing numbers of operatives with at least part of the plan, and using the services of outsiders. The more complex the plan, the more conspirators are necessary, the more outside resources need to be acquired, and the greater the likelihood of detection and betrayal... Usually, the lone amateur is detected in the course or preparing for his mission. He is most likely to succeed in his native country, where he is able to blend in and where he knows how to acquire resources without being noticed. A lone bomber operating in a foreign country is much harder to imagine. Carrying out simultaneous attacks in two foreign countries is extremely difficult to execute. The chances of detection are enormous." (SGIU, 8/10/98)

[redacted]

[redacted]

Bombing Analysis
Lessons Learned

The Good News

Very few Americans were killed

The embassies suffered relatively light structural damage: most deaths were in the building next to the Nairobi embassy (which collapsed)

The existence of the East African cell was known and it was under intense scrutiny

The East African cell was feeling the heat of scrutiny: Fazul wrote that they were "at 100% danger"

Meanwhile, several other bombings (e.g., Albania) seem to have been pre-empted

Following the bombings, the U.S. launched a massive campaign to expose and destroy bin Laden's terrorist network, which led to a series of captures and has kept bin Laden from launching additional attacks (SGIU, 10/13/98)

We were quick to identify the perpetrators and have been aggressive in building a case against them

We have kept bin Laden from launching additional attacks (SGIU, 10/13/98)

"...if this action was... bin Laden's best shot, it really wasn't much."

(SGIU, 8/10/98)

[redacted]

OFFICIAL USE ONLY

Bombing Analysis
Lessons Learned

The bottom line

We cannot act on all of the many thousands of warnings (and warning signs) that we receive: To do so would place control of U.S. installations in the hands of terrorists

Some bombings slipped through the cracks, but many others were prevented

Lots of innocent Africans were killed, but this could have been done anywhere

The biggest impact is on our perceptions: we perceive that we are unsafe (based on the African bombings) even though the facts may suggest otherwise

Just because we are targets does not mean that we are unsafe

We tend to have zero tolerance, meaning that even small numbers of casualties are unacceptable

However, if we view terrorism as an ongoing war, in which some level of casualties is unavoidable, then the events on and around August 1998 can be viewed as a demonstration of our strengths, as opposed to a demonstration of our weaknesses

[redacted]

[redacted]

Bombing Analysis

Indications and Warnings

Several indications and warnings preceding the East African bombings. This section contains an analysis of the early pieces of intelligence and what we might learn from them after the fact.

1. The computer letter (August 1997)

Background: A letter was discovered on the computer of Wadih el Hage after the August 1997 raid on el Hage's home in Kenya

Value: Evidence of an active cell

Action: The existence of the cell was already known and it was the target of active disruption; for example, el Hage was told to leave the country

Shortcomings: No hints of a bomb plot or other specific threats

Possible Failure: None. Uncovering this letter and other evidence by means of an aggressive counter-terrorist program is a sign of intelligence at its best.

Lesson: Active disruption operations such as those that led to the uncovering of this evidence are a valuable counter-terrorist tool

[redacted]

[redacted]

Bombing Analysis
Indications and Warnings

2. Informant tip #1 (Summer 1997)

Background:

- In the summer of 1997 the CIA received a tip from an informant that the Nairobi branch of an Islamic charity, the Al Haramain Foundation, was involved in terrorism and was planning specific attacks against the U.S. Embassy in Nairobi (PBS Online, "Warnings to the FBI")

- The tipster had walked into the U.S. Embassy in Nairobi in September 1997 and claimed that seven Arabs who worked for the charity had connections with a bin Laden terror group

- Other reports say that in the summer 1997, the intelligence service of another country turned over an informant to the CIA who said that the Nairobi branch of the Islamic charity known as the Al Haramain Foundation was plotting terrorist attacks against Americans and that the informant eventually warned that the group was plotting to blow up the American Embassy in Nairobi (NYT, 1/9/99)

[We will assume here that these reports refer to the same informant, with some confusion as to how the informant came to the attention of American authorities]

Value: Evidence of a cell AND of a plot against the embassy

[redacted]

Bombing Analysis
Indications and Warnings

2. Informant tip #1 (Summer 1997), continued

Action 1: By 31 October Kenyan police arrested nine Arabs connected to the charity and seized the group's files (PBS Online, "Warnings to The FBI")

Action 2: The CIA sent a counterterrorism team to investigate, but they found no evidence of a bomb plot (PBS Online, "Warnings to The FBI")

Action 3: The nine employees of the charity were later deported (in late 1997) and the investigation was dropped (PBS; PBS Online, "Warnings to The FBI")

Shortcomings: No evidence specifically of a bomb plot

Possible Failure: The CIA investigation team wanted to interrogate the suspects but the CIA Station Chief objected (PBS Online, "Warnings to The FBI")

Lesson: In retrospect, it appears as though the suspects should have been interrogated by the investigation team, which might have revealed more information that might have been used to prevent the bombings

[redacted]

Bombing Analysis
Indications and Warnings

3. Informant tip #2 (November 1997)

Background:

- In November 1997 Mustafa Mahmoud Said Ahmed, an Egyptian, walked into the U.S. Embassy in Nairobi and warned that unnamed terrorists planned to car bomb the compound
- He claimed that the plan was to detonate a truck bomb in the parking garage of the embassy (PBS Online, "Warnings to The FBI")
- He admitted that he had taken part in surveillance of the embassy, including taking photos (PBS Online, "Warnings to The FBI")
- He was grilled for days, and provided details of the attack, but was believed to be making up the tale
- A warning was issued that said that Ahmed was probably making up the story, but could be telling the truth or could be approaching the embassy to check its security
- In response, extra guards were posted at the front and back of the building and a letter was sent to Madeleine Albright warning that the embassy was vulnerable to car bombs
- Ahmed was later arrested in connection with the bombing in Dar es Salaam
- In March 1998 a team from Diplomatic Security and the Foreign Building Office, which handles embassy leases and construction projects, arrived in Nairobi to conduct a security review (NYT, 1/9/99)

Value: Specific evidence of a bomb plot, the target, and details of the plan

Action 1: Warning issued
Action 2: Extra guards posted
Action 3: Letter to Albright
Action 4: Security review conducted

[redacted]

[redacted]

Bombing Analysis
Indications and Warnings

3. Informant tip #2 (November 1997), continued

Difficulty 1: Many such warnings are received at U.S. facilities annually, many of which are false alarms
Difficulty 2: It is difficult to gauge the sincerity and motives of human informants
Difficulty 3: No government can allow its policies to be dictated by threats (i.e., it cannot allow people to shut down its facilities at will with simple proclamations)

Possible Failure 1: The investigation may not have given sufficient weight to the credibility of the informant
Lesson 1: In retrospect it appears as if more resources, perhaps to include polygraph examination, should have been devoted to the interrogation of the informant

Possible Failure 2: There is no mention of active surveillance of the informant and his contacts
Lesson 2: Aggressive surveillance of the informant and his contacts might have turned up details of, and preparations for, the eventual bombings

Possible Failure 3: The warnings and letter may not have been sufficient to motivate effective changes
Lesson 3: In retrospect it appears as if the warning should have been used to push through effective changes, such as a wider buffer zone around the embassy, an embassy relocation or other changes

[redacted]

[redacted]

Bombing Analysis
Indications and Warnings

4. CIA warnings

Background:

- The CIA repeatedly told the State Department in Washington and in the Nairobi embassy that there was an active terrorist cell in Kenya connected to bin Laden (NYT, 1/9/99)
- In fact, the CIA investigated at least three terrorist threats in Nairobi in the year before the bombings and took one seriously enough to send a counterterrorism team from CIA headquarters (see Informant tip #1 above)
- Intelligence officials briefed Ambassador Bushnell about the presence of the group in early 1997 but told her there was no evidence of a specific threat against the embassy or American interests in Kenya (NYT, 1/9/99)

Value: Evidence of a cell
Action: The cell was the target of active disruption; for example, the raid on el Hage's home and when el Hage was told to leave the country

Shortcoming #1: There had been no information or intelligence to warn of the actual attack (RARB)
Shortcoming #2: Although a number of intelligence reports had cited alleged threats, they were largely discounted because of doubts about the sources; because they were imprecise, changing, and non-specific; and because actions taken by intelligence and law enforcement authorities were believed to have dissipated the threat (RARB)

Possible Failure: It might be alleged that more aggressive pressure on the suspects could have led to more useful information, that the cell should have been penetrated, or that that the various suspects should have been the subject of more aggressive surveillance in order to learn about their activities
Lesson: In retrospect it appears as if the disruption activities were insufficient and that they might better have been replaced or augmented by active penetration and surveillance operations

[redacted]

[redacted]

Bombing Analysis: Findings

Physical security at the sites generally met or exceeded levels prescribed by the DoS for posts at medium or low threat levels (RARB)

However, these standards were insufficient to protect against large vehicular bombs (RARB)

Neither embassy building met the DoS standard for a 100 ft setback/standoff zone: Because both were "existing office buildings" occupied before this standard was adopted, a general exception had been made (RARB)

The widespread use of such exceptions reflects the reality of funding levels that are inadequate to replace sub-standard buildings rapidly (RARB)

Security systems and procedures at both sites were properly implemented (RARB)

- In Nairobi the bomber failed to penetrate the embassy's outer perimeter because local guards refused to open the gates (RARB)
- In Dar es Salaam the bomber also failed to penetrate the perimeter, stopped by guards and blocked by an embassy water truck (RARB)

Neither site's Emergency Action Plan anticipated a car bomb scenario: Therefore, personnel were not trained to react properly and guards did not have adequate equipment (RARB)

In general, the DoS has systematically failed to recognize the threat posed by vehicle bombs and to react accordingly (RARB)

[redacted]

[redacted]

Bombing Analysis: Findings

There has been a collective failure of the US government for a decade to provide adequate resources to reduce the vulnerability of US diplomatic missions to terrorist attacks (RARB)

There was no credible intelligence that provided immediate warning of the bombings (RARB)

Some intelligence was discounted because of doubts about the sources (RARB)

Some intelligence, while taken seriously, was imprecise, changing, and non-specific (RARB)

Actions by intelligence and law enforcement authorities to confront and disrupt suspect persons and groups were believed to have dissipated the threat (RARB)

Intelligence has allowed the US to thwart a number of similar terrorist threats (RARB)

[redacted]

[redacted]

Bombing Analysis: Recommendations

Recommendations of the RARB

Provide a "special alarm signal" to warn of large exterior bombs (RARB)

Institute duck-and-cover practice drills

Provide special equipment to perimeter guards to counter vehicular bombs

Assume that all posts are potential targets of vehicular bombs

Improve perimeter stand-off

Improve counter-surveillance

Close posts for which adequate enhancements cannot be made

Provide training and equipment, where needed, to local governments and their police forces

Place more weight on terrorism in the DoS "Composite Threat List"

Increase the number of posts with full-time Regional Security Officers

Augment the number of Marine Security Guard Detachments

Provide Regional Security Officers with training on terrorism, terrorist methods, explosives, etc.

Reduce the number of embassies by establishing regional embassies

Review physical security standards on a priority basis

When building new chanceries abroad, collocate all US government agencies in the same compound

Obtain funding for capital building programs

[redacted]

Bombing Analysis: Recommendations

Recommendations of the RARB (continued)

Clarify responsibilities for security

Encourage better coordination among persons with security responsibilities

Ensure that a single high-ranking officer is accountable for all security matters

Build public support for increased resources for foreign affairs

Advise all posts of the threats posed by WMD

Provide crisis management training for mass casualty and mass destruction incidents

Establish a revitalized program for on-site crisis management training

Create and exercise a team and equipment package configured to assist in post blast crises

Acquire a modern, reliable, air-refuelable Foreign Emergency Support Team aircraft

Improve procedures for mobilizing aircraft and aircrews to provide more rapid and effective assistance

Ensure that all posts have emergency communications, excavation tools, medical supplies, emergency documents, next of kin records, and other safety equipment at secure off-site locations

Enhance the flow of intelligence

Assign a State Department official to the Counter Terrorism Center

The FBI and DoS should consult on ways to improve information sharing

[redacted]

Analysis: The Islamic Bomb

There are apprehensions that Islamists might assume power in Pakistan and that, if this were to happen, Pakistan could join into a federation with the Afghan Taliban (JIR, Mar 1999, p. 32)

- A considerable part of the power base for Prime Minister Nawaz Sharif was made up of various fundamentalist groups (JIR, Mar 1999, p. 32)
- Pakistan's Pathan tribesmen would strongly support an Islamic government (JIR, Mar 1999, p. 32)

If this were to happen, Arab Afghans would naturally lobby strongly for a nuclear war against Israel (JIR, Mar 1999, p. 32)

Arabs find it very difficult to understand why sanctions were imposed on Pakistan after its nuclear tests (which was effectively forced to respond to Indian tests) and not on Israel (JIR, Mar 1999, p. 34)

- In Muslim eyes, this is further evidence of a double standard in Washington (JIR, Mar 1999, p. 34)

If India and Pakistan sign the Comprehensive Test Ban Treaty (neither had signed at the time of this survey), then Israel will remain as the only nuclear power that is not a party to the treaty – further evidence for Arabs that the real threat comes from Israel (JIR, Mar 1999, p. 34)

[redacted]

[redacted]

Analysis: Solutions

Any state harboring bin Laden could take the following overt actions

- Arrest and hold him
- Arrest and try him (in a real trial or in a "show" trial meant to exonerate him)
- Arrest and extradite him
- Expel him

However, overt acts might raw criticism from bin Laden supporters

Any state harboring bin Laden could take secret steps

- Arrange secretly for him to move out, ostensibly of his own free will
- Secretly expel him
- Deliver him secretly to another country
- Arrange secretly for another nation to learn of his whereabouts (after which he could be apprehended or killed)
- Arrange secretly for him to be assassinated by his enemies
- Secretly kill or incapacitate him
- Keep him incommunicado so that he ceases to get media attention and ceases those activities which draw criticism and international pressure

The advantage of secrecy is that the nation might hope to avoid criticism from domestic bin Laden supporters

[redacted]

[redacted]

Analysis
Targeting bin Laden

The advantages of targeting bin Laden

- It would send a message of resolve
- It would serve justice
- It might diminish his capability for future strikes
- It might act as a deterrent
- He may not be replaceable

"There [are] a finite number of people who can plan and organize a transnational terrorist organization. Theoretically, there's an infinite number of people you could recruit as vehicle bombers, although I really don't believe that either. But history shows that when you cut off the heads of an organization, the total command structure, it dies."

Neil C. Livingstone, a private terrorism expert:

[redacted]

[redacted]

Analysis
Targeting bin Laden

The disadvantages of targeting bin Laden

- He may be replaceable, requiring a sustained and widespread follow-on
- It may only make him a martyr
- It may inflame further violence

Livingstone supports his assertion above (previous page) with an example that required multiple killings around the world, making it obvious that no one death alone was sufficient:

"Israel did that [cut off the heads of an organization] when it went after the Black September movement in the early 1970s. Israel didn't hit the rank and file, it hit the leadership all over the world. And Black September ceased to exist."

"US cruise missile strikes... failed to kill the Saudi but succeeded spectacularly in galvanizing Pakistan's Islamic hardliners while reinforcing bin Laden's image as an Islamic Che Guevara"

Jane's Intelligence Review, Jan 1999, p. 36

[redacted]

[redacted]

Analysis
Targeting bin Laden

"If the U.S. is perceived by Arabs to be using a double standard and a heavy hand against Arab interests, then the terrorists will find more understanding among people who perceive the U.S. as an aggressor."

Khalid Abdalla, chief representative of the Washington office of the 22-nation Arab League

"We have to have a political and diplomatic strategy to attack him without aggrandizing him"

A US counter-terrorism official, (NYT, 2/8/99)

The missiles inflicted little lasting damage but helped to make Mr. Bin Laden a "revered figure" in the Islamic world

A US counter-terrorism official, (NYT, 2/8/99)

"What was served by the cruise missile attacks? You've inflated one individual to an enormous extent. Why would you want to create more like him? Such acts only help him proliferate."

Mohammad Saddique Kanju, Deputy Foreign Minister of Pakistan (NYT, 2/8/99)

Protests After the Al Shifa

[redacted]

[redacted]

Analysis
Targeting bin Laden

"I know the guy.. and he's not that mighty... But the United States has created a hero out of him."

Ghazi Salah el-Din, Information Minister of Sudan (NYT, 2/8/99)

"You can kill Osama bin Laden today or tomorrow; you can arrest him and out him on trial in New York or in Washington. If this will end the problem – no. Tomorrow you will get somebody else."

Ahmed Sattar, an aide to Sheik Omar Abdel Rahman, (NYT, 4/13/99)

In November 1979 a mob of 10,000 Pakistanis, inflamed by rumors that American troops had entered Mecca, stormed the U.S. Embassy in Islamabad: two American officials and two Pakistani employees died (NYT Op-Ed, 8/13/99)

- A good example of the willingness of militant Muslims to believe anti-American rhetoric

"Not since Che Guevara's face was a ubiquitous presence on the walls of America's college dormitories has a revolutionary figure been blown so far out of proportion"

Milt Bearden, former CIA chief in Pakistan, arguing that the hype and hysteria surrounding Osama bin Laden exacerbates U.S./Muslim frictions and serves to make bin Laden a hero (NYT OP-Ed, 8/13/99)

"Well, there was somebody before bin Laden, and there will be somebody after bin Laden."

Terrorism expert Brian Jenkins (WP, 7/29/99)

[redacted]

[redacted]

Analysis: Solutions

American stratagems to block bin Laden's access to bank accounts, cut his connections to terrorist cells, and sever his links to political supporters have not succeeded (NYT, 2/8/99)

The Taliban have been deeply divided over their decision to host bin Laden: bin Laden is a hero in Afghanistan, but his presence has also been costly (SGIU, 3/16/99)

The name of Osama bin Laden is a top choice for baby boys born in the North West Frontier Province of Pakistan with more than 500 baby boys named Osama between August 1998 and July 1999 (JTWR, 7/8/99)

In addition, businesses and public institutions bearing his name have also sprung up, such as the Osama Poultry Farms, Osama Bakery, an Osama drug store, several Osama clothing stores and the Osama Public School: people were impressed by the courage bin Laden has shown in challenging the US and speaking out for oppressed Muslims (JTWR, 7/8/99)

"Rewards are offered, defectors are encouraged, sources are paid, diplomatic muscles are flexed, and as a consequence, terrorist activities are thwarted"

Brian M. Jenkins, terrorism expert (WP, 2/17/99)

On pressuring the Taliban to give up bin Laden: "To treat the Afghan refusal to extradite Osama bin Laden differently [than the French case of Ira Einhorn or the Israeli case of Samuel Scheinbein] seems to many in the Islamic world like just another example of American cultural arrogance"

Milt Bearden, former CIA chief in Pakistan, NYT Op-Ed, 8/13/99

The Saudis have made it clear that they feared bringing bin Laden back to Saudi Arabia because he could become a martyr figure to Saudi dissidents (NYT, 10/18/98)

[redacted]

[redacted]

Conclusions

1. TERRORISM IS NOT DEAD

Like the Aum Shinrikyo cult, the bin Laden terrorist network demonstrates that the threat of terrorism has not diminished

- Neither the collapse of the Soviet Union, nor the decline of traditional terrorist groups (such as the Red Brigades, RAF, JRA, PIRA, PLO, etc.), has brought an end to terrorism

Threats may evolve from unexpected sources

- The Aum threat arose from an obscure religious cult
- The Afghan resistance turned to bite the hand that fed them
- Bin Laden was initially dismissed as a "Gucci terrorist" with a fat wallet and a big mouth

2. TERRORISM IS A GLOBAL PHENOMENON

Modern threat groups think globally: Both Aum and bin Laden had followers worldwide

Threat groups can reach out to strike at a broad range of targets in unexpected places

[redacted]

[redacted]

Conclusions

3. RELIGION PLAYS A STRONG ROLE IN MODERN TERRORISM

Religion is a powerful motivational factor

Religion is a protective shield which complicates counter-terrorism

- Mosques and religious leaders spread the fiery rhetoric
- Religious organizations (such as charities, scholarship organizations, and refugee centers) are used to finance terrorism
- They also provide a steady supply of would-be terrorists by identifying key individuals and sending them abroad for training
- These religious organizations provide a ready supply of would-be terrorists who can be called upon to provide local manpower in support of terrorist operations: they act as a "holding pen"

4. KILLING IS AN EXPLICIT GOAL OF MODERN TERRORISTS

The deaths of innocents do not deter terrorists

- Aum sought to spark the end of the world
- Bin Laden seeks to target all Americans everywhere

Body counts are the goal of modern terrorists (as opposed attention-getting schemes)

Weapons of Mass Destruction appeal to modern terrorists

[redacted]

[redacted]

Conclusions

5. MODERN TERRORISM IS NOT EASILY COUNTERED

Bin Laden has been involved in terrorism for many years and linked to many acts and yet has survived repeated attempts to have him killed or detained

Acts linked to bin Laden and his cohorts demonstrate that terrorists are not easily deterred

- The risk of death does not significantly deter terrorism (as evidenced by the suicides)
- The risk of apprehension does not deter terrorism (as evidenced by the heavy pressure under which the Nairobi cell operated)

Despite repeated attacks over a period of many years, the truck bomb remains a very potent weapon and remains difficult to defend against

Despite repeated warnings over a period of many months, the Nairobi bombing was not prevented

- Raw intelligence, which looks damning in hindsight, can be very difficult to authenticate at the time
- With intelligence information, it can be difficult to separate the wheat from the chaff
- Even with good intelligence, it is not always possible to prevent an attack
- Even with good intelligence, it is not easy to quickly enact changes that might mitigate the effects of a possible attack

The terrorist can always seek out the weakest targets (although that may NOT have been the motivating factor behind the choice of the African embassy targets)

[redacted]

[redacted]

Conclusions

6. THE BIN LADEN THREAT IS SIGNIFICANT

The bin Laden threat demonstrates several strengths:

- A huge following from which losses can quickly be replaced: bin Laden is said to command forces numbering 3,000 and has influence over many thousand more
- Even bin Laden himself may be replaceable (especially given his close ties to many other well-led terrorist organizations)
- Multi-national facilities and ties
- Numerous front companies
- Significant amounts of available funding
- Potential access to chemical weapons
- State support of many types, especially safe haven

Although he is being cast as a free-lancing independent renegade, bin Laden has had links for years with Sudan, Iran, and the Afghan Taliban

On the other hand, the lack of a clear nation-state player in bin Laden's attacks complicates the ability of a country to strike back

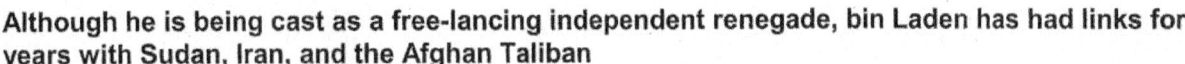

[redacted]

[redacted]

The Bottom Line

Bin Laden is not a new threat: He has direct or indirect ties to many terrorist events in recent years

Yesterdays friend may be tomorrow's enemy

There were many warning signs before the African bombings, but not a lot that we could do

Terrorism can be unpredictable: Who would have predicted the bin Laden phenomena?

The reach of terrorists is truly global

Bin Laden taps a bottomless reservoir of ethnic and religious discontent and funnels it against the U.S.

Religion is a powerful motivating factor in modern terrorism

Religiously-motivated terrorists will kill indiscriminately

[redacted]

[redacted]

Abbreviations Used for Sources

ABCN	ABC News
AP	Associated Press
AWST	Aviation Week & Space Technology
BBCN	BBC News
CNN	CNN News and CNN Interactive (website)
CRS	Congressional Research Service
CS	Corporate Security
CTSR	Counterterrorism & Security Reports
DOE TSD	Department of Energy Terrorism and Security Developments report
ECON	The Economist
FYEO	For Your Eyes Only
FYEOX	For Your Eyes Only Express
ICT	Institute of Computer Technology

[redacted]

Abbreviations Used for Sources

IHT	International Herald Tribune
IPIN	Indigo Publications Intelligence Newsletter
JCSI	Journal of Counterterrorism & Security International
JDW	Jane's Defence Weekly
JIR	Jane's Intelligence Review
JIRP	Pointer, a monthly supplement to JIR
JTWR	Jane's Terrorism Watch Report
LAT	Los Angeles Times
MDNC	MDN Consulting, International Travel Bulletin Newsletter, Daily Intelligence Summary
MSNBC	Microsoft, National Broadcasting Corporation
NYT	New York Times
PBS	Public Broadcasting Service

[redacted]

Abbreviations Used for Sources

RARB	U.S. State Department, "Report of the Accountability Review Boards on the Embassy Bombings in Nairobi and Dar es Salaam on August 7, 1998", January 1999
SGIU	STRATFOR Global Intelligence Update, STRATFOR, Inc., Austin, TX
TIME	TIME Magazine
TST	The Sunday Times
USDCNY	U.S. District Court, Southern District of New York
USNWR	U.S. News & World Report
USAT	USA Today
USIA	United States Information Agency
WND	World Net Daily
WP	Washington Post
WTC	World Tribune.com

[redacted]

www.ingramcontent.com/pod-product-compliance
Lightning Source LLC
Chambersburg PA
CBHW060303010526
44108CB00042B/2617
9781608881284